JAPAN
IN CRISIS

D1607391

With the Compliments

of

Dr. Hahm Chaibong
President,
The Asan Institute for Policy Studies

THE ASAN INSTITUTE for POLICY STUDIES

JAPAN IN CRISIS

WHAT WILL IT TAKE FOR JAPAN TO RISE AGAIN?

Edited by **Bong Youngshik and T.J. Pempel**

First published 2012 by The Asan Institute for Policy Studies
First Published in the United States in 2013 by
PALGRAVE MACMILLAN®—a division of St. Martin's Press LLC,
175 Fifth Avenue, New York, NY 10010.

Palgrave Macmillan is the global academic imprint of the above companies
and has companies and representatives throughout the world.

Palgrave® and Macmillan® are registered trademarks in the United States,
the United Kingdom, Europe and other countries.

ISBN (hardcover): 978–1–137–35743–4
ISBN (paperback): 978–1–137–35744–1

Library of Congress Cataloging-in-Publication Data is available from the
Library of Congress.

A catalogue record of the book is available from the British Library.

First Palgrave Macmillan edition: September 2013

10 9 8 7 6 5 4 3 2 1

EDITORS

Bong Youngshik

Bong Youngshik is a Senior Research Fellow and the Director of the Center for Foreign Policy at the Asan Institute for Policy Studies. Before joining the Asan Institute, Dr. Bong was an Assistant Professor at American University's School of International Service in Washington, DC from 2007 to 2010. He was also a Freeman Post-Doctoral Fellow at Wellesley College and Assistant Professor of Korean Studies at Williams College in Massachusetts. His research focuses on the interplay between nationalism and security issues including Dokdo and other island disputes in Asia, anti-Americanism and ROK-US alliance. He holds a Ph.D. and an M.A. in Political Science from the University of Pennsylvania and a B.A. from Yonsei University.

T.J. Pempel

T.J. Pempel is the Jack M. Forcey Professor of Political Science at the University of California, Berkeley. He served as the Director of the Institute of East Asian Studies from 2002 until 2006. His research focuses on comparative politics, Japanese political economy, and Asian regional issues. His most recent publications include, *Security Cooperation in Northeast Asia* (New York: Routledge, 2012, Co-editor with Lee Chung Min) and "Soft Balancing, Hedging, and institutional Darwinism: The Economic-Security Nexus and East Asian Regionalism" (*Journal of East Asian Studies*, 2010). He received his Ph.D., M.A., and B.S. from Columbia University.

CONTENTS

PART 4 TOWARD A MULTICULTURAL SOLUTION?

 **PART 5** IMPROVING RELATIONS WITH THE ASIA-PACIFIC NEIGHBORS

PREFACE

Japan's decline since the economic bubble burst in the early 1990s has been as spectacular and as confounding as its rise during the preceding decades. Once a model of rapid economic development and good corporate governance, Japan has since become a case study on how political and economic missteps and missed opportunities can lead to precipitous national decline. "Japan Inc.'s" inability to re-group after the "lost-decade," is a lesson on the importance of sound politics for a sound economy, among other things. The fall from grace of many of Japan's industrial giants such as Sony and Sharp has revealed the limits of Japanese corporate culture and governance structure. The Tohoku earthquake and the Fukushima nuclear disaster revealed not only the vulnerability of some of the most advanced industrial installations to the wrath of nature, but also how much political and bureaucratic ineptitude can add to the people's suffering.

For South Korea, its closest neighbor, former colony and one-time would-be emulator, the drama of Japan's triumphs and tribulations have been especially poignant. Ever since its independence from Japan in 1945, catching up with Japan became a national imperative for South Korea. At the same time, Japan became the model as well as a major source of technology transfer and capital investment for the development of South Korean industry. By the middle of the last decade, South Korea succeeded in catching up in certain sectors. By 2009, Samsung Electronics' operating profit was more than twice the combined operating profit of Japan's nine largest consumer electronics companies. In 2012, South Korea's credit rating became higher than that of Japan for the first time in history.

However, South Korea can hardly rest on its laurels as there are striking similarities between South Korea's growth trajectory and Japan's. South Korea's birth rate is the lowest among the OECD countries and its population is ageing at an even faster rate than Japan's. Welfare populism has become a political imperative even as welfare spending is already beginning to skyrocket. South Korean politics is proving to be as divisive and polarizing as Japan's. Learning from Japan has become an imperative, albeit for different reasons than in the past.

Japan's decline has profound implications for the region's geopolitics as well. Once the lynchpin of prosperity and security of East Asia, Japan's alliance with the US has begun to fray. It has become an object lesson in alliance (mis)management. More importantly, the relative decline of Japan (and the US) has coincided with the rise of China and North Korea's nuclear armament. That Japan needs to contribute its fair share to the maintenance of peace in this region is obvious. Whether it has the political will and sophistication to overcome historical issues and settle territorial disputes that continue to plague its relations with its neighbors all the while reasserting its role as a major power will prove crucial for the region's power balance.

Despite the immediacy as well as the importance of these issues surrounding Japan, they have yet to receive the full treatment that they deserve. The Asan Japan Conference of 2011 was planned to fill this gap. I would like to take this opportunity to thank all the participants to the conference, especially Professor T.J. Pempel for taking on the arduous task of editing the present volume. Most of all, I would like to thank Dr. Bong Youngshik, Director of the Center for Foreign Policy Studies, and Mr. Lee Ji Hyung (John), the center's program officer, for seeing this project through to completion.

Hahm Chaibong
President, The Asan Institute for Policy Studies
Seoul, November 2012

INTRODUCTION

T.J. PEMPEL

This volume is the result of a conference held by the Asan Institute for Policy Studies in November 2011. Organized in the aftermath of the crisis presented by the triple disaster that struck the Tohoku region of Japan the previous March 11, the conference had as its overarching theme "Japan in Crisis: What Will It Take for Japan to Rise Again?" Many authors began by addressing the question of what it would take for Japan to "recover" from 3/11 but, while that disaster was on everyone's mind, it was just the latest in a series of challenges that have plagued the country since the bursting of its economic bubble at the end of the 1980s.

To most of the chapter writers, for Japan to "rise again" would mean recovery not simply from the triple disaster—the March 2011 earthquake, tsunami, and nuclear meltdown—but from 20-plus years of almost unilateral economic stagnation, political fumbling, and deterioration in the country's regional and global influence. Returning to the halcyon heyday of Japan's economic successes in the 1970s and 1980s might be too much to wish for, but the authors were largely in agreement that recreating a sense of optimism about the future direction of the country's economy and politics would surely be essential to any meaningful "rise."

The most obvious concerns to many were dealing with the series of troubles associated with 20 years of slow-to-no economic growth; one of the industrial world's largest levels of public-sector debt; decades of unbalanced national budgets with debt repayment taking an ever larger segment of those budgets; an aging population and the rising health and welfare costs associated with that demographic shift; rising unemployment and underemployment, particularly among the country's youth; and declining labor and capital productivity—to name only the most obvious of the country's more formidable problems.

But Japan's lost two decades reflected more than economic troubles. The lethargic political response from Tokyo to the crisis of 3/11 seemed but the most recent manifestation of the deeper problems within the country's politics and the political system's persistent inability to generate effective problem-solving leadership. The country's prime ministers and cabinets had the shortest tenure within the 20-plus rich democracies in the Organisation for Economic Co-operation and Development (OECD), agencies seem to devote as much energy to turf battles as to resolving the country's monumental structural problems, policy stumbles and fumbles were frequent, and citizen trust in politics was laughably low.

Japanese society confronted problems of rapid aging and declining birth rates. But few solutions seemed palatable, including serious moves toward gender equality in the workplace, a less xenophobic resistance to immigration, or granting full citizen rights to Japan's long-suffering Korean minority.

Adding to Japan's myriad troubles were problems in its foreign relations. Its alliance with the United States showed signs of mutual frustration; Japan's Asian neighbors, but most especially South Korea and China, remained deeply mistrustful of its trajectory; and even cooperation on regionally common problems such as disaster preparation have been slow to develop.

Such an array of problems would be monumental for any country to confront. Dealing with all of them as a prelude to a new rise would likely confine Japan to immobility. Clearly some of the problems were hardly unique to Japan, and far more manageable to solve than what the country's and the outside world's often hyperventilating media might suggest. Nor did the conference participants have any illusions that some magic wand could be found that would eradicate them all with a wave.

Most of the chapter writers addressed quite specific dimensions of the current problems areas and went on to offer tangible and pragmatic proposals for action. Yet the range of the chapters and the problems they address make it obvious that any path toward reversing some of the worst trends of the past two decades will be strenuous to navigate and not without considerable painful departures from the path Japan now treads.

Starting with Fukushima

The first chapter is by Masakatsu Ota, Senior Writer, *Kyodo News*. Ota provides extensive analysis of the problems surrounding the nuclear meltdown following 3/11. He is particularly critical of two prevailing conceits. The first was the overwhelming belief by the political, business, and scientific communities in the safety of the nuclear plants, a phenomenon that he calls the "overshadowing myth" of nuclear safety. Key players in the nuclear industry and their supposed regulators within government shared such a strong conviction that the plants were safe that they became collectively vulnerable to the second problem, namely, failure to plan adequately for the kind of disaster that eventually occurred. In particular, though there was precedent for believing that a tsunami of nine meters or more could occur in the region, Tokyo Electric Power Company (TEPCO) officials and engineers in charge of disaster planning chose to dismiss such evidence and to rely on far less conservative (and less costly) models.

The result was that neither TEPCO nor the Japanese government handled the disaster well. Citing a post-crisis report by the independent government Investigation Committee on the Accident at Fukushima Nuclear Power Stations of Tokyo Electric Power Company, Ota highlights several key failures in the wake of the disaster. For example, the off-site nuclear response center quickly became dysfunctional because of loss of telecommunication infrastructure; power cuts; shortages of food, water, and fuel; elevated radiation levels in the building, which was not equipped with air cleaning filters; and so on. The Nuclear Emergency Response Headquarters in the Prime Minister's Office provided only a "disorganized and uncoordinated" response. Information was poorly collected and distributed to relevant agencies and to the public. Due to the tsunami, many monitoring systems for radiation were washed away, making it impossible to gain adequate monitoring data. And despite the many pictures showing calm and organized citizens at emergency shelters, the report was critical of the official disorganization and confusion at these shelters.

Further, Ota notes, right in the middle of one of postwar Japan's greatest single crises, the political leadership was engaged in petty bickering. The most symbolic political fiasco involved a harsh internal power struggle within the Democratic Party of Japan (DPJ) from the end of May to the beginning of June 2011, which ultimately resulted in the change of prime ministers from Naoto Kan to Yoshihiko Noda. As Ota notes, most ordinary people in Japan perceived this political tug-of-war during such a real national crisis as another unsurprising exposure of so-called "Third-Grade Japanese politics."

In the immediate aftermath of the 3/11 crisis, many people remained confident in the long-term future of nuclear power. But as Ota points out, the dissembling by TEPCO and by government officials generated increasingly negative sentiments among the Japanese public toward nuclear energy as well as a rising mistrust of the government and of the DPJ.

The Political Economy of Slow Growth

The next two chapters are by Gregory Noble and William Grimes, professors at Tokyo University and Boston University, respectively. Each analyzes Japan's longstanding economic problems from their respective vantage points as political economists. Using 3/11 as his starting point, Noble notes that the difficulties in dealing with the economic aftermath of that triple disaster will indeed be serious but that Japan faces more problematic longer-term difficulties, including the accumulated public debt, lingering deflation, and a suite of problems related to rapid demographic aging. Both Noble and Grimes identify the demographic problem as the taproot from which other problems grow. As Noble puts it, one of the country's most ominous trends is that "[t]he ratio of working-age adults to both children and old people reached 9.1 in 1965 in the midst of the miraculous growth period. By 2011, however, that figure had fallen to 2.5. The government projected it to hit 1.8 by 2025 and just 1.2 by 2050."

Thus, as Japan's aged become an ever larger proportion of the total population, the cost of providing them with services such as retirement and health care also increases. Yet in Japan social security is not actuarially based and hence 20 percent of its costs are now being funded out of general funds. Furthermore, as both authors underscore, the government has been paying for the rising costs of such programs largely by deficit finance. This in turn has meant that an ever-rising share of the government's budget has been devoted to debt service. Grimes points out that, since 1998, the annual Japanese central government deficits have equaled 4 to 10 percent of gross domestic product (GDP) and thus "[t]o say that the Japanese government is spending beyond its means is a major understatement." The result is that, as is well known in international financial circles, Japanese national government debt is over 200 percent of GDP.

This fiscal problem continues and is exacerbated by the nation's paltry tax revenues. As Noble points out, tax revenues in 2011 were no higher than they had been a quarter of a century earlier, despite considerable increases in population for most of that period as well as overall gains in GDP. Additionally, since 1997 Japan has been facing deflation, which has spawned "reverse bracket creep," further undercutting the government's tax revenues.

Yet Grimes sees some reasons for believing that the debt problem, which is so frequently cited as problematic, might continue to be managed and that conditions might not be as bleak as the oft-quoted doomsday figures might suggest. Net government debt is lower than absolute debt, interest rates remain low, the debt is in yen, and most of that debt is held by Japanese citizens or institutions. Japan is, for now at least, immune from foreign pressures to raise interest rates, nor is its currency at as much risk as if its debts were to foreigners. Thus he suggests, "one does not need to be a fiscal alarmist to see 2020 as an appropriate rough deadline for bringing Japan back into primary fiscal balance. This is in fact the basis for the fiscal reduction plans proposed by the Japanese government." But, as Noble points out, it is not at all clear that current Japanese citizens, and most importantly its institutions, will be willing to continue holding their low-interest debt indefinitely, or even until 2020.

Looking ahead, both authors offer some hope for reversing the downward trajectory of these interconnected problems. Noble points out that overproduction is likely to end by 2013, leading to increased demand for labor, a break in the deflationary cycle, and higher tax revenues. Even so, this reversal will continue to clash with the broader negative consequences of the demographic shifts.

He argues that, as a consequence, only substantial policy shifts can begin to deal with the longer-term economic difficulties. Grimes shares this view. Both authors point out that Japan is a low-tax country compared to other industrial democracies. The Japanese government has in recent years shown an ability to enact various difficult reforms, but clearly the present political structures have not been conducive to raising taxes as an approach to solving Japan's chronic debt overhang and dealing with the structural problems associated with an aging population.

Grimes is crisp in his formulation of the political difficulties, citing three key dimensions to the political challenge: (1) there are no winners from deficit reduction in the short run; most taxpayers will face higher taxes and/or social security premiums, while not seeing increases in benefits or services. (2) The second dimension is intergenerational; older citizens who would be the ones most harmed by reduced social services vote at higher rates than younger citizens. (3) Rural areas, which are most favored by electoral malapportionment, are also disproportionately populated by the elderly. Noble adds that there are additional political difficulties likely to impede reform, including the frequency of elections, the rapid change in cabinets and prime ministers, and bicameralism, which is picked up later in detail in Jun Saito's paper.

Grimes concludes that Japan is not facing a fiscal crisis for some time to come because there is plenty of potential to expand government revenues, and the problem can be addressed through a combination of incremental policy shifts rather than requiring sudden and drastic austerity measures, but that "the political obstacles are daunting indeed."

Agreeing with Grimes that, unlike the countries of the Eurozone, Japan has an independent currency and net national savings, which so far have spared the country from financial crises, Noble points out that Japan's very immunity has been a mixed blessing: "[u]nlike citizens in many European countries, Japanese voters have not seen the devastation that financial crises can wreak."

Hurdling Political Obstacles

Tetsundo Iwakuni, a former parliamentarian, largely agrees that Japan's problems can be laid at the door of the political establishment. He resonates with Ota in highlighting what he sees as the inept political response to the crisis in Fukushima. His sweeping indictment, however, goes well beyond the 3/11 disaster. In the aftermath of the disaster, he argues, a fundamental flaw in Japanese governance became apparent: the flaunting of authority, but no assumption of responsibility. From his perspective, Japan's problems run far deeper than a poor response to one disaster: he contends that Japan's "'governance crisis' has been developing for many years now—the confusion brought on by a lack of leadership, lack of established procedures, lack of planning, and lack of information, together with a general ethos of self-preservation and finger-pointing, have in fact become an entrenched mode of governance in Japan."

Most legislators are criticized for jockeying for power rather than serving the public interest. In Iwakuni's view, legislators' lack of attention to the public leaves the nation's top bureaucrats with far greater control over actual decision making, though they are not necessarily responsible to the public in their actions. Most damningly, he suggests that with no fewer than 18 prime ministers in the last 25 years, most function simply as pawns. In his terse formulation, the prime minister is not a "leader" but merely a "reader," reciting statements given to him by bureaucrats whenever he deals with legislators' questions in the parliament. Nor does he see the DPJ as having made much progress in its promise to exert political control over the bureaucracy. Lack of expertise on the part of the DPJ cabinet ministers left most of them beholden to the bureaucratic officials who allegedly were their subordinates.

Like Noble and Grimes, Iwakuni also underscores the overrepresentation of the rural areas in the electoral system, and he criticizes the weakness of the judiciary in failing to enforce more equal representation. He bolsters his criticism of Japanese politics by noting that media polls now indicate that the Japanese people's trust in their politicians has fallen to as low as 15 percent. "People ranked their trust in doctors at 81 percent, teachers at 58 percent, whereas the politicians ranked below fortune-tellers, who came in at 20 percent," he writes.

For Iwakuni, the solution lies largely in greater citizen involvement in politics. This would include a stronger role for the general citizenry in choosing party leaders through a more extensive primary system rather than the relatively closed process by which parties choose their leaders today. He is also encouraged by the rise in citizen participation that has emerged in the wake of 3/11. In many respects, the failure of the governmental world to respond more effectively left the door open for greater activism from citizens in the form of anti-nuclear protests, volunteerism in clean-up efforts, or in citizen use of radiation detection units to dispute claims that particular areas were "safe" from nuclear dangers. As he sees it, such moves suggest that "Japanese civil society is maturing to the point where it can demand accountability from the country's leaders."

Jun Saito, a political science professor at Yale University, also highlights problems in Japanese politics and the slowness with which it responds to crises. But his target is quite specific. He provides an analysis of what has become a major impediment to political decision making in today's Japan, that is, the revolving stream of prime ministers replaced on a seemingly annual basis and the so-called "twisted Diet," where Japan's two houses of parliament have majorities from competing parties. Both impede effective governance and the ability of governments to make unpopular decisions. At present, though the DPJ government has a majority in the more powerful Lower House, the Liberal Democratic Party (LDP) and its Komei ally have a blocking majority in the Upper House. As each side jousts for maximum political advantage, the LDP-Komei group has essentially blocked most DPJ policy proposals, making it all but impossible for the government to enact legislation.

Saito points out how unusual such a situation is in most parliamentary democracies, even those with bicameral parliaments. Bicameralism, he notes, has an inherent structural bias toward the status quo. However, usually an upper house has severe restrictions on its abilities to impede government-initiated legislation. In the Japanese case, however, it is virtually only the budget that cannot be blocked by the Upper House. The result is that, in Japan, an Upper House majority opposition can successfully create reputational damage for the incumbent cabinet, which in turn reduces cohesion within the Lower House majority coalition, leaving the prime minister vulnerable to the ongoing need to ensure his party's chances in the next election. The process, Saito argues, is equivalent to impeachment in presidential systems, which he notes would usually require a super-majority in legislatures.

Even worse, once majority control over the two chambers is split in a parliamentary system, agents within the political system incorporate the expectation that the current government's tenure is an ephemeral one. The incumbent prime minister faces insurmountable governance issues, including the enhanced probability of bureaucratic sabotage against policies that work counter to the bureaucrats' parochial self-interest.

This problem, though structural, proved largely irrelevant during the long dominance of the LDP, which held majorities in both houses. And even after it lost control of the Upper House in 1989, the LDP was often able to craft compromises with small parties in the Upper House to push through its legislation.

In the wake of the 1994 electoral reforms, however, Saito notes, the weights of urban and rural districts were rebalanced. Some shift away from the prior rural bias within the Lower House occurred, but that in the Upper House remains at perhaps an even greater level. Thus the median legislators in the two chambers now represent two different constituencies and two alternative policy preferences. Until such time as the institutional causes of this clash are removed, Saito concludes, it is unlikely that Japan will be able to avoid ongoing bicameral confrontation.

Toward a Multicultural Solution?

Kim Mikyoung, a professor at Hiroshima City University and the Hiroshima Peace Institute, tackles the issue of "Japan rising" through an examination of problems associated with Zainichi Koreans. For the most part these are ethnic Koreans who have been long-time residents of Japan, usually descendants of Koreans who immigrated to Japan after Korea's colonization or else those forced to work in Japan during World War II. This issue is particularly salient, Kim notes, because, given Japan's shrinking population, many have argued that one potential solution is a loosening of barriers against immigration and a move toward greater multiculturalism and social pluralism. Yet, as Kim notes, Japanese law has posed major barriers preventing such individuals from gaining Japanese citizenship and in the interim they are subjected to substantial legal and cultural barriers to full integration along with substantial discrimination at the public level.

As she notes, immigration control remains strict in Japan, but foreigners are currently being admitted in relatively small numbers, mostly as unskilled workers in two rather broad categories, ethnic repatriates (mostly Brazilians and Peruvians of Japanese descent) and vocational trainees (mostly Chinese and Southeast Asians). Though the foreign population in Japan rose roughly 48 percent from 1995 to 2005, the foreign total still represents well below two percent of the national population and is concentrated in a few of the country's larger cities. Ethnic Koreans constitute nearly 30 percent of Japan's total minority population. Kim notes, "the experience of ethnic minorities in Japan suggests that the road to multiculturalism is going to be bumpy. Accepting foreigners as a substitute for the dwindling Japanese labor force is a separate issue from acknowledging them as rightful co-inhabitants of the land. The latter is the policy domain of the government, whereas the former entails the cultural tolerance of the Japanese people."

Kim criticizes the overall resistance by the Japanese public to a welcoming integration of those who are ethnically or culturally different. Japan continues to demonstrate an underlying strength to the Nihonjinron contentions about the alleged uniqueness of the Japanese people. The Japanese government, business elites, and journalists continue to perpetuate the myth of ethnic homogeneity while images of cultural nationalism remain strong in literature and the moral education textbooks.

Thus, government policies perpetuate stereotypes of the "ideal Japanese family" as being a Japanese man and a Japanese woman who are married and have two Japanese children. Ironically, however, many Japanese employers resist hiring non-Japanese for any but the most menial labor, and Japanese public opinion polls show a strong proportion of Japanese continuing to express dislike for Koreans and Chinese. However, since the 1980s, some 80 percent of Zainichi Koreans have been marrying Japanese and resident Koreans now enjoy generally higher incomes than the median Japanese worker.

Improving Relations with the Asia-Pacific Neighbors
During the heyday of Japan's prosperity, the country was everyone's best friend. The United States looked for job-creating investments, for "voluntary restrictions" on Japanese exports that threatened American markets, and for greater contributions to the cost and substance of its defense. Economic ties with China were bolstered by Japan's willingness to break with Europe and the United States by relatively quickly ending sanctions imposed following the 1989 Tiananmen Square massacre and by substantial but rarely acknowledged development assistance. Much of the rest of Asia looked to Japan for investments, technology, and regional leadership toward the rest of the world while many European countries swallowed slices of their cultural pride and, like the United States, looked to Japan for investments and even lessons in corporate culture. Much of that has changed with the end of the Cold War, a deepening of intra-European linkages, the rapid rise of China, and 20 years of economic lethargy for Japan.

Kazuhiko Togo, a former ambassadorial-level foreign service official and now a professor, links Japan's declining regional and global role to the country's failure to develop a national consensus around its collective national goal. Such a goal was present during the phenomenal economic expansion as Japanese collectively mobilized toward achieving the goal of making Japan an "economic giant." But since achieving economic success in the 1980s, Japan has struggled to find a new banner under which to advance collectively. Togo proposes the Shizuoka motto of "Rich Country, Virtuous Country, and the Country of Mount Fuji," which, he believes, adds both a moral and an aesthetic dimension to Japan's reorientation.

With that slogan in mind, he then addresses the complex regional and global conditions faced by Japan, most notably a rising and increasingly aggressive China, an America anxious to retain its alliance with Japan but frustrated by many Japanese actions, a region uncertain about how best to forge closer economic ties, a Russia anxious to forge a new Eurasian strength, and a South Korea that remains skeptical of many Japanese actions. To deal effectively with the complex new conditions in the region, Togo argues for closer Japan-South Korea relations. These two "middle powers," he argues, should focus on common problems and work to advance regional economic structures, perhaps even common security arrangements.

The path forward, he acknowledges, will not be easy, given the remaining territorial issues, historical memory residues, and the perennial problem of North Korea and eventual reunification of the peninsula. But with a combination of goodwill and strategic calculation by both sides, he is convinced that cooperation is possible. And from such cooperation, Japan could well return to a position of enhanced regional and global diplomatic leadership.

One of the areas in which Japan has not been as proactive as one might have wished is in regional disaster preparedness, as Dr. Kim Sok Chul of the Korea Institute of Nuclear Safety points out in his chapter. Starting from the 3/11 disaster, the government's handling of which is examined in detail by Ota and criticized by both Ota and Iwakuni, Kim notes the many ways in which the disaster quickly became a transboundary problem but that Japan's neighbors, most especially South Korea and China, reacted to the crisis from a lack of adequate information about the ongoing nature of the problem and experienced social disruptions as a consequence. Reactions to the disaster itself were consequently misguided, but, more importantly, Japan's relations with the two countries were damaged as a result.

Kim proposes a specific trilateral disaster preparation mechanism, something he labels a regional situation awareness model, that would be created and implemented among Japan, South Korea, and China.

It would aim to deal with any future crises, including not just nuclear disasters but also climate change problems, pandemics, and other transboundary problems. Kim notes that East Asia has already made some progress on cross-border cooperation for problems such as regional haze; efforts are also being advanced to deal with potential nuclear terrorism. For him, responses to such region-wide problems must be treated as regional public goods that transcend any particular national interest, as a consequence of which regional cooperation is a must. This is particularly the case because China, South Korea, and Japan together contain 22 percent of the world's population and account for 20 percent of global GDP, and currently 64 nuclear power plants are in operation and 44 units are under construction within those three countries; together these account for 20 percent and 71 percent of the world's nuclear power plants in operation or under construction, respectively.

Kim's model involves the creation of a regional epistemic community through a three-stage cognitive process—(1) regional situation perception, (2) comprehension prediction and decision making, and (3) a collective mental model. The first step, regional situation perception, involves securing timely and correct awareness of the basic facts of any developing situation; gaining and sharing such information is crucial for effective disaster management. From this, it becomes possible to attempt to predict how the disaster will unfold and to reach common multinational decisions as to how best to cope with the expected problems. Finally, the "mental model" involves a variety of mechanisms to ensure collaborative reactions to any crisis. Among other things, this might include an experts group deployed from each country, integrated detection-monitoring across the region, and institutional arrangements at the bilateral or multilateral levels to ensure early notification and to provide disaster management support.

Ultimately, legally binding agreements need to be put in place, Kim argues, and these can be started through the trilateral summit headquarters now situated in Seoul. Moreover, he notes that any such trilateral agreement must also work toward cooperation beyond the three countries, including, for example, coordination with Association of Southeast Asian Nations (ASEAN).

Michael Auslin, Director of Japanese Studies at the American Enterprise Institute, follows with an analysis of the changing bilateral alliance relationship between Japan and the United States. Auslin notes the exceptional contribution of the bilateral US-Japan security alliance to the military stability in East Asia, which also provides a secure context within which the economic dynamism in the region can be promoted. The end of the Cold War eliminated a major threat within the region, but more recently both China and the Democratic People's Republic of Korea (North Korea) have been perceived by both American and Japanese defense planners as potential threats to the region's long history without shooting wars. Yet from an American defense planner's perspective, "restrictions on collective self-defense, as well as the general inviolability of Article 9 of the Japanese Constitution, continued to limit the amount of joint planning the allies could do and raised concerns in Washington that Japan would employ its military only under narrow circumstances."

American military skepticism toward Japan was by no means helped by the continual fumbling of issues surrounding the US Marine base at Futenma, an issue addressed by Togo as well. Despite an agreement to relocate the Marines to a new facility at Henoko and despite tentative plans for that transfer, the new DPJ government of Prime Minister Yukio Hatoyama announced that it wished to renegotiate the existing arrangements, largely to meet campaign promises to the Okinawan voters.

Not only did the DPJ seek renegotiation of the agreement, but, as Auslin notes, it sought to take complete control of the negotiations, "thereby cutting experienced bureaucrats out of the loop and endangering the long-standing working relations between Tokyo and Washington. These moves led to months of protracted negotiations with Washington, in which working relations became strained." Hatoyama's efforts were widely perceived, particularly in Washington, as little more than a monumental fumbling of a delicate bilateral issue by a political novice, and eventually Hatoyama found it necessary to resign in favor of Naoto Kan. But Washington's doubts about the DPJ have continued. Although the Futenma issue continues to fester, Auslin notes that both sides have been anxious to prevent any one such issue from poisoning the broader relationship.

Meanwhile the American defense establishment has applauded Japan's new National Defense Program Guidelines of 2010, in which Tokyo has committed to a new security paradigm of "dynamic deterrence," a doctrine that includes a strategic focus on its southwestern islands, the East China Sea, and the broader Asian commons as areas of primary concern. Moreover, Auslin notes, "Japan recently built its first overseas base since World War II, at Djibouti, which has been viewed as a testimony to Tokyo's commitment to protect its interests while providing public good from which its partners may benefit." But ironically he goes on to note that, though Washington has applauded such moves, they may also "portend a relationship in which Washington cannot take Tokyo's support or participation for granted, even as both approach shared security concerns from a national perspective. Instead, both sides will have to decide the best means of interaction after each has chosen a particular policy, even over concerns that are shared."

For the most part, however, Auslin sees the hard power dimensions of the bilateral alliance as driven by close and continued cooperation around a shared set of strategic objectives. As he notes, "the costs and difficulties of maintaining the alliance are far outweighed by the benefits the alliance continues to bring to Japan, the United States, and Asia as a whole." That said, however, he reminds readers that the broader bilateral relationship, with its interests in political, economic, and social cooperation, remains far more ambiguous.

T.J. Pempel, a professor of political science at the University of California, Berkeley, closes the volume by picking up the concerns noted by Auslin by suggesting that one way for Japan to improve several dimensions of its relations with the United States would be to participate early and actively in negotiations for the Trans-Pacific Partnership (TPP). He contends that the TPP could provide a liberalizing jolt to Japan's excessively rigid economy and a challenge to the entrenched veto groups so resistant to economic change that were examined by both Noble and Grimes.

Pempel analyzes four trends that he suggests militate in favor of this course of action. First, as has been widely noted, East Asia, including Northeast Asia, has become increasingly interdependent economically as a consequence of enhanced cross-border investment and trade and the development of regional production networks. Yet, as Togo also laments, Japan, which in earlier years was a key driver of this integration, has surrendered its prior leadership to a now regionally dominant China.

A good deal of Japan's decline as a regional economic leader has been due to its slowness to liberalize its domestic economy and its reluctance to move quickly to embrace the bilateral free trade agreements (FTAs) that have driven trade policy for so many countries in East Asia in the last decade. As Pempel notes, Japan has indeed entered into several FTAs (or as Japan prefers, Economic Partnership Agreements or EPAs); however, most of Japan's partners have been peripheral players in Japan's total trade profile, with the result that "only 14 percent of Japan's exports are covered by existing FTAs (or EPAs) compared to 56 percent for ASEAN, 45 percent for Hong Kong, 25 percent for China, and 28 percent for South Korea." And of course this lack of liberalization is congruent with the kind of economic rigidity that has been noted by so many others, both in this volume and elsewhere.

As Asian interdependence has risen, East Asia's dependence on the US market for the region's exports has diminished. This has been especially true for Japan, which now finds China as its major export market while the United States, which used to take 36-39 percent of Japan's exports, now receives far less than half that amount. The risk, as he sees it, is parallel to that articulated by Auslin, namely that the bilateral US-Japan relationship risks moving from its prior multidimensional cooperation and interdependence to one that is far more dependent on a joint military and security vision but not much more.

And finally as his fourth main point he notes that Japan joining the TPP would resonate with the Obama administration's explicit efforts to reengage with or pivot toward East Asia. The United States has recently endeavored to return foreign policy to its pre-Bush multidimensionality, including an engagement with East Asian regional institutions such as the East Asia Summit and a strong commitment to using American economic prowess as a diplomatic tool.

Sound as engagement with the TPP might be in the abstract, however, Japan has been stymied by political resistance from both the main opposition parties as well as from within its own DPJ ranks, obstacles that were identified by Grimes, Noble, and Iwakuni as well. The result has been that negotiations have proceeded quickly without Japan as of this writing, and negotiators are targeting the Asia-Pacific Economic Cooperation (APEC) forum meeting in November 2012 as the time for completion and a formal announcement of the TPP's launch. Japan, Pempel notes, may well be able to join the TPP at some later date, with all the potential benefits noted above—closer economic ties to the United States, greater economic leadership in East Asia, breaking the logjam of anti-liberalization forces at home, and the like. But delay will clearly be costly, denying Japan a role in drawing up the rules by which it might eventually be bound and, perhaps more importantly, depriving Japan of the chance once again to rise to a leadership role in the Asia-Pacific region.

As should be clear from this sketch, the chapters in this volume cover considerable territory with a variety of diverse perspectives. All agree on the desirability of a more vibrant and self-confident Japan—one that has been able to rise from the ashes of its two lost decades. But they also agree on how formidable some of the remaining obstacles to such a transformation continue to be. Yet it is only first by correctly identifying and naming the problems that decision makers can expect to move forward to solutions. We hope that our efforts have identified some of the main targets for change so that Japan's leaders and its citizens can move forward to forge a stronger and more self-confident Japan able to regain a meaningful role in creatively and effectively engaging with the rest of the world.

CHAPTER 1 Masakatsu Ota

The Fukushima Nuclear Crisis and Its Political and Social Implications

PART 1

STARTING WITH FUKUSHIMA

CHAPTER
01

THE FUKUSHIMA NUCLEAR CRISIS
AND ITS POLITICAL AND SOCIAL IMPLICATIONS

Masakatsu Ota

●

Masakatsu Ota is a Senior Writer at *Kyodo News* and an Adjunct Fellow for the Program on Global Security and Disarmament at the University of Maryland. Dr. Ota reports on nuclear related issues and Japan-US security relation. He served in the Hiroshima and Osaka branch offices of *Kyodo News* and was a correspondent in Washington, DC. He has written a number of Japanese books, including *Nichibei Kaku Mitsuyaku no Zenbo* [The Whole Picture of the US-Japan Secret Nuclear Deal] (Tokyo: Kabushiki Kaisha Chikuma Shobo, 2011) and *Atomikku gosuto* [Atomic Ghosts] (Tokyo: Kodansha, 2008). He received his Ph.D. in Policy Studies from the National Graduate Institute for Policy Studies (GRIPS) in Tokyo and B.A. in Political Science from Waseda University.

On March 11, 2011, Japan, the only nation attacked with nuclear weapons in the entirety of human history, abruptly got caught in another tragic, nationally traumatizing event, Hibaku—a Japanese word that means people and societies suffering from massive nuclear or radioactive fallout—without the slightest prior notification or pre-warning.

Following Hiroshima and Nagasaki back in 1945, and a Japanese fishing vessel, the Daigo Fukuryu Maru (Lucky Dragon No. 5), which was victimized by the US nuclear test near Bikini Atoll in 1954, the nuclear accident in Fukushima is the fourth Hibaku experience for the nation, which is internationally well known for its extraordinarily strong anti-nuclear sentiment.

Since the fateful day of the latest Hibaku, the Government of Japan (GOJ), the Tokyo Electric Power Company (TEPCO, a main operator of the Fukushima Daiichi nuclear power plant), and Japanese citizens and residents, especially in the surrounding regions, have each made hard and dedicated efforts to contain and recover from the unprecedented "Triple Crisis"—the destructive earthquake, a gigantic tsunami, and a gradually mitigated but ongoing nuclear disaster.

As one of the journalists who has covered this historical challenge and the present ongoing crisis, I would like to share my observations in order to tentatively summarize the political and social implications for the nation, which still has great potential to move on.

Interesting "Sea Change" and Political Fiasco

Dr. Tatsujiro Suzuki, the vice-chairman of the Japan Atomic Energy Commission, recently described the fateful day of March 11 in a succinct way, saying that "the day became one of historic proportions, forever to be remembered for a nuclear accident unprecedented in both scale and time frame."[1] As Dr. Suzuki pointed out, its "scale and time frame" has uniquely characterized this nuclear disaster in a way that illustrates some interesting political and social implications.

The scale of the crisis and its correlated social effects are so vast and profound that a strongly negative and accursed image of nuclear

---

1 Tatsujiro Suzuki, "Deconstructing the Zero-Risk Mindset: The Lessons and Future Responsibilities for a Post-Fukushima Nuclear Japan," *Bulletin of the Atomic Scientists* 65, no. 5 (2011): 9–18.

energy was decisively imprinted on the minds of the Japanese general public, which has viewed anything related to things "nuclear" with special sensitivities and bitterness for more than 60 years since the nuclear catastrophes in Hiroshima and Nagasaki. This anti-nuclear mindset has been clearly demonstrated in several opinion polls since the March 2011 accident.

According to an opinion poll conducted by the *Kyodo News* between March 26 and March 27, 2011, 39.5 percent of responders answered that they would like to see a new energy policy that calls for reducing the number of existing nuclear power plants in the future. Surprisingly, only 7.2 percent chose a policy option of immediately eliminating whole nuclear power plants, and 40 percent opted for maintaining the status quo. Before the accident, roughly 30 percent of Japan's entire energy consumption came from nuclear energy.[2] It seems fair to say that an initial reaction by the Japanese public after the accident was relatively modest and composed.

However, we can see an interesting "sea change" as the crisis turned into a prolonged struggle in the eyes of many Japanese citizens. In another poll by the *Kyodo News* in mid-May 2011, 47 percent of responders answered that they support a policy change to reduce the number of nuclear power plants all over the country. An additional 39.5 percent chose the status quo. Compared to the earlier poll, 7.5 percent more people have shifted toward a "Less Nuclear Energy World." This trend was accelerated by a sensational statement by then Prime Minister Naoto Kan, who publicly announced "Datsu-Genpatsu"(脱原発)—nuclear energy phase-out—in July. About a week later, a new poll found 70.3 percent of responders supporting the "Datsu-Genpatsu" policy set by Mr. Kan.[3]

We can observe that the extension of the time frame and the expan-

---

2 "Shincho/hitei ha 46% ni zoka" [Cautious and negative opinion increased to 46%], *Kyodo News*, March 27, 2011.

3 "Hamaoka genpatsu teishi, 66% ga hyoka" [66% positive on suspension of Hamaoka nuclear power plants], *Kyodo News*, May 15, 2011; "'Datsu-genpatsu' 70% sansei" [70% support phasing-out nuclear power], *Kyodo News*, July 24, 2011. Also, see "Seikatsusya no genshiryoku hatsuden ni taisuru ishiki" [Consumers' perception of nuclear power plants], Mitsubishi Sogo Kenkyujo, September 20, 2011. In this poll, 50.4 percent disapproved of policy that promotes nuclear energy, while only 13.5 percent approved.

sion of the scale of the crisis have left the general public more frustrated and distrustful toward the GOJ and TEPCO, both of which floundered during the early development of the crisis. Delays in troubleshooting and increasingly uncertain prospects of the situation gradually created an unfavorable and negative public receptiveness to the future role of nuclear power itself.

These generally negative sentiments toward nuclear energy echo the prevailing mistrust of the GOJ and its leading majority party, the Democratic Party of Japan (DPJ), among the Japanese public. There were a few important and decisive moments that strengthened this negative public psychology as the entire nation sought to overcome the unprecedented events and prioritize recovering and reconstructing its vast devastated regions hit by the tsunami and earthquake.

The most symbolic political fiasco was a harsh and ugly internal power struggle in the DPJ that could be seen from the end of May to the beginning of June 2011, which consequently resulted in the change of prime ministership from Kan to Yoshihiko Noda, Kan's finance minister. Most ordinary people in Japan considered this political tug-of-war during the middle of a perceived unprecedented crisis as just another unsurprising demonstration of the poor quality and unchanging nature of what critics called "Third-Grade Japanese politics."

Just two years prior, the Japanese public had elected the DPJ with a landslide majority in the Lower House of the Diet, sending a clear message and strong hope for change. However, after watching this political "Kabuki play," most voters, especially those who had voted for the DPJ, felt betrayed and abandoned.[4] A political implication brought in by these events is significant and profound, because, for many years, a majority of Japanese citizens acknowledged that the DPJ would be a reasonable and good alternative to replace the Liberal Democratic Party of Japan (LDP), which had controlled Japanese politics and decision making for more than 50 years. But, the internal political battle in the face of this real national crisis vividly demonstrated to the Japanese public how

---

4 A polling survey done by *Kyodo News* at the end of June 2011 showed that the DPJ had lost 4.0 points of its approval rating, dropping to 21.9 percent from the previous survey. The approval rating of the minority, the LDP, was 22.8 percent. See "Kan naikaku shij 23% ni kyuraku" [Approval rating of Kan cabinet rapidly dropped to 23%], *Kyodo News*, June 29, 2011.

self-interested and nasty Japanese politics can be.

In other words, the DPJ, a party formed as a political marriage of convenience designed simply to take power from the LDP, showed its true colors, because it had put "politics" ahead of "policies." There must be no argument that policies rather than politics must be prioritized when such a huge number of people suffer severely and seek urgent help from public authorities.

The GOJ's mishandling of the crisis response, especially at the early stage, and its incorrect management of the political scene has undermined public trust in its right to hold higher office. It is difficult to see any positive reversal of this general mindset among Japan's current political leaders in the foreseeable future. Worse, we should be concerned that their behavior is likely to weaken political cohesion among Japanese citizens, national leaders, and policymakers in the future.

Overshadowing Myth and Lack of Preparation
The aftermath of the crisis also revealed the unsavory nature of Japan's "Genshiryoku Mura" (原子力ムラ)—the small and exclusive circle of interests linked to the nuclear energy sector. Such revelations have almost irreversibly solidified the negative attitudes of the Japanese public toward nuclear power. One of the most important factors created by its nature and character is the so-called "Nuclear Power Safety Myth" (原子力安全神話), a zero-risk mindset that avoided looking squarely at the possibility of a severe nuclear accident.

An interim report published by an independent governmental investigative body unequivocally demonstrates how dominantly and robustly this ingrained mindset came to overshadow nuclear safety policies and crisis management guidance that had been established by both the central governments and the nuclear industry for almost half a century.

The report, issued at the end of 2011 by the Investigation Committee on the Accident at Fukushima Nuclear Power Stations of Tokyo Electric Power Company, provides several noteworthy facts correlated with the "Nuclear Power Safety Myth."[5] All of these facts strongly indicate how seriously nuclear safety procedures and nuclear crisis management systems had been hollowed out by long-term biases and the "business-as-usual" behavior of nuclear stakeholders.

Several crucial findings from the report are quoted below with my own additional analyses.

Finding 1: Loss of Functionality at the Off-Site Center

According to the "Act on Special Measures Concerning Nuclear Emergency Preparedness and the Nuclear Emergency Response Manual of the Government," once a nuclear accident occurs, a local nuclear emergency response headquarters is to be established close to the accident site to serve as the center of the emergency response coordination. A local response headquarters (Off-Site Center) is to be located at a local standing facility for emergency responses and measures. In the case of the Fukushima Daiichi Nuclear Power Plant, its Off-Site Center was located about five kilometers from the plant, but it could not function as intended.

This Off-Site Center had to be evacuated because of the loss of telecommunication infrastructure; power cuts; shortages of food, water, and fuel; elevated radiation levels in the building, which was not equipped with air-cleaning filters; and so on. In a nutshell, the Off-Site Center lost its ability to function because it was not assumed that nuclear disasters might strike simultaneously with an earthquake. Another reason for its dysfunction is that its building structure was not designed to withstand elevated radiation levels, even though it was intended for use in nuclear emergencies.[6]

---

5 "Chukan houkoku" [Interim report], Tokyo Denryoku Fukushima Hatsudesho ni okeru Jiko Chosa/Kensho Iinkai [Investigation Committee on the Accident at Fukushima Nuclear Power Stations of Tokyo Electric Power Company], December 26, 2011, http://icanps.go.jp/111226HonbunGaitou.pdf. Also see its English summary, Investigation Committee on the Accident at Fukushima Nuclear Power Stations of Tokyo Electric Power Company, "Executive Summary of the Interim Report," December 26, 2011, http://icanps.go.jp/eng/120224SummaryEng.pdf.

6 "Chukan houkoku" [Interim report], 4.

Finding 2: Disorganized and Uncoordinated Responses by the Nuclear Emergency Response Headquarters at the Prime Minister's Office

Once a nuclear disaster occurs, the Nuclear Emergency Response Headquarters (NERHQ) is to be established at the Prime Minister's Office with the prime minister as its head; its role is to execute emergency responses. Officials of relevant ministries and agencies at the director-general level are to assemble at the Crisis Management Center of the Government, located on the underground floor of the Prime Minister's Office, and to form an emergency data-gathering team. The team is expected to collect the information each ministry has obtained and co-ordinate their views with flexibility.

However, at the time of the accident, decisions on emergency responses were made primarily by the NERHQ, which is located on the fifth floor of the Prime Minister's Office. All relevant ministers and the chairman of the Nuclear Safety Commission of Japan convened there. Senior executives of TEPCO were also present.

The emergency team members on the underground floor could hardly catch up with the discussions taking place at the NERHQ on the fifth floor. Even though an integrated response by the entire government was of critical importance, there was insufficient communication between the NERHQ and the emergency data-gathering team in the basement.[7]

In other words, indispensable coordination for smooth crisis-management operation among senior levels of the GOJ did not occur at the initial stage of the accident because of a lack of serious advance preparedness.

Finding 3: Poor Information Collection

The Nuclear Emergency Response Manual stipulates that in an emergency, nuclear operators report relevant information to the Emergency Response Center (ERC) at the Ministry of Economy, Trade and Industry (METI), which is supposed to provide NERHQ within the Prime Minister's Office with appropriate information related to the accident.

However, at the time of the accident in Fukushima, there was no

---

7 Ibid., 5–6.

such smooth flow of information. The Nuclear Industry Safety Agency (NISA) staff and others at the ERC were aware of the need for prompt information collection and forwarding, but they were unable to do so because they had failed to install their own teleconferencing system in ways that were compatible with the one extensively used by TEPCO. Also, NISA did not dispatch its members to TEPCO headquarters for information gathering. In the end, they failed to be proactive in effective information collection at the time of the evolving crisis.

Collection of accurate and the most up-to-date information is a prerequisite for timely and appropriate decision making.[8] But there was no flexible and tactful operation for prompt information collection during the initial period of the crisis. This inflexibility and inactiveness almost surely came from the lack of preparation for an emergency response, which was never assumed or exercised before this nuclear disaster took place.

Finding 4: Loss of Radiation-Level Monitoring Capability

Monitoring data on environmental radiation levels is indispensable for preventing extended radiation exposure and planning evacuation of local residents. But during the early stages of the accident in Fukushima, as a result of many monitoring posts having been washed away by the tsunami or having become inoperative due to power cuts, the monitoring system lost substantial portions of its capabilities. In addition, in the initial stage of responses to the accident, there was confusion over the utilization of monitoring data. In particular, the government lacked a willingness to make the monitoring data promptly available to the public. Even when some data were made public, they were only partial disclosures.

In general, in order to maintain their indispensable functionality, any monitoring systems for nuclear disasters should be designed to survive severe circumstances like ones created by the tsunami and earthquake on March 11. Also, appropriate measures are supposed to be taken by envisioning the so-called "complex disasters" like the case of

---

8 Ibid., 6.

Fukushima.[9] However, necessary measures were not designed or taken before the accident. It seems that the "Nuclear Power Safety Myth," which avoids imagining serious consequences such as losing monitoring capability, must be seen as one of the root causes for the failure to establish and restore the early monitoring systems.

Finding 5: Disorganized Decision Making During Evacuation of Residents and Confusion at Localities

During the early period of the disasters, the central government issued instructions for evacuation several times. These decisions were made at the NERHQ, located on the fifth floor of the Prime Minister's Office, only on the basis of the information and views of the senior members of relevant ministries and TEPCO. There is no evidence that any official representing the Ministry of Education, Culture, Sports, Science and Technology, which is in charge of the System for Prediction of Environmental Emergency Dose Information (SPEEDI), was present at the NERHQ.

The SPEEDI system was designed to play an important role in planning for the prevention of radiation exposure as well as for the evacuation of local populations. But there is no evidence that SPEEDI was utilized in the decision making process. The investigative committee emphasized this lost opportunity, saying it should be pointed out as problematic that any thought of utilizing the SPEEDI system was totally missing in planning the evacuation strategy.

Also, a series of instructions given by the GOJ for evacuation did not promptly reach all of the relevant local governments subject to the evacuation areas that had been declared by the central government. Worse, the instructions were not sufficiently specific or detailed, bringing about a confusion at local levels in making decisions to evacuate, locating evacuation destinations and following actual evacuation procedures.[10]

This evidence also points to the prevalence of the myth of nuclear safety that had become ingrained in the government and in the electric

9 Ibid., 9–10.
10 Ibid., 11–13.

power companies. Both the GOJ and TEPCO had never fully envisioned any potential occurrence of severe nuclear accidents nor made their best advance efforts to prepare for containing or mitigating such disasters.

Suspicion of Negligence—Dismissal of Prior Risk Assessments

This ingrained "Nuclear Power Safety Myth" seems to be not only an obstacle against taking precautionary measures to contain a potential gigantic crisis and arranging for well-organized crisis management at the time of severe nuclear accidents, but it was also a grave root-cause for fatal negligence of scientific indications that could have avoided the tremendous loss of lives and assets that took place.

Several years before such a huge tsunami hit off the coast of Fukushima on March 11, 2011, a few internal scientific assessments were conducted by TEPCO specialists aimed at predicting the potentiality of a severe level of tsunami that might reach the Fukushima Daiichi Nuclear Power Plant. But all of these assessments, which could have been utilized as important indications of future serious tsunami disasters if a nuclear station operator chose to do so, were dismissed by senior officials of the nuclear power division at the headquarters of TEPCO.

As early as 2006, civil engineering specialists at TEPCO calculated the probability of a large tsunami hitting the Fukushima coast area by using a relatively modern risk-analysis measure, called "Probabilistic Safety Assessment" (PSA). Even though the original purpose of this study was to verify the effectiveness of the PSA method for tsunami risk calculation, its preliminary result was remarkable and suggestive.

According to an academic paper published by TEPCO specialists at the International Conference on Nuclear Engineering (ICONE) in Miami, Florida, held in July 2006, an estimated tsunami hazard curve showed that the probability for the occurrence of a tsunami larger than TEPCO's original assumption, 5.7-meters-high, was roughly 10 percent at maximum in 50 years. The paper also indicated that the probability of a tsunami higher than 10 meters was roughly one percent at maximum.[11]

One veteran senior nuclear specialist who was informed of this assessment after 3/11 made insightful comments in my interview with him in October 2011:

> This assessment based on PSA indicates a drastic increase in the probable occurrence of a larger tsunami than TEPCO's original assumption. TEPCO should have taken some emergency measures, which could be taken without tremendous difficulty in terms of social and financial costs.... They could have taken some interim measures like strengthening the water-tightness of key equipment inside the reactor and turbine buildings and deploying emergency diesel generators at higher places than the nuclear reactor or turbine buildings. But no overall effort was made under the authority of TEPCO senior leaders.[12]

According to this veteran specialist, a 10-meter-level tsunami would inevitably result in fatal consequences for nuclear reactors at the Fukushima Daiichi plant because these reactors were not designed to survive a high-level tsunami. That means that no precautionary measures were established that could protect minimum functioning of an independent cooling system if the reactors got caught in a severe tsunami. In other words, even though it was a low possibility, a tsunami higher than 10 meters would trigger a nightmare scenario of reactor meltdown almost automatically unless other back-up arrangements like early deployment of emergency batteries and key equipment were promptly and appropriately introduced.[13]

A TEPCO civil engineering specialist team conducted two other

---

11 Toshiaki Sakai, Tomoyoshi Takeda, Hiroshi Soraoka, and Ken Yanagisawa, "Development of a Probabilistic Tsunami Hazard Analysis in Japan," Proceedings of ICONE14, International Conference on Nuclear Engineering, Miami, Florida, United States, July 2006. Also see Masakatsu Ota, "Souteicho no tsunami gojunen ni 10%" [Larger tsunami than TEPCO's assumption occurring 10% in fifty years], Kyodo News, October 18, 2011.

12 Interviews with a TEPCO nuclear specialist on the condition of anonymity, October 4 and 12, 2011.

13 Ibid. According to the safety principles of the International Atomic Energy Agency, meltdown of a reactor should be minimized to less than once in 100,000 years.

notable tsunami assessment studies in 2008. Both studies applied data and analyses of past gigantic tsunamis that had previously hit off the coast of northern areas of Fukushima to offer future risk assessments. The specialist team used recorded data of the Meiji Sanriku Tsunami, which severely hit Iwate Prefecture, located about 200 kilometers north of Fukushima, in 1896, in order to gauge the extent of possible damage on the Fukushima Daiichi and Daini Nuclear Power Plants if the same level of tsunami were to occur. Its calculated assessment shows that Daiichi could be hit by a maximum 15.7-meters-high tsunami, almost three times as high as TEPCO's original assumption, 5.7 meters.[14]

At the end of 2008, another assessment was conducted internally by TEPCO civil engineering specialists. This study was based on a calculated source model of the Jogan Tsunami in 1869, which hit Miyagi Prefecture, located 100 kilometers north of Fukushima. This tsunami source model, back-calculated from the data of geological surveys on the ground, was not completely established in an academic and practical sense. But this model was provided by a tsunami specialist outside TEPCO in an effort to enhance risk assessment for the Fukushima nuclear plants. The study estimated a maximum 9.2-meters-high tsunami, another indication of a tsunami larger than any in TEPCO's original assumptions.[15]

But none of these assessments were taken into serious consideration inside the nuclear branch of TEPCO, because key decision makers there strongly believed that such extraordinary tsunamis were too unrealistic to ever occur, judging that it would not be necessary to take any concrete precautionary measures to deal with them as possibilities. There were some internal technical debates about building a higher coastal levee which was estimated to cost tens of billions of Japanese yen and to take four years to construct. But senior officials of the TEPCO nuclear branch showed no serious interest in this back-up option, referring these important assessments to the Japan Society of Civil Engineers

---

14 "Fukushima genshiryoku jiko chosa hokokusho; Chukan houkoku" [Investigative report of the Fukushima nuclear accident; Interim report], Tokyo Denryoku Kabushiki Gaisha (TEPCO), http://www.tepco.co.jp/cc/press/betu11_j/images/111202c.pdf, 10–11; "Chukan houkoku" [Interim report], 395–396.

15 "Fukushima genshiryoku jiko chosa hokokusho; Chukan houkoku" [Investigative report of the Fukushima nuclear accident; Interim report], Tokyo Denryoku Kabushiki Gaisha (TEPCO), 10.

for further detailed studies.[16]

As TEPCO emphasized, it seems these tsunami assessments in 2006–2008 were still tentative and at the trial stage, because the PSA method in tsunami study itself was not established as an adequate and complete procedure and the Jogan Tsunami source model used for the study was not formally consolidated.[17] However, the salience of such tsunami assessments for disaster planning is undeniable in terms of nuclear safety. As the aforementioned veteran engineer pointed out, it is possible to say that TEPCO missed opportunities to take some practical responsive measures that could have mitigated the ultimately severe consequences caused by a larger tsunami.

But TEPCO did not initiate any concrete actions to take advantage of these critical opportunities in order to beef up protective measures on the ground at the Fukushima Daiichi plant. Thus, the long shadow of the "Nuclear Power Safety Myth" seems to have affected crucial decision making inside TEPCO before the gigantic tsunami actually took place on March 11, 2011.

Conclusion

In this paper, I explained three specific factors that have significant political and social implications for the Japanese public in the long term. These factors are:

1. The internal political fiasco just a few months after the unprecedented nuclear disasters.
2. TEPCO's hollowed nuclear safety procedures and the GOJ's impractical crisis management systems that became clear to the public through post-disaster investigations.
3. Suspected negligence in not taking adequate precautionary measures as the result of dismissing the possibility of a gigantic tsunami that had been predicted through the PSA method.

---

16 "Chukan houkoku" [Interim report], 396–398; Masakatsu Ota, "Toden setusbi tanto busho ugokazu" [TEPCO nuclear branch did not take action], *Kyodo News*, November 28, 2011.

17 "Fukushima genshiryoku jiko chosa hokokusho; Chukan houkoku" [Investigative report of the Fukushima nuclear accident; Interim report], Tokyo Denryoku Kabushiki Gaisha(TEPCO), 10–11.

Already, some of these factors have generated negative public receptiveness toward nuclear power itself. One clear vindication is nationwide debate on restarting suspended nuclear power reactors after routine technical checks. On May 5, 2012, all 50 reactors across Japan were shut down for the first time in about 40 years. Just a few months after 3/11, pro-nuclear bureaucrats at the METI initiated efforts to improve the national environment in an effort to prevent power utility companies from having to confront their nightmare scenario—the complete shutdown of all reactors in a nation that had relied so heavily on nuclear power. But the reality, even after one year, remains stark and severe for them. The most recent poll just after the shutdown of all reactors showed that a full 54 percent of the public opposed any restarting of the Ohi nuclear power plant in Fukui Prefecture, with only 29 percent supporting its restart.[18]

In terms of policymaking and consensus building, the reaction of the general public must remain a key element for consideration. Especially in developing the future nuclear and energy policies of Japan, this dimension would have some special significance because of the nation's unique "nuclear footprint" in the past 70 years after World War II.

Of course, besides the three factors noted above, there are other important elements that have to be considered in an effort to deepen our understanding of the future implications brought about by the Fukushima nuclear disasters. For example, it is important to be wary of the now-exposed nature of the "Genshiryoku Mura," which stands as a symbol of a culture of collusion among both private and public nuclear stakeholders, the financially rooted connection between influential politicians and nuclear industries, and the historical collaboration among nuclear industries, pro-nuclear scholars, and a pro-nuclear mass media.

However, at this moment, the three factors elaborated above are major leading elements fostering the strong public mood of "Datsu Genpatsu"—nuclear energy phase-out. That mood rests on a loss of public confidence in nuclear safety policies and seems to be expanding, with the public inclined to pursue alternative mixes of energy sources.

18 "Ohi genpatsu saikado 'hantai' 54%" [54% oppose restart of Ohi nuclear power plant], *Asahi Shimbun*, May 21, 2012.

The fourth Hibaku for this nation, which was triggered by the massive tsunami and earthquake and exacerbated by a series of human errors before and after 3/11 both by TEPCO and the public authority, is likely to intensify the country's anti-nuclear atmosphere in the short run and solidify this social trend in the long run.

This prevailing anti-nuclear trend is also associated with the so-called NIMBY—"not in my back yard"—feeling among ordinary Japanese citizens. This NIMBY phenomenon has been manifested by the fact that almost all local governments are now hesitant to accept radioactive debris from Fukushima, even for interim deposit.

Noda's administration made a decision to push the export of nuclear components and related technologies later in 2011, and has tried to clearly differentiate its nuclear export policy from its domestic nuclear energy policy.[19] Nuclear exports by big Japanese industries like Toshiba, Hitachi, and Mitsubishi could become one future source of sustainable growth, a goal supported by a majority of Japanese people. However, the economic benefits produced by nuclear exports would not necessarily guarantee another "sea change" of Japanese public opinion, especially on domestic nuclear energy policies.

Also, there has been another argument that tries to give additional rationales to sustain the long-term national nuclear policy that had been established by the former majority party, the LDP, which dominated the Japanese political scene for more than 50 years. That argument rests on the claim that national defense demands require the current national nuclear fuel-cycle policy, including reprocessing of spent fuels used by reactors. Some conservative politicians and hardcore defense-minded bureaucrats in the GOJ advocate retention of the current national policy, which allows nuclear reprocessing and the production of huge amounts of plutonium. They claim that such a policy would provide "a potential nuclear deterrent" for Japan, which currently has no nuclear weapons as the result of its adherence to the Nuclear Non-Proliferation Treaty (NPT).

---

19 In December 2011, the Japanese Diet, both the Upper and Lower Houses, endorsed bilateral nuclear cooperation agreements with four nations—Vietnam, Jordan, Russia, and South Korea. At the voting, more than two dozen members of the majority DPJ bolted from the party's decision to support ratification of the four agreements.

Japan in Crisis

Since the Fukushima nuclear accident occurred, the Yomiuri Shinbun, a leading major national daily in Japan, has twice published editorials supporting the current nuclear policy for precisely this strategic reason.[20] But such an opinion, which would violate Japan's longstanding nuclear taboo, has never enjoyed wide-ranging support from the Japanese public. So, even from the national strategic defense viewpoint, it is unlikely that the anti-nuclear energy trend would be reversed soon.

The Fukushima nuclear crisis and Japan's day of "historic proportions," with all of its political and social implications, may force Japanese political leaders and the entire public not only to rethink and redefine the country's future perspectives, but also to redesign its overall national strategy by forcing the leadership to consider some fundamental questions regarding its national philosophy and grand vision: What kind of nation should we pursue in the long term?[21]

This of course is a gigantic theme that this paper cannot elaborate upon in any succinct manner. However, a few implications discussed above, most notably the negative receptiveness toward nuclear power as an energy source and a growth vehicle and the undermining of Japanese public trust toward political leadership, suggest some directions for further debate.

---

20 "Musekininna syusho no seisaku minaoshiron" [Irresponsible policy review by prime minister]," *Yomiuri Shimbun*, August 10, 2011; "Tenbo naki 'datsu genpatsu' to ketsubetsu wo" [Farewell to unrealistic "nuclear energy phase-out"], *Yomiuri Shimbun*, September 7, 2011.

21 Suzuki, "Deconstructing the Zero-Risk Mindset: The Lessons and Future Responsibilities for a Post-Fukushima Nuclear Japan," 9–18.

References

Asahi Shimbun. "Ohi genpatsu saikado 'hantai' 54%" [54% oppose restart of Ohi nuclear power plant]. May 21, 2012.

Investigation Committee on the Accident at Fukushima Nuclear Power Stations of Tokyo Electric Power Company. "Executive Summary of the Interim Report." December 26, 2011. http://icanps.go.jp/eng/120224SummaryEng.pdf.

Kyodo News. "'Datsu-genpatsu' 70% sansei" [70% support phasing-out nuclear power]. July 24, 2011.

———. "Hamaoka genpatsu teishi, 66% ga hyoka" [66% positive on suspension of Hamaoka nuclear power plants]. May 15, 2011.

———. "Kan naikaku shij 23% ni kyuraku" [Approval rating of Kan cabinet rapidly dropped to 23%]. June 29, 2011.

———. "Shincho/hitei ha 46% ni zoka" [Cautious and negative opinion increased to 46%]. March 27, 2011.

Mitsubishi Sogo Kenkyujo. "Seikatsusya no genshiryoku hatsuden ni taisuru ishiki" [Consumers' perception of nuclear power plants]. September 20, 2011.

Ota, Masakatsu. "Souteicho no tsunami gojunen ni 10%" [Larger tsunami than TEPCO's assumption occurring 10% in fifty years]. *Kyodo News*, October 18, 2011.

———. "Toden setusbi tanto busho ugokazu" [TEPCO nuclear branch did not take action]. *Kyodo News*, November 28, 2011.

Sakai, Toshiaki, Tomoyoshi Takeda, Hiroshi Soraoka, and Ken Yanagisawa. "Development of a Probabilistic Tsunami Hazard Analysis in Japan." Proceedings of ICONE14, International Conference on Nuclear Engineering, Miami, Florida, United States, July 2006.

Suzuki, Tatsujiro. "Deconstructing the Zero-Risk Mindset: The Lessons and Future Responsibilities for a Post-Fukushima Nuclear Japan." *Bulletin of the Atomic Scientists* 65, no. 5 (2011).

Tokyo Denryoku Fukushima Hatsudesho ni okeru Jiko Chosa/Kensho Iinkai [Investigation Committee on the Accident at Fukushima Nuclear Power Stations of Tokyo Electric Power Company]. "Chukan houkoku" [Interim report]. December 26, 2011. http://icanps.go.jp/111226HonbunGaitou.pdf.

Tokyo Denryoku Kabushiki Gaisha (TEPCO). "Fukushima genshiryoku jiko chosa hokokusho; Chukan houkoku" [Investigative report of the Fukushima nuclear accident; Interim report]. http://www.tepco.co.jp/cc/press/betu11_j/images/111202c.pdf.

Yomiuri Shimbun. "Musekininna syusho no seisaku minaoshiron" [Irresponsible policy review by prime minister]. August 10, 2011.

———. "Tenbo naki 'datsu genpatsu' to ketsubetsu wo" [Farewell to unrealistic "nuclear energy phase-out"]. September 7, 2011.

PART 2

THE POLITICAL ECONOMY
OF SLOW GROWTH

CHAPTER 02

JAPAN'S ECONOMIC CRISIS:
MORE CHRONIC THAN ACUTE—SO FAR

Gregory W. Noble

●

Gregory W. Noble is a Professor at the Institute of Social Science, University of Tokyo, where his research focuses on comparative political economy in East Asia. Prior to this position, Dr. Noble taught at the San Diego and Berkeley campuses of the University of California. He was also a Research Fellow in the Department of International Relations at the Research School of Pacific and Asian Studies, Australian National University. His recent publications include, *Political-bureaucratic Alliances for Fiscal Restraint in Japan* (Tokyo: University of Tokyo Press, 2011) and "The Decline of Particularism in Japanese Politics" (*Journal of East Asian Studies*, 2010). He received his Ph.D. from Harvard University.

J apan's crisis of 2011 stunned the world, as a massive earthquake followed by an equally massive tsunami killed more than 20,000 people in the poor northeast region, left hundreds of thousands homeless, and overwhelmed the defenses of many of Japan's electric power plants, leading to power shortages and a meltdown at the Fukushima No. 1 nuclear power plant. The government's faltering response to the nuclear meltdown further shocked the world. For many, both in Japan and abroad, these multiple crises seemed to symbolize and exacerbate Japan's longer-term problems, including the decline of rural areas and the incompetence of the political system, which seemed even less capable under the Democratic Party of Japan (DPJ) than it had in the waning years of the Liberal Democratic Party (LDP) regime that had ruled Japan for almost all of the five decades before the DPJ gained control of the cabinet in 2009. Partisan transformation, far from leading to reform and renewal, seemed to have worsened Japan's many woes, and the crisis in the northeast seemed to provide definitive proof of that failure.

This perception of abject failure in the face of crisis is not fully justified. If the government's response to the meltdown at the Fukushima No. 1 nuclear power station was indeed inept, much of the blame lay at the feet of the old policymaking system inherited from the LDP. Moreover, notwithstanding the impatience and exasperation of Japan's infamously critical electorate and mass media, from a comparative perspective, many aspects of recovery after the tsunami proceeded remarkably smoothly and effectively.

In contrast, Japan's longer-term problems, including the accumulated public debt, lingering deflation, and many problems related to rapid demographic aging, are indeed serious. The pressure on government expenditures is intense, but the slow-growing economy fails to provide adequate tax revenues. Aging also contributes to two other serious long-term problems: the decline in Japanese savings rates, which eventually will make it difficult to sustain payments on the country's massive public debt, and pressures on the employment system, which are contributing to economic rigidity and an increasing polarization of income and security. Japanese political and corporate leaders have carried out a number of important reforms, but structural weaknesses in Japan's political system make it even more difficult than usual to mount an adequate response to these chronic conditions. By the time Japan's excess savings dry up, in perhaps half a decade, Japan's accumulated public debt, already the highest in the developed world, will have grown even more astronomical. It could set off a massive financial crisis.

Crisis Response: Not as Bad as Advertised, and Not All the Fault of the DPJ

If the government's response to the nuclear crisis at Fukushima was indeed worrisome, the performance of the Japanese government in dealing with homelessness and rebuilding actually was, from a comparative perspective, quite good.[1] First, despite the immense destructive power unleashed by the magnitude-nine shake, few buildings toppled after the earthquake, suggesting that Japanese building codes were rigorous and well enforced. The rebuilding of key roads in the northeast was remarkably quick and effective. The British newspaper the *Daily Mail* reported on March 24, 2011, that "[t]he picture of gaping chasms in a Japanese highway [a photo frequently reprinted around the world] demonstrated the power of the March 11 earthquake. Now the astonishing speed of reconstruction is being used to highlight the nation's ability to get back on its feet. Work began on March 17 and six days later the cratered section of the Great Kanto Highway in Naka was as good as new."[2] According to the Secretary-General of the Organisation for Economic Co-operation and Development (OECD), "the Japanese people greeted tragedy with pride, dignity, perseverance and will power. The recovery of supply chains in the car and electronic device industries was unexpectedly quick. . . . The Japanese government committed 19 trillion yen (4% of GDP) over five years as part of the reconstruction efforts. As a result, less than a year after the disaster, GDP has almost reached its pre-

1 See Ota chapter, this volume.

2 Mail Foreign Service, "The Japanese Road Repaired SIX Days After It Was Destroyed by Quake," *Daily Mail*, March 24, 2011, http://www.dailymail.co.uk/news/article-1369307/Japan-tsunami-earthquake-Road-repaired-SIX-days-destroyed.html.

earthquake level. . . . This has been an amazing come-back."[3]

Foreigners were struck by the orderly and remarkably civil way Japanese government and society acted to help the hundreds of thousands of refugees. Naturally, delays and problems of coordination were also common, but they paled in comparison to the massive foul-ups following the much smaller Hurricane Katrina disaster in the United States in 2005, or the immense loss of life and delayed response to China's giant Sichuan earthquake in 2008. A month after the earthquake and tsunami, Malka Older, a Japan team leader with extensive international experience working for the International Mercy Corps, told the Los Angeles Times on April 14, 2011, "I've never seen anything like it, how all this came together so fast for these people."[4] Japanese reporters bitterly assailed their government's "bureaucratic logic" for the slow and inconsistent pace of construction of temporary housing for refugees, but their own data actually showed how remarkably quick and effective the response really was, especially given the heated debates about where the housing should be built and how it should relate to long-term reconstruction of the region (for example, how far back from the coast new buildings should be recessed). Construction began barely a week after the earthquake, and by the end of May—less than two months after the massive destruction unleashed by the tsunami—the completion rate for temporary housing was almost 50 percent in Miyagi Prefecture, and nearly 70 percent in Iwate Prefecture.[5]

The response of Japan's government and society to the threat of electrical blackouts also proved effective. In addition to the Fukushima nuclear plant, many other nuclear generating plants happened to be offline at the time of the tsunami, and the government closed others for emergency inspections. The tsunami also damaged a number of thermal

---

3 Organisation for Economic Co-operation and Development, "An Amazing Come-Back: Working Together for a Strong Recovery and Sustainable Growth in Japan," accessed June 14, 2012, http://www.oecd.org/document/39/0,3746,en_21571361_44315115_49920423_1_1_1_1,00.html.

4 John M. Glionna, "To Japan Quake Survivors, Temporary Homes Feel Like Heaven," Los Angeles Times, April 14, 2011, http://articles.latimes.com/2011/apr/14/world/la-fg-japan-quake-housing-20110414.

5 Toshihide Aikawa, "Kasetsu jūtaku kensetsu tachiokure no ura ni chiiki jitsujō naigashiro no 'kan nor onri'" [Behind the delay in construction of temporary housing: "Bureaucratic logic" that ignores local realities], Shūkan Daiyamondo, 2011, 13–14.

power plants in the northeast. Yet Japan reacted with orderly and effective conservation measures, such as limiting the use of air conditioners and moving some automobile production to the weekends. Blackouts and brownouts were minimal, as was the economic burden of curtailed industrial operations.

Finally, despite Japan's divided government and recurrent partisan conflict, as well as divisive debates about how to rebuild a region already in deep decline before the tsunami, the political parties came together to pass a series of supplemental budgets totaling hundreds of billions of dollars to clear rubble, repair roads, construct temporary housing, support small businesses and the unemployed, and begin long-term reconstruction.

Thus, the DPJ government's response to the various crises engendered by the earthquake and tsunami was not nearly as feckless as portrayed by Japan's always-critical media and public opinion, especially considering the difficulties governments everywhere face in reacting to massive catastrophes, and the unfortunate legacy of collusive nuclear oversight inherited from the LDP.

Long-Term Ills: Rising Costs for Social Welfare and Debt Servicing

Japan's longer-term problems—its chronic ills—are, however, sobering. Japan shares with most, if not all, advanced democracies serious structural problems, including increasing economic polarization, vulnerability to rising energy prices, and difficulties in competing with lower-cost rivals such as China and South Korea. Japan's biggest problem, however, is slow and uncertain economic growth, which in turn reflects to a significant degree the aging of Japan's shrinking population. The ratio of working-age adults to both children and old people reached 9.1 in 1965 in the midst of the miraculous growth period. By 2011, however, that figure had fallen to 2.5. The government projected it to hit 1.8 by 2025 and just 1.2 by 2050.[6] According to the World Bank, Japan's dependency ratio for old people—the share of the population over 64 years old—rose from 25 percent in 2000 to 35 percent in 2010, the highest

---

6 "Japan's Fiscal Condition," Ministry of Finance, December 2011.

and most rapidly growing ratio in the world.[7]

Aging, in turn, has contributed to a rapid growth in social welfare expenditures, which in Japan are dominated by spending on old people rather than children and families, or the poor, disabled, and unemployed; by 2011, pensions, long-term care for the elderly, and health care (much of it for old people) accounted for nearly three-quarters of all expenditures on social welfare.[8] Back in 1975, social welfare as a whole accounted for only a quarter of general or policy expenditures—all spending except debt servicing and transfers to local governments—in the central

Figure 1: UN's "Medium Variant" Estimation of Japanese Age Composition
Total population by major age groups

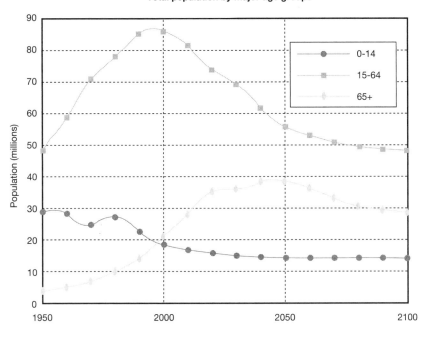

Source: United Nations, "World Population Prospects: The 2010 Revision," accessed June 14, 2012, http://esa.un.org/unpd/wpp/index.htm.

7 World Bank, "Age Dependency Ratio, Old (% of Working-Age Population)," accessed July 9, 2012, http://data.worldbank.org/indicator/SP.POP.DPND.OL.

8 Margarita Estévez-Abe, Welfare and Capitalism in Postwar Japan (Cambridge: Cambridge University Press, 2008).

government's General Account budget.[9] As late as 2000, the ratio was only about 35 percent. Yet by 2011 social welfare accounted for over half of all policy spending.[10] The "natural increase" attributed to aging accounted for at least one trillion yen per year, or about one percent of the budget.[11] For 20 years—from 1990 to 2010—spending on national defense, education, and science; the local allocation tax grant; and miscellaneous "other" items remained flat. Public-work spending escalated in the 1990s, but then declined even more sharply in the first decade of the new millennium. Only spending on social welfare increased.[12]

Table 1: Social Welfare Expenditures as Share of All Policy Spending (trillion yen; %)

	1970	1980	1990	2000	2011
General Account Policy Expenditures (A)	6.0	30.7	35.4	38.1	54.1
Social Welfare Expenditures (B)	1.1	8.2	11.6	16.8	28.7
B/A	19.0%	26.7%	32.8%	34.9%	53.1%

Note: Initial budget base. Policy expenditures [ippan saishutsu] = General Account spending – (debt service + transfer payments to local governments).
Source: "Zaisei no kenzenka ni muketa kangaekata ni tsuite" [Thoughts on heading toward healthier finance], Zaiseiseidotō Shingikai, Zaisei Seido Bunkakai, accessed June 14, 2012, http:// www.mof.go.jp/about_mof/councils/fiscal_system_council/sub-of_fiscal_system/report/ zaiseia231209/00.pdf.

It is important to point out, however, that while Japan is highly indebted, overall Japanese spending has not been high by OECD standards, nor has it increased particularly quickly in recent years. In fact, Japanese leaders have exerted considerable effort to limit spending and

---

9 "Shakai hoshō kankei yosan" [Social welfare-related budget], Ministry of Finance, accessed June 14, 2012, http://www.mof.go.jp/budget/budger_workflow/budget/fy2012/seifuan24/yosan012.pdf.

10 "Zaisei no kenzenka ni muketa kangaekata ni tsuite" [Thoughts on heading toward healthier finance], Zaiseiseidotō Shingikai, Zaisei Seido Bunkakai, accessed June 14, 2012, http://www.mof.go.jp/ about_mof/councils/fiscal_system_council/sub-of_fiscal_system/report/zaiseia231209/00.pdf.

11 Yasuhiro Terasawa, "Heisei 23 nendo shakai hoshō yosan: Genkai ga mieta zaigen no nenshutsu" [The budget for social insurance expenditures in F.Y. 2011: Limits to squeezing out revenues come into view], Rippō to Chōsa 303 (February 2011): 77–85.

12 "Wagakuni no zaisei jijō (Heisei 24 nendo yosan seifuan)" [Our country's financial situation (F.Y. 2012 government budget proposal)], Ministry of Finance Budget Bureau, December 2011.

Japan in Crisis

reduce waste.[13] Spending on public works, very high during the rapid growth period and then again in the 1990s as an attempt to stimulate the economy after the bursting of the financial bubble, came down sharply, despite howls of protest from Japan's legion of construction firms and declining regions such as the northeast. Spending on agriculture and small-business promotion also declined. Similarly, starting with Prime Minister Hashimoto in the mid-1990s, the Japanese government steadily and forcefully cut back on expenditures in the Fiscal Investment and Loan Program, the infamous "second budget" funded by postal savings and government pension funds.[14] Finally, for all the talk in Japan of wasteful bureaucrats, the number of civil servants in Japan is remarkably low compared to that in other advanced democracies; their total number has not increased since the mid-1960s; and their pay is, if anything, slightly on the low side.[15] The DPJ has largely continued the restriction of expenditures, though it has received little credit for its discipline because spending patterns have been distorted by the need to respond to two crises: the international financial crisis set off by the "Lehman shock" of 2008–2009, which sharply reduced Japanese exports, and the tsunami of 2011.

One other expenditure, however, is increasing ominously: service on the government's debt. The combination of growing social welfare expenditures and expensive economic stimulus packages in the 1990s contributed to a huge and ever-accumulating deficit. (Depending upon the observer, the stimulus packages were either a waste of money or indispensable but still inadequate to deal with the massive financial shock following the collapse of the financial bubble in 1990).[16] At first, debt repayment was not a problem. Slack demand in the 1990s and outright deflation in the early 2000s reduced interest rates to record-low levels,

---

13 Gregory W. Noble, "The Decline of Particularism in Japanese Politics," *Journal of East Asian Studies* 10, no. 2 (2010): 239–273.

14 Gregory W. Noble, "Front Door, Back Door: The Reform of Postal Savings and Loans in Japan," *Japanese Economy* 33, no. 1 (2005): 107–123.

15 Toshihiro Ihori, *"Saishutsu no muda"* no kenkyū [Research on "wasteful expenditures"] (Tokyo: Nihon Keizai Shimbunsha, 2008), 13.

16 Richard C. Koo, *The Holy Grail of Macroeconomics: Lessons from Japan's Great Recession*, rev. ed. (Singapore: John Wiley, 2009).

and eased the cost of debt service. Despite the huge run-up in debt in the 1990s, the costs of servicing the debt actually decreased for many years, fatally weakening the political will to deal with the chronic debts.

Despite ever-lower interest rates, however, interest paid on bond issues finally turned up in 2006 and continues its inexorable rise.[17] By 2012 the total cost of debt servicing accounted for just under a quarter of all spending in the General Account budget.[18] As interest rates finally bottom out and the government continues to rely on issuance of new bonds to cover half of all expenditures, the share of the budget occupied by debt servicing can only increase. The International Monetary Fund (IMF) estimates that, based on current trends, outstanding Japanese government debt will surpass the total household assets within a decade.[19]

Slow Growth of GDP and Tax Revenue

If Japanese policymakers have managed so far to offset some of the pressures from the ever-rising social welfare spending on the elderly by cutting other expenditures with unexpected vigor, why does Japan suffer such immense budget deficits? A glance at Japanese General Account budget documents provides a clear answer: in 2011, tax revenues were no higher than they had been a quarter of a century earlier, despite considerable increases in population (until 2005) and gross domestic product (GDP).[20] Through the 1980s, vigorous economic growth provided rapidly increasing revenues, even though Japan's tax base is narrow and riddled with exemptions, and the burden of taxation falls heavily on the most successful large companies.[21] Tax revenues peaked in 1990 at 60.1 trillion yen; expenditures increased proportionately less, to 69 trillion

---

17 International Monetary Fund, "Outlook and Strategy for Reviving Growth in Japan," September 8, 2011, http://www.mof.go.jp/about_mof/councils/fiscal_system_council/sub-of_fiscal_system/proceedings/material/zaiseia230908/01_1.pdf.

18 "Wagakuni no zaisei jijō (Heisei 24 nendo yosan seifuan)" [Our country's financial situation (F.Y. 2012 government budget proposal)], Ministry of Finance Budget Bureau, December 2011.

19 "Zaisei no kenzenka ni muketa kangaekata ni tsuite" [Thoughts on heading toward healthier finance].

20 "Wagakuni no zaisei jijō (Heisei 24 nendo yosan seifuan)" [Our country's financial situation (F.Y. 2012 government budget proposal)], Ministry of Finance Budget Bureau, December 2011.

21 Sven Steinmo, The Evolution of Modern States: Sweden, Japan, and the United States (Cambridge: Cambridge University Press, 2010).

yen, and Japan seemed on the road to fiscal recovery. Then the financial bubble burst, and by 2007, revenue slipped to 51 trillion yen. After the Lehman shock, revenue slumped even more disastrously to 38.7 trillion yen in 2009, below the level of 1979.

Revenue recovered only slightly to 42.4 trillion yen in the initial budget draft for 2012. Expenditures, meanwhile, surged after the Lehman shock to 101 trillion yen in 2009 before dropping sharply to 90.3 trillion yen in 2012. Thus, while population aging is indeed exerting upward pressure on expenditures, and exogenous shocks such as the Lehman Brothers crisis and the Fukushima earthquake have temporarily exacerbated deficits, the most pressing problem is complete stagnation in tax revenues extending now a full generation.

Collapsing tax revenues, in turn, reflect slow and uncertain economic growth after the bursting of the financial bubble, and the repeated tax cuts enacted in the late 1990s and early 2000s in an attempt to counteract the ensuing downturn. From 1997, Japan fell into deflation, creating a kind of "reverse bracket creep," further undermining tax revenues. In 2010, nominal GDP was lower than it had been in 1994. Corporate profits, and thus revenues from the corporate tax, did not begin to recover from the "balance sheet recession" until well into Koizumi's term as prime minister in the mid-2000s.[22]

While weak tax revenues and demographic aging have combined to exert tremendous pressure on Japanese budget balances, the most immediate economic problem has been a mismatch between excess production capacity and shrinking demand. The contraction of the working-age population beginning in the mid-1990s did not immediately become a major constraint on economic activity because the collapse of the bubble left many firms with excess capacity and thus excess workers. In the "balance sheet recession," managers were more concerned with cutting debt and saving their companies (and executive positions) than with pursuing investments in profitable new opportunities.[23] As a result, aggregate investment dropped sharply. From 1990 to 2010, gross fixed capital investment in Japan declined by more than one-third,

22 "Financial and Economic Statistics Monthly," Bank of Japan, February 2012.

23 Koo, *The Holy Grail of Macroeconomics: Lessons from Japan's Great Recession*.

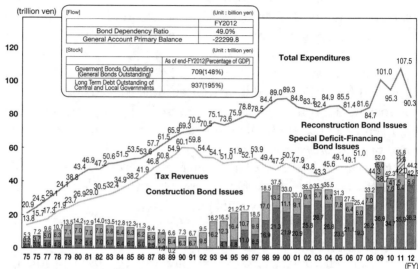

Figure 2: Japanese Government's Total Expenditures

(Note 1) FY1975-2010: Settlement, FY2011: 4th Revised budget, FY2012: Draft budget

(Note 2) AD-hoc deficit-financing bonds (approx, 1 trillion yen) were issued in FY1990 as a source of funds to support peace and reconstruction efforts in the Persian Gulf Region.

(Note 3) Reconstruction bonds (approx.11.6)trillion yen are issued in FY2011, which are used as a temporary means until when the finacial resources are secured by the revenues including the special tax for reconstruction. Measures and projects for reconstruction from the Great East Japan Earthquake, expected to be implemented within the first five years (FY2011-FY2015), would be financed by reconstruction bonds issuance.

(Note 4) General Account Primary Balance is calculated based on the easy-to-use method of National Debt Service minus Government Bond Issues, and is different from the Central Government Primary Balance on an SNA basis.

Source: "Japan's Fiscal Condition," Ministry of Finance, December 2011.

amounting to a drop of almost 12 percent of GDP. Virtually all sectors experienced declining investment. The decrease in the government sector reflected primarily sustained efforts to reduce the level of public works from their peak in the late 1990s. The drop in private residential construction reacted to the speculative overbuilding of the bubble period, as well as the drop in incomes in the late 1990s and early 2000s. Private nonresidential investment, primarily by Japan's manufacturing sector, recovered after 2003, but then slumped again in the wake of the Lehman shock, and then the Fukushima crises.[24]

In the mid-2000s, during the latter half of Koizumi's prime ministership, firms finally disposed of most of their excess capacity, and demand for labor strengthened briefly, but with the Lehman shock, excess

---

24 "Tankan Summary," Bank of Japan, December 15, 2011.

Japan in Crisis

capacity reappeared yet again. From 2001 to 2010, real GDP grew at an average of only 0.75 percent per year, even less than Japan's low and unstable rate of growth in hourly labor productivity, thus depressing demand for labor.[25]

To be sure, gross fixed capital investment has declined in most advanced industrial democracies, and a good case can be made that Japan's traditional investment rate was excessively high, the product of particularistic politics and a defective corporate governance system that indulged far too many marginal or even unprofitable investments. Even if readjustment to a lower rate of investment was rational in the long run, however, the speed and persistence of decline placed a heavy deflationary weight on the Japanese economy. Huge government budget deficits only partly lightened that burden, and at a high cost to the government's long-term solvency.

Starting in 2013 or 2014, excess capacity should finally disappear, and the labor market should begin experiencing more sustained shortages.[26] This should exert upward pressure on wages and thus increase household incomes and consumption, helping Japan to break out of the deflationary cycle. Yet, over the longer run, the decline of the workforce-age population in both absolute and relative terms will tend to reduce income, investment, GDP, and tax revenue. Even before the Fukushima catastrophes, OECD analysts estimated Japan's potential rate of growth in economic output at less than one percent per year.[27] The shift of consumer demand to health and elder care also means that many of the new jobs will appear in relatively labor-intensive sectors resistant to increases in productivity and incomes.

The combination of slow growth and aging citizens is decimating Japan's once-healthy savings rate. In the early 1990s, Japanese households saved about 15 percent of their income, double that of American

---

25 "Gross Domestic Product," Ministry of Internal Affairs and Communications, Statistics Bureau, accessed July 10, 2012, http://www.stat.go.jp/data/getujidb/zuhyou/c01-3.xls; "Productivity Statistics," Japan Productivity Center, accessed June 14, 2012, http://www.jpc-net.jp/eng/ stats/index.html.

26 "Tankan Summary," Bank of Japan.

27 Luiz de Mello and Pier C. Padoan, "Promoting Potential Growth: The Role of Structural Reform," Organisation for Economic Co-operation and Development, Economics Department Working Paper no. 793, July 20, 2010.

households, but by 2008 (the latest year for which comparable data are available) Japan trailed the United States 2.3 percent to 4.2 percent.[28] On current trends, Japanese household saving is likely to turn negative within the next five years.[29] The Ministry of Finance will have to sell bonds not just to Japanese but also to foreigners, who have more investment options and will demand higher interest rates. Debt-servicing costs will surge, and may enter a deadly upward spiral.[30]

To be sure, households are not the only source of savings: since emerging from the recession, Japanese corporations have raised their savings rates, and they own hundreds of billions of dollars in assets abroad. Those assets produce profits that can come back to Japan as income. The stream of income should help keep Japan's current account in the black even as household savings continue to shrink. In a pinch, companies could sell some of the assets.

Nothing guarantees, however, that Japanese corporations will continue seeing their interests as largely congruent with those of Japanese society and the Japanese government, not least because the share of foreign ownership of companies on the Tokyo Stock Exchange has been climbing steadily, reaching nearly 27 percent of total market value in 2010.[31] As the mountain of debt pressing on the slow-growing Japanese economy grows, stockholders will have to ask why they should repatriate funds back into such a risky and low-growing environment. Even if they were moved by patriotic sentiments, or by appeals and arm-twisting from the Japanese government, they would face a serious collective action dilemma: if many firms yield to temptation and keep their funds abroad, firms that do repatriate funds could lose them to a crisis or a surge of inflation resulting from a sharp drop in bond prices. Already, the leading Japanese business magazines are beginning to carry articles

---

28 Organisation for Economic Co-operation and Development, "OECD Factbook 2011-2012," accessed June 14, 2012, http://www.oecdilibrary.org/economics/oecd-factbook_18147364.

29 Kazuyoshi Nakata, "Nihon no kakei chochikuritsu no chōkiteki na dōkō to kongo no tenbō" [Long-term trends and future prospects of Japan's household savings rate], *Kikan Seisaku/Keiei Kenkyū* 1 (2009): 113–128.

30 Martin Feldstein, "Japan's Savings Crisis," *Project Syndicate*, September 24, 2010, http://www.project-syndicate.org/commentary/japan-s-savings-crisis.

31 "2010 Share Ownership Survey," Tokyo Stock Exchange, accessed July 10, 2012, http://www.tse.or.jp/english/market/data/shareownership/b7gje60000003t0u-att/e_bunpu2010.pdf.

on the dangers—and appeal—to both companies and individual investors of capital flight.[32] For the moment, those articles are not terribly persuasive: the amounts of money moving abroad are not unusual, nor are the incentives powerful. The seemingly inexorable growth of public debt, however, raises the possibility that before too many years, bond prices could suffer a devastating shock.

The Employment Dilemma

Accumulated debt, deflation, and population aging have combined to exacerbate the rigidity of Japan's employment system, and undermine efforts to accelerate the pace of economic transition and stimulate growth of tax revenue. Japanese-style employment practices, such as seniority wages, company unions, and long-term employment, are controversial and many see them as outmoded. Scholars traditionally emphasized that "permanent employment" emerged in full form only in the postwar period, was mostly limited to males in large firms, and was often an ambiguous understanding rather than an enforceable agreement.[33] Neo-classical economists were never fond of permanent employment, and after the bursting of the financial bubble in the early 1990s, they became even more critical of permanent employment for reducing economic flexibility and limiting the employment opportunities of women, the young, and the elderly.[34] Since the bursting of the bubble economy and the steady increase in temporary or part-time "irregular" employees, who now account for over one-third of the workforce, many economists and business executives have come to ridicule permanent employment as a "delusion."[35]

In fact, their views better deserve the title "delusion," or perhaps "wishful thinking." Permanent employment still has powerful roots in

---

32 See, e.g., the cover story "Shisan tōhi" [Asset flight] in *Nikkei Bijinesu*, February 13, 2012.

33 Robert E. Cole, "The Theory of Institutionalization: Permanent Employment and Tradition in Japan," *Economic Development and Cultural Change* 20, no. 1 (1971): 47–70.

34 Naohiro Yashiro, *Rōdō shijō kaikaku no keizaigaku: Seishain "hogo shugi" no owari* [The economics of labor market reform: The end of "protection" of regular workers] (Tokyo: Tōyō Keizai Shinpōsha, 2009).

35 "Shūshin koyō to iu gensō wo suteyo: Sangyō kōzō henka ni atta koyō shisutemu ni tenkan wo" [Abandon the illusion of permanent employment: Shifting to an employment system suited to changes in industrial structure], National Institute for Research Advancement, 2009.

Japan. Employment patterns have changed somewhat, of course, but by no means completely: company unions have declined, but while seniority wages have come under considerable strain, they have by no means been completely replaced by "merit" wages.[36] Long-term employment, in particular, has deep roots in Japan's Constitution (Articles 25 and 27) and legal structure. Even small firms must meet a demanding "four conditions" test before dismissing "regular" workers.[37] Mass hiring of new school graduates (shinsotsu ikkatsu saiyō) has, if anything, grown stronger, and mid-career hires remain limited.[38] In sharp contrast to the Anglo-American model of employment and the famed fluidity of Silicon Valley, mobility of research and development personnel in Japan is extraordinarily low.

It is true that the permanent employment system faces tremendous pressure. Back in the high-growth period of the 1950s and 1960s, long-term employment for core workers was attractive to employees and relatively economical for companies: young workers accepted low initial wages in return for the prospect of steady promotions and steep salary increases. In the 1970s and 1980s, however, workers grew better educated and the rate of promotion and wage increases stalled; "permanent employment" came to seem as much shackle as lifesaver, impeding the progress of the most talented and aggressive employees and forcing workers to stick with their employers no matter what. For companies, the salary profile grew more burdensome as inexpensive entry-level workers aged into well-paid middle managers with fewer and fewer younger employees under them. Companies reacted by forcing some employees to retire early and by hiring a wide variety of temporary and part-time employees—some actually performing for extended periods virtually the same jobs as core employees—at roughly half the wages. The resulting lightening of employment expenditures and increased flexibility contributed to the improvement in corporate finances noted above, but at a high cost to workers, especially those who left school after the mid-

36 Harald Conrad, "From Seniority to Performance Principle: The Evolution of Pay Practices in Japanese Firms since the 1990s," *Social Science Japan Journal* 13, no. 1 (2010): 115–135.

37 Akira Okuyama, *Rōdō hō* [Labor law] (Tokyo: Shinsei-sha, 2006).

38 "'Shin sotsu saiyō' no chōryū to kadai" ["Employment of new graduates"—Trends and Issues], Recruit Works Institute, November 2010, 6–8.

1990s. Unions have protested wage stringency and the shift to irregular workers, but they cover an ever-shrinking share of the workforce (18.5 percent in 2010; MHLW 2011). Stagnant income for workers means stagnant domestic demand for companies' products and services, exacerbating the deflationary spiral in a kind of financial "anorexia."[39]

As permanent employment has shrunk, however, the alternatives to it have grown increasingly unappealing: working part-time or temporary jobs for low wages, with little hope of graduating to more lucrative and challenging career positions, and with little support from a restrictive and stingy system of unemployment insurance. Surveys show that young workers have rediscovered the merits of permanent employment: the proportion of new employees supporting the permanent employment system, once in steady decline, has reached all-time highs in recent years.[40] Political parties are also reluctant to undermine permanent employment further. Policy revisions under Prime Minister Koizumi that allowed temporary employment agencies to expand their ambit to include placements in the manufacturing sector created a strong backlash. Similarly, repeated calls to reduce or eliminate the tax breaks directed at housewives married to permanent workers have fallen on deaf ears.

Thus, while the system of long-term employment has been compressed, it is far from gone, and social and political support for it is, if anything, growing. Unfortunately, permanent employment exacerbates the rigidity and stasis of Japan's low-growth economy. Companies find it difficult to shutter or sell under-performing divisions. Well-educated and highly skilled employees such as engineers and researchers are still overwhelmingly covered by permanent employment, and without access to skilled employees, it is difficult to create or expand new firms.

In the early 2000s, it seemed that things were finally turning around, partly thanks to an unprecedented (though in comparative perspective still modest) boom in inward foreign investment and increasing diversity and flexibility of capital markets. New firms appeared and

---

39 Richard Katz, *Japanese Phoenix: The Long Road to Economic Recovery* (Armonk: M.E. Sharpe, 2003).

40 "2011 nendo shin nyū shain no kaisha seikatsu chōsa" [Survey of the company lifestyles of new employees, 2011], Sangyō Nōritsu Daigaku, June 2011.

were listed on new high-tech stock exchanges, venture capital suddenly expanded, and mergers and acquisitions soared.[41]

Just as scholars grew excited by Japan's newfound dynamism, however, the boom collapsed. Virtually all indicators, from inward direct foreign investment to mergers to venture capital, began to turn down even before the Lehman shock, and have remained depressed or grown even more dismal since then.[42] Would-be entrepreneurs attract few colleagues and even fewer with experience in founding or growing companies. In a recent survey of 23 advanced countries, barely six percent of Japanese respondents perceived entrepreneurial opportunities, by far the lowest share in any country and less than one-sixth the average; only 26 percent of Japanese viewed entrepreneurship as a good career choice, again by far the lowest response, and well under half the average.[43]

As for those largely excluded from the permanent employment paradigm, such as women and less-educated people, they are surprisingly resistant to calls to strengthen Japan's system of unemployment and social welfare so as to make it realistic to move away from permanent employment. Apparently, decades of living under the particularistic LDP policy regime led them to conclude that if they supported a "high tax, high benefit" model, they would pay higher taxes (particularly consumption taxes) but would fail to receive more benefits in return.[44]

The Response of the Political System:
Steady but Still Insufficient Reform

One can argue that Japan's demographic and economic problems, while daunting, are not categorically different from those of other aging countries, particularly in Europe, and that with only modest reforms Japan

---

41 Ulrike Schaede, *Choose and Focus: Japanese Business Strategies for the 21st Century* (Ithaca: Cornell University Press, 2008).

42 Gregory W. Noble, "Party Dynamics and the Myth of the Myth of Permanent Employment" (paper prepared for delivery at the Joint Conference of the Association for Asian Studies and the International Convention of Asia Scholars, Honolulu, Hawaii, United States, March 31–April 3, 2011).

43 Donna J. Kelley, Slavica Singer, and Mike Herrington, "GEM 2011 Global Report," *Global Entrepreneurship Monitor*, accessed June 14, 2012. http://www.gemconsortium.org/docs/download/2201.

44 Shogo Takegawa, "Liberal Preferences and Conservative Policies: The Puzzling Size of Japan's Welfare State," *Social Science Japan Journal* 13, no. 1 (2010): 53–56.

could maintain itself quite well.[45] Japan has done an excellent job of restraining the cost of health care while supporting the longest-lived population in the world, and the burden of pensions will not keep increasing indefinitely—demographic projections suggest that by the middle of this century the share of the elderly in Japan's population will begin to decline. This optimistic perspective is a useful reminder that Japan's problems are not inherently insoluble, and that aging is not Japan's only problem: so far, deflation has been more of an impediment to growth, while the rising cost of health care is a function not just of aging but also of expensive technological advances.

Nonetheless, the optimistic view rests on some bold assumptions. For example, some of the techniques Japan has used to restrain budgetary expenditures so far, such as cutting public works and reducing reimbursement to physicians and hospitals, cannot continue indefinitely. More important, the optimistic view slides all too quickly over the huge gap in tax rates between Japan and Europe, and Japan's much higher burden of accumulated government debt. As of 2009, the ratio of tax revenues to GDP in the five largest European economies (Germany, France, the United Kingdom, Italy, and Spain) averaged 37.6 percent, more than 10 percentage points higher than the share of taxes in Japan's economy.[46] Moreover, Japan faces a far larger overhang of debt: in 2010 gross government financial liabilities equaled 200 percent of Japan's GDP, more than double the 98 percent average of all OECD countries, itself well over the 90 percent danger line identified by Reinhart and Rogoff.[47] Much of Japan's debt is held by domestic banks; if increasing indebtedness shakes confidence in the government's credibility, Japanese banks could find their assets shrinking before their eyes, leading to a credit crisis. If Japan is to maintain even its current modest welfare state in the face of a still-aging society and regain some semblance of balance in its public finances, it will need to prune expenditures, improve efficiency, and above all raise taxes sharply.

45 John C. Campbell, "The Political Economy of Aging in Japan" (presentation, Contemporary Japan Group, Institute of Social Science, University of Tokyo, January 26, 2012).

46 Organisation for Economic Co-operation and Development, "Total Tax Revenue as Percentage of GDP," accessed June 14, 2012, http://www.oecd.org/dataoecd/13/38/46721091.xls.

47 Organisation for Economic Co-operation and Development, "OECD Factbook 2011-2012," 1-9.

It is certainly not the case that the Japanese political system is completely incapable of reform. Since the LDP first lost control of the Lower House of the Diet in 1993, many reforms have passed, including electoral and campaign laws that strengthen parties and the Cabinet relative to party backbenchers; regulatory relaxation in many areas, such as telecommunications; and increased flexibility of labor (albeit at the cost of increased inequality). Japanese companies have also undertaken some reforms, such as paring down debt and moving cautiously away from the "one-set" mentality toward a focus on areas of competitive strength.

It is difficult to deny, however, that significant structural obstacles impede the kind of reform that will be necessary to meet the country's pressing problems. Those obstacles include a bicameral legislature that does not give the prime minister the right to carry out (or threaten) double-dissolution elections; a "second-chance" electoral system that allows candidates to run simultaneously in both single-member and proportional electoral districts, thus weakening party discipline; and excessive frequency of elections, so that leaders are always afraid to take bold initiatives.

Some structural features, such as bicameralism and the lack of the right of double dissolution, are fixed by the Constitution, which is virtually impossible to revise. Reforms could change some structures, however, such as eliminating intra-party elections or at least lengthening the tenure of party presidents, and revising the system of local elections to make them less like yet another referendum on national politics. Prime ministers could learn from Australia and make greater use of "same day elections" (that is, dissolve the Lower House to meet a regularly scheduled Upper House election) so as to create stronger policy mandates and a longer period between elections for voters to become accustomed to new policies.

Some evidence also suggests that politicians are learning how to use the existing political system more effectively. Prime Minister Noda, for example, shows a keen awareness of the necessity to balance strong leadership with constant attention to maintaining the loyalty of his party's skittish backbench members. Similarly, while electoral incentives give the opposition parties strong incentives to block the ruling party from claiming victory even on desirable reforms, the DPJ and its rivals have learned to cooperate gingerly on some issues, such as financing public works to rebuild the northeast, or creating a new "feed-in tariff" system to encourage the use of renewable energy and reduce the monopolistic control of the regional electric power utilities.

The real test will be raising taxes. Virtually no one conversant with Japanese economic policy denies that in the long run taxes will have to increase significantly to support pensions and medical care and at least slow the growth in public debt. The timing and composition of tax increases, however, are subjects of intense debate: should the government cut expenditures even more aggressively before hiking taxes? Should it wait until deflation has clearly receded before raising the consumption tax? Should it raise income taxes more and consumption taxes less? Elite conflict over the details of tax policy and the ever-present tendency of politicians to delay unpopular measures naturally affect public opinion. Surveys show that a strong majority of voters reluctantly accepts that a tax increase is "necessary."[48] Yet when Noda's government actually formally proposed implementing small, incremental increases in the tax rate beginning in 2014—precisely the cautious approach recommended by the IMF—a similar majority opposed the hikes.[49]

One reason voters lack urgency is that so far they have been spared acute financial crises. Japan has been largely immune from the discipline (admittedly episodic and often abrupt) provided by international investors. Japan has excess savings (first from households, and now from the corporate sector), so it does not rely on overseas borrowing. For now, at least, Ministry of Finance officials in charge of selling Japanese government bonds still view foreigners mostly as speculators to be fought off rather than as indispensable purchasers of excessive debt.[50] Unlike Greece or Spain, Japan has its own, freely floating currency: when times are

---

48 "Shōhi zōzei 'hitsuyō' 63%, Yomiuri yoron chōsa" [Yomiuri opinion survey: 63% say consumption tax increase is "necessary"], *Yomiuri Shimbun*, January 29, 2012.

49 International Monetary Fund, "Outlook and Strategy for Reviving Growth in Japan;" "Shōhi zōzei, hantai 6 wari, Mainichi Shimbun yoronchōsa" [60% opposition to increasing the consumption tax— *Mainichi Shimbun* opinion survey], *Mainichi Shimbun*, April 2, 2012.

50 Junichi Nakajima (Section Chief, Debt Management Policy Division, Financial Bureau, Ministry of Finance), interview by author, February 24, 2011.

---

hard, depreciation of the yen stimulates exports, while in good times, a stronger yen discourages inflows of inflationary hot money. In contrast, researchers have found that in Europe, countries that have experienced painful financial crises are more likely to undertake difficult reforms.[51] For all the talk of Japan's crisis or crises, in some ways, Japan's problem is that it suffers from a dearth of constructive crises—sudden, acute shocks that would motivate the country to take resolute action before a sovereign debt crisis or banking collapse imposes devastating consequences.

Conclusion

An air of despair and distrust in government pervades Japan, as Iwakuni vividly describes in chapter 4 of this volume. In light of the scale of the disaster in 2011 and the failings of the DPJ government in dealing with the Fukushima nuclear crisis, the disappointment is understandable. To many Japanese, the partisan transformation seems to have made a bad situation worse, though many failings, notably the lack of an independent nuclear regulator, date back to the days of LDP dominance. Japan is also plagued by deep structural problems, particularly a huge budget deficit resulting in part from a Japanese version of divided government. As Saito's chapter emphasizes, Japan's bicameral parliamentary system leaves the prime minister (unlike the prime minister in Australia) without the right to dissolve the Upper House in case of irresolvable conflict.

In the short run, the situation is not necessarily as grim as it appears. In a comparative perspective, Japan's response to the aftermath of crisis (housing refugees and rebuilding the northeast) actually looks quite vigorous. Lack of confidence in government reflects not just actual failures, but also the exceptionally, and perhaps unrealistically, high expectations of Japanese citizens.[52]

Nor is Japan's admittedly awkward version of bicameralism necessarily an insuperable obstacle. In Australia, for example, recent prime ministers have rarely resorted to the right of dual dissolution, but in-

---

51 Mark Hallerberg, Rolf Rainer Strauch, and Jürgen von Hagen, *Fiscal Governance in Europe* (Cambridge: Cambridge University Press, 2009).

52 Lawrence M. Friedman, *Total Justice* (New York: Russell Sage Foundation, 1994).

stead have voluntarily dissolved the lower house to coincide with the fixed elections of the Senate, thus creating strong policy mandates and a greater space between elections. This approach allowed conservative Prime Minister John Howard to survive the introduction of an initially unpopular goods and services tax in 1999. Japanese prime ministers could also call "same day" elections, as Prime Minister Nakasone did to great effect in 1986, and as the DPJ has said it would like to do.

Moreover, the policy preferences of the major parties may converge on some issues, as they have over promotion of alternative energy, and seems to be occurring in the effort to create a more independent nuclear regulatory agency. Even as the LDP seeks partisan gain by frustrating and weakening the ruling DPJ, it accepts the need for tax increases, not least because, otherwise, as soon as the LDP gained power, inadequate revenue would force it to impose highly unpopular expenditure cuts. Indeed, the real gap in preferences is less between the DPJ and the LDP and more between party leaders and nervous backbenchers in each party.[53] William Grimes' chapter notes three scenarios that could lead to an agreement, and there is room to trade concessions in other policy areas, such as redistricting the Diet to meet court orders to reduce malapportionment, in order to get action on taxes. From the LDP's perspective, it would be better to cut a deal and let the DPJ take the brunt of public wrath. Thus, as Grimes notes, it is quite possible for Japan to bring its budget back into balance by 2020 or so.

Possible does not mean inevitable, however: more alarming scenarios are also possible, and as time passes, they grow more likely. As Grimes notes, older voters, among the biggest losers in tax increases, are numerous and prone to vote. Unlike citizens in many European countries, Japanese voters have not seen the devastation that financial crises can wreak. As noted above, Japan's potential growth rate is low, and pervasive insecurity is further undermining entrepreneurship and structural transformation, so that it will be difficult for Japan to grow out of its fiscal problems. The temptation to procrastinate will remain strong even as debt continues to pile up at a ferocious rate. Even if currently

---

53 "Jimin chōrō noshiaruku" [LDP elders swagger], *Asahi Shimbun*.

proposed legislation passes, the consumption tax will not begin to rise until 2014, and only to a total rate of 10 percent in late 2015, which will not be enough to close the fiscal gap. Moreover, to gain the grudging acquiescence of the DPJ's backbenchers, Prime Minister Noda vaguely promised not to implement the tax until the Japanese economy sustains a two percent real growth rate—a level of vitality it has not displayed since the bursting of the financial bubble 20 years ago, and is unlikely to attain for any extended period in the foreseeable future.

Optimists take great comfort in pointing out that the vast majority of government debt is held by Japanese investors at extremely low interest rates, making a sovereign debt crisis unlikely for the next decade. Recently, however, that complacency has given way to increasing concern in the business community. A collapse of confidence in Japanese public finance would create not a sovereign debt crisis but a banking crisis as the value of assets held by the major Japanese financial institutions would suddenly crater. At the moment, Japan has too much gloom and not enough genuine urgency. Perhaps scholars and the media can help contribute to showing that action is necessary and possible.

References

Aikawa, Toshihide. "Kasetsu jūtaku kensetsu tachiokure no ura ni chiiki jitsujō naigashiro no 'kanno ronri'" [Behind the delay in construction of temporary housing: "Bureaucratic logic" that ignores local realities]. *Shūkan Daiyamondo*, 2011.

American Chamber of Commerce in Japan. "Charting a New Course for Growth: Recommendations for Japan's Leaders." Accessed June 14, 2011. http://iis-db.stanford.edu/res/2323/ACCJ_CHARTING_A_NEW_COURSE_FOR_GROWTH.pdf.

Asahi Shimbun. "Jimin chōrō noshiaruku" [LDP elders swagger]. May 22, 2012.

Bank of Japan. "Financial and Economic Statistics Monthly." February 2012.

———. "Tankan Summary." December 15, 2011.

Campbell, John C. "The Political Economy of Aging in Japan." Presentation at the Contemporary Japan Group, Institute of Social Science, University of Tokyo, January 26, 2012.

Cole, Robert E. "The Theory of Institutionalization: Permanent Employment and Tradition in Japan." *Economic Development and Cultural Change* 20, no. 1 (1971).

Conrad, Harald. "From Seniority to Performance Principle: The Evolution of Pay Practices in Japanese Firms since the 1990s." *Social Science Japan Journal* 13, no. 1 (2010).

de Mello, Luiz, and Pier C. Padoan. "Promoting Potential Growth: The Role of Structural Reform." Organisation for Economic Co-operation and Development, Economics Department Working Paper no. 793, July 20, 2010.

Estévez-Abe, Margarita. *Welfare and Capitalism in Postwar Japan.* Cambridge: Cambridge University Press, 2008.

Feldstein, Martin. "Japan's Savings Crisis." *Project Syndicate*, September 24, 2010. http://www.project-syndicate.org/commentary/japan-s-savings-crisis.

Friedman, Lawrence M. *Total Justice.* New York: Russell Sage Foundation, 1994.

Glionna, John M. "To Japan Quake Survivors, Temporary Homes Feel Like Heaven." *Los Angeles Times*, April 14, 2011. http://articles.latimes.com/2011/apr/14/world/la-fg-japan-quake-housing-20110414.

Hallerberg, Mark, Rolf Rainer Strauch, and Jurgen von Hagen. *Fiscal Governance in Europe.* Cambridge: Cambridge University Press, 2009.

Ihori, Toshihiro. "Saishutsu no muda" no kenkyū [Research on "wasteful expenditures"]. Tokyo: Nihon Keizai Shimbunsha, 2008.

International Monetary Fund. "Outlook and Strategy for Reviving Growth in Japan." September 8, 2011. http://www.mof.go.jp/about_mof/councils/fiscal_system_council/sub-of_fiscal_system/proceedings/material/zaiseia230908/01_1.pdf.

Japan Productivity Center. "Productivity Statistics." Accessed June 14, 2012. http://www.jpc-net.jp/eng/stats/index.html.

Katz, Richard. *Japanese Phoenix: The Long Road to Economic Recovery.* Armonk: M.E. Sharpe,

2003.

Kelley, Donna J., Slavica Singer, and Mike Herrington. "GEM 2011 Global Report." *Global Entrepreneurship Monitor*. Accessed June 14, 2012. http://www.gemconsortium.org/docs/download/2201

Koo, Richard C. *The Holy Grail of Macroeconomics: Lessons from Japan's Great Recession*, rev. ed. Singapore: John Wiley, 2009.

Mail Foreign Service. "The Japanese Road Repaired SIX Days After It Was Destroyed by Quake." *Daily Mail*, March 24, 2011. http://www.dailymail.co.uk/news/article-1369307/Japan-tsunami-earthquake-Road-repaired-SIX-days-destroyed.html.

Mainichi Shimbun. "Shōhi zōzei, hantai 6 wari, *Mainichi Shimbun* yoron chōsa" [60% opposition to increasing the consumption tax—*Mainichi Shimbun* opinion survey]. April 2, 2012.

Ministry of Finance. "Japan's Fiscal Condition." December 2011.

——. "Nihon no zaisei kankei shiryō" [Japan's financial-related data]. September 2011.

——. "Shakai hoshō kankei yosan" [Social welfare-related budget]. Accessed June 14, 2012. http://www.mof.go.jp/budget/budger_workflow/budget/fy2012/seifuan24/yosan012.pdf.

Ministry of Finance Budget Bureau. "Wagakuni no zaisei jijō (Heisei 24 nendo yosan seifuan)" [Our country's financial situation (F.Y. 2012 government budget proposal)]. December 2011.

Ministry of Internal Affairs and Communications, Statistics Bureau. "Gross Domestic Product." Accessed July 10, 2012. http://www.stat.go.jp/data/getujidb/zuhyou/c01-3.xls.

Nakajima, Junichi. (Section Chief, Debt Management Policy Division, Financial Bureau, Ministry of Finance), interview by author, February 24, 2011.

Nakata, Kazuyoshi. "Nihon no kakei chochikuritsu no chōkiteki na dōkō to kongo no tenbō" [Long-term trends and future prospects of Japan's household savings rate]. *Kikan Seisaku/Keiei Kenkyū* 1 (2009).

National Institute for Research Advancement. "Shūshin koyō to iu gensō wo suteyo: Sangyō kōzō henka ni atta koyō shisutemu ni tenkan wo" [Abandon the illusion of permanent employment: Shifting to an employment system suited to changes in industrial structure]. 2009.

Nikkei Bijinesu. "Shisan tōhi" [Asset flight], February 13, 2012.

Noble, Gregory W. "The Decline of Particularism in Japanese Politics." *Journal of East Asian Studies* 10, no. 2 (2010).

——. "Front Door, Back Door: The Reform of Postal Savings and Loans in Japan." *Japanese Economy* 33, no. 1 (2005).

——. "Party Dynamics and the Myth of the Myth of Permanent Employment." Paper prepared for delivery at the Joint Conference of the Association for Asian Studies and the International Convention of Asia Scholars, Honolulu, Hawaii, United States, March 31–April

3, 2011.

Okuyama, Akira. *Rōdō hō* [Labor law]. Tokyo: Shinsei-sha, 2006.

Organisation for Economic Co-operation and Development. "An Amazing Come-Back: Working Together for a Strong Recovery and Sustainable Growth in Japan." Accessed June 14, 2012. http://www.oecd.org/document/39/0,3746,en_21571361_44315115_49920423_1_1_1_1,00.html.

———. "OECD Factbook 2011-2012." Accessed June 14, 2012. http://www.oecd-ilibrary.org/economics/oecd-factbook_18147364.

———. "Total Tax Revenue as Percentage of GDP." Accessed June 14, 2012. http://www.oecd.org/dataoecd/13/38/46721091.xls.

Recruit Works Institute. "'Shin sotsu saiyō' no chōryū to kadai" ["Employment of new graduates"—Trends and issues]. November 2010.

Reinhart, Carmen M., and Kenneth S. Rogoff. "Growth in a Time of Debt." *American Economic Review*: *Papers & Proceedings* 100, no. 2 (May 2010).

Sangyō Nōritsu Daigaku. "2011 nendo shin nyū shain no kaisha seikatsu chōsa" [Survey of the company lifestyles of new employees, 2011]. June 2011.

Schaede, Ulrike. *Choose and Focus: Japanese Business Strategies for the 21st Century*. Ithaca: Cornell University Press, 2008.

Steinmo, Sven. *The Evolution of Modern States: Sweden, Japan, and the United States*. New York: Cambridge University Press, 2010.

Takegawa, Shogo. "Liberal Preferences and Conservative Policies: The Puzzling Size of Japan's Welfare State." *Social Science Japan Journal* 13, no. 1 (2010).

Terasawa Yasuhiro. "Heisei 23 nendo shakai hoshō yosan: Genkai ga mieta zaigen no nenshutsu" [The budget for social insurance expenditures in F.Y. 2011: Limits to squeezing out revenues come into view]. Rippō to Chōsa 303 (February 2011).

Tokyo Stock Exchange. "2010 Share Ownership Survey." Accessed July 10, 2012. http://www.tse.or.jp/english/market/data/shareownership/b7gje60000003t0u-att/e_bunpu2010.pdf.

United Nations. "World Population Prospects: The 2010 Revision." Accessed June 14, 2012. http://esa.un.org/unpd/wpp/index.htm.

World Bank. "Age Dependency Ratio, Old (% of Working-Age Population)." Accessed July 9, 2012. http://data.worldbank.org/indicator/SP.POP.DPND.OL.

Yashiro, Naohiro. *Rōdō shijō kaikaku no keizaigaku: Seishain "hogo shugi" no owari* [The economics of labor market reform: The end of "protection" of regular workers]. Tokyo: Tōyō Keizai Shinpōsha, 2009.

Yomiuri Shimbun. "Shōhi zōzei 'hitsuyō' 63%, Yomiuri yoron chōsa" [Yomiuri opinion survey: 63% say consumption tax increase is "necessary"]. January 29, 2012.

Zaiseiseidotō Shingikai, Zaisei Seido Bunkakai. "Zaisei no kenzenka ni muketa kangaekata nit-

suite" [Thoughts on heading toward healthier finance]. Accessed June 14, 2012. http://
www.mof.go.jp/about_mof/councils/fiscal_system_council/sub-of_fiscal_system/re-
port/zaiseia231209/00.pdf.

CHAPTER
03

JAPAN'S FISCAL CHALLENGE:
THE POLITICAL ECONOMY OF REFORM

William W. Grimes

●

William W. Grimes is the Department Chair of International Relations at Boston University. Dr. Grimes was a Visiting Researcher at the University of Tokyo, the Japanese Ministry of Finance, and the Bank of Japan. He is also a life member of the Council on Foreign Relations and a Research Associate for the National Asian Research Program, a joint project conducted by the National Bureau of Asian Research and Woodrow Wilson International Center for Scholars. He has published numerous articles on Japanese political economy, East Asian regionalism, and US-Japan relations. His recent publications include, "The Future of Regional Liquidity Arrangements in East Asia: Lessons from the Global Financial Crisis" (*The Pacific Review*, 2011) and *Currency and Contest in East Asia* (Ithaca: Cornell University Press, 2009). He earned his Ph.D. from Princeton University, MPA from the Woodrow Wilson School of Public and International Affairs, and B.A. from Yale University.

The year 2011 was an *annus horribilis* for Japan. The Tohoku earthquake, tsunami, and subsequent nuclear crisis were of course by far the worst of events of a bad year, but there was plenty of bad economic and political news to go around. Not only did the economic and human dislocations of the tsunami reverberate much longer than most had initially envisioned, Japan also shed its fifth prime minister in as many years, underwent a loss of confidence in the nuclear power plants that provided 30 percent of the nation's electricity, saw an acceleration of fiscal deterioration and an apparent outsourcing of manufacturing, witnessed continuing legislative gridlock and confusion over rebuilding and restructuring, began a potentially wrenching debate over the character of Japanese economic policy in the form of the proposal to enter the Trans-Pacific Partnership, and ended the year with the nation's first annual trade deficit in over 30 years. While there were bright spots, including the dignity and resilience of the Japanese people in the face of what was arguably one of the most devastating natural disaster in recorded history, as well as the effective coordinated response by corporations to the massive reduction in electrical power and the effective response of the US-Japan alliance to the Tohoku disaster, these successes paled in comparison with the losses suffered by the Japanese people.

It is by no means surprising that the word "crisis" was in the air in domestic and international commentary on Japan in 2011. This chapter focuses on Japan's economic situation, which has been disappointing for nearly two decades now. Although not all of Japan's problems are economic in nature, nearly all either have economic implications or will be costly to address. Therefore, any examination into the phenomenon of "Japan in Crisis" must address Japan's economic challenges directly.

In the wake of the triple crisis, it has been said that Japan is in an economic crisis. This is not correct—yet. While Japan certainly faces significant challenges, including an aging society, stagnant economic growth, and a grim fiscal picture, the moment has not yet arrived in which those adverse trends lead to an actual crisis, such as a breakdown of the financial system, large-scale unemployment, or an inability to fund the activities of the national government. But the negative trends have been accentuated—and their solutions made more difficult—by the Tohoku disaster and the global financial crisis that preceded it. The time has come to take seriously the possibility that an economic crisis in Japan may occur.

This chapter will focus on the seemingly inexorable build-up of Japanese public debt, which has increasingly become a topic of domestic and international concern. Indeed, Japan's fiscal situation has come to the point where an actual crisis has become plausible in the medium term; thus, it is essential to think carefully about causes, possible solutions, and obstacles to effective action. Moreover, Japan's grim fiscal picture is both a result of its other problems and a problem in its own right, providing an illuminating window into nearly all of Japan's economic challenges.

Japan's fiscal challenges remain manageable in principle, although addressing them effectively will certainly be difficult. That is the good news, such as it is. The bad news is that solving those challenges will require effective political leadership, which appears to be in short supply in Tokyo. By "leadership," I mean the ability to forge coalitions that can make decisions about how to address long-term policies that will stick. There are two separate points embedded in this conception. First, policies to address Japan's long-term fiscal problems will be painful to many groups in the short run, which means that decisions must be made about who will lose and to what extent. This is in sharp contrast to the political choices that are available during times of healthy growth.[1] Second, policies aimed at long-term problems will be ineffective if they are constantly reopened, reconsidered, and reversed; sadly, that is a pretty good summary of how Japanese politics has been operating in the post-Koizumi era.

This leadership deficit is not a phenomenon of group-based culture or a failure of imagination. I argue that it is structural in nature and, as such, the Japanese political system is simply ill-equipped to permit effective leadership. Nonetheless, this paper seeks to outline a grand bargain that has the potential to work politically as well as economically in rising

---

1 For a classic statement of the "politics of productivity," see Charles S. Maier, "The Politics of Productivity: Foundations of American International Economic Policy after World War II," *International Organization* 31, no. 4 (Autumn 1977): 607–633.

to meet the challenge of fiscal sustainability.

The Nature of the Fiscal Challenge

In the 2010 Upper House election, Naoto Kan led the Democratic Party of Japan (DPJ) with a platform that called for a consumption tax, based on his stated fear that Japan could become the next Greece. The result was the loss of the coalition's majority in the Upper House less than a year after its historic landslide victory in the Lower House election. Clearly, raising the consumption tax was not a winning platform with the electorate. Nonetheless, with Japan's gross government debt at 230 percent of gross domestic product (GDP)—far outstripping Greece or Italy—it appeared that the warning was not out of line.[2]

In analyzing the nature of Japan's potential economic crisis, it is easy to allow the extraordinary gross debt ratio to become the sole focus of attention. However, to adequately evaluate the problem of Japan's fiscal sustainability, it is essential to start with an accurate picture of the current situation, how Japan got to this point, and how the debt picture might evolve under reasonable projections of economic growth.

There can be no mistaking the vastness of the Japanese government's debt. Official Ministry of Finance figures state outstanding general government debt (Japanese Government Bonds, or JGBs; Financing Bills, or FBs; and Treasury Bills) at over ¥1,100 trillion (approximately $14 trillion), which exceeds even the public debt of the US federal government.[3] This enormous burden has been accumulating for nearly 40 years, albeit with many variations in annual deficits and at a much more rapid rate since 1999 (and even more so since 2009). Since 1998, annual Japanese central government deficits have been equivalent to 4 to 10 percent of GDP, and have funded 40 to 55 percent of spending from the General Account budget.[4] To say that the Japanese government is spending beyond its means is a major understatement.

---

2 This is the IMF figure. The Ministry of Finance issues a separate data series that pegs 2011 debt at 181 percent of nominal GDP.

3 "Statistical Yearbook of Japan 2011," Statistical Research and Training Institute, Statistics Bureau, Ministry of Internal Affairs and Communications, accessed May 18, 2012, http://www.stat.go.jp/english/data/nenkan/index.htm.

4 See International Monetary Fund, *International Financial Statistics*.

Japanese deficits are the result of trends of both rising expenditures and contracting revenues. While it is not essential for the purposes of this paper to dig deeply into government budgets, there are four key factors that have worsened Japan's debt problem. On the expenditure side, efforts to address Japan's post-bubble financial and economic woes (public works spending and costs related to nationalization of banks and resolution of non-performing loans) dominated rising spending in the 1990s.[5] Since around the year 2000, however, the bulk of rising spending has been in expenditures related to social security (national pensions and health insurance)—social security spending reached 27 percent of GDP by fiscal year (FY) 2008, having risen in nominal terms by about 150 percent from FY 1990, a period in which nominal GDP actually decreased.[6] This trend reflects the aging of Japanese society, which is a long-term trend that offers little hope for reversal—the share of elderly (65 years and older) in the Japanese population has increased from 12 percent in 1990 to about 23 percent today; during the same period, the ratio of national pensions to GDP has doubled from 7 percent to 14 percent.[7]

On the revenue side, general account tax revenues fell an astounding 30 percent in nominal terms over the same period. This can be explained by two factors. First, fiscal stimulus plans in the 1990s permanently reduced effective income tax rates (mostly by significantly raising deductions—as of 2011, only about 50 percent of Japanese wage earnings were subject to income tax, compared to 75 to 80 percent for most OECD countries).[8] Meanwhile, revenues were also hit by deflation, weak corporate profits, and anemic economic growth.

Looking at these trends would appear to offer little cause for opti-

5 See Adam Posen, Restoring *Japan's Economic Growth* (Washington, DC: Peterson Institute of International Economics, 1998); William W. Grimes, *Unmaking the Japanese Miracle: Macroeconomic Politics 1985-2000* (Ithaca: Cornell University Press, 2001).

6 "Statistical Handbook of Japan 2011," Statistical Research and Training Institute, Statistics Bureau, Ministry of Internal Affairs and Communications, accessed May 18, 2012, http://www.stat.go.jp/english/data/handbook/index.htm.

7 "Statistical Yearbook of Japan 2011," Statistical Research and Training Institute.

8 These data are from a proprietary analysis by an asset management firm, based on publicly available statistics from the Japanese National Tax Agency and the Organisation for Economic Co-operation and Development.

mism. Excessive public works expenditure—long a staple of the Japanese political economy—was largely squeezed out (at the macro level) under the Koizumi and Abe governments, so the key issue on the expenditure side is the need to provide pensions and health care to an inexorably aging society. On the revenue side, Japanese officials face the "Catch-22" that raising tax rates will likely have a negative impact on economic growth, which will at least partly offset the positive effect on revenues. Meanwhile, the combination of a technologically advanced economy that is well beyond the "catch-up" developmental period (and thus the potential for rapid growth in productivity) with an aging society (and thus a declining labor force) means that Japan's long-term growth potential does not offer prospects for simply growing out of its deficits and debt, as it essentially did in the 1980s.[9]

That said, the fiscal sustainability picture is not unrelievedly bleak, for four reasons. First, Japan's net debt is significantly lower than its gross debt. For example, Japan's foreign reserves of approximately $1 trillion are financed through short-term FBs that appear in the gross debt figures, but they are fully offset by the foreign reserve assets. There are a variety of other examples where the Japanese government essentially owes itself money, and the government also holds significant financial assets in the form of stock in privatized or quasi-public companies. While computing net debt is less straightforward than computing gross debt, the International Monetary Fund (IMF) estimate is that Japan's net debt is around 125 percent of GDP, not including physical assets (real estate, forest land, etc.) that could in principle be sold. This is still at the top of the range for advanced economies, but it is not in a league of its own.[10]

Second, interest rates are extraordinarily low in Japan. As of January 2012, 10-year JGBs were yielding returns of only about one percent, and even 30-year bonds were yielding below 2 percent. Thus, debt service is affordable (albeit still comprising about 22 percent of general account spending), despite the size of debt relative to both GDP and

---

9 Junko Kato, *The Problem of Bureaucratic Rationality: Tax Politics in Japan* (Princeton: Princeton University Press, 1994).

10 International Monetary Fund, "Tensions from the Two-Speed Recovery: Unemployment, Commodities, and Capital Flows," *World Economic Outlook*, April 2011, http://www.imf.org/external/pubs/ft/weo/2011/01/pdf/text.pdf.

government revenues. The absence of even a hint of inflationary pressure suggests that those rates are unlikely to rise significantly unless there is a crisis of confidence among debt holders.

Third, Japanese government debt (and corporate debt, for that matter) is held almost entirely in yen. This makes it unlike any of the countries hit by the Asian financial crisis between 1997 and 1998, as well as non-Eurozone countries that were rattled by the global financial crisis between 2008 and 2010. Meanwhile, unlike Greece and other Eurozone countries, Japan's central bank operates on the basis of stabilizing the currency and economy of Japan alone; in the event of a crisis, the Bank of Japan would be in a position to provide essentially unlimited yen liquidity to finance the government's needs.

Fourth, to return to the point about a potential crisis of confidence among debt holders, 95 percent of Japanese government debt (and a much higher share of corporate debt) is owned by Japanese entities and households. There has been some debate about the extent of and reasons for domestic bias of savers in general and Japanese savers in particular, but there has been only the most marginal of movement by Japanese savers into foreign assets to date and there is little reason to expect a sudden shift.[11] This is particularly true of the major players in Japanese debt markets—banks, insurance companies, public entities (such as Japan Post and the pension trust fund), and the Bank of Japan.[12]

The continued ability of the Japanese government to fund its debt domestically, in yen and at low interest rates, has been extraordinary indeed. JGB markets have proven to be remarkably impervious to forces that have rocked other sovereigns, with no meaningful interest rate spikes or funding difficulties even in the face of ratings downgrades and spikes in prices of CDs. This stability has even given rise to a rueful saying inside Japan's foreign investment community: "[y]ou're not really a

---

11 The home bias is noted repeatedly in a report prepared by the International Monetary Fund at the request of the G20. See International Monetary Fund, "Japan Sustainability Report 2011," accessed May 18, 2012, http://www.imf.org/external/np/country/2011/mapjapanpdf.pdf.

12 I will not attempt to justify this assertion in this paper. For a concise explanation, see "Final Report of the 2011 Symposium on Building the Financial System of the Twenty-First Century: An Agenda for Japan and the United States," Harvard Law School Program on International Financial Services, November 4–6, 2011.

trader until you've been burned shorting JGBs."[13] Meanwhile, the yen has again come to be seen as a safe haven in the midst of the Eurozone crisis, despite the awfulness of 2011 and popularly noted fiscal similarities to Greece and Italy. As the Bank for International Settlements reported in early 2012, "[i]nternational banks cut their loans to fellow lenders and governments in Italy, France, and Spain in the third quarter [of 2011], hoarding German, Japanese, and US bonds instead."[14]

Despite the calm prevailing in Japan's government debt market, all of the factors that contribute to its stability are contingent in nature. While I will not attempt to analyze the motivations of Japanese debt holders continuing to invest in JGBs, it is worth thinking about their capacity to do so. From 2007 to 2010, over 90 percent of newly issued JGBs were purchased by Japanese banks.[15] This was made possible by strong growth in deposits and declining private-sector lending. Leaving aside prospects for renewed growth in lending, the continued growth of yen deposits depends ultimately on whether Japan as a whole remains a net saver—in other words, whether Japanese current account surpluses persist. Given the long history of foreign governments and analysts viewing Japanese surpluses as a problem to be solved, it sounds strange to worry about Japan ever running current account deficits; nevertheless, that is the logic of an aging society such as Japan's in which an increasing proportion of the population continues to consume but is no longer producing economic added value.

Thus, a key question for predicting the Japanese government's ability to issue more and more debt is whether—or when—Japan shifts into current account deficit. There are, of course, many uncertainties and assumptions involved in making such projections, but many economists see Japan as a trade deficit country somewhere between 2016 and 2020, and a current account deficit country (i.e., net capital importer) a few years later. Although the crossover point will not necessarily (or even probably) be a tipping point at which Japan will plunge into a Greek-

13 Ibid.

14 Boris Groendahl, "Banks Cut Loans to France and Italy, Pile into Bunds, Treasuries, BIS Says," *Bloomberg*, January 26, 2012, http://www.bloomberg.com/news/2012-01-26/banks-cut-loans-to-france-and-italy-pile-into-bunds-treasuries-bis-says.html.

15 See Bank of Japan Flow of Funds statistics, http://www.boj.or.jp/en/.

style debt crisis, it is hard to deny that the danger of such a crisis, or at least of severe market-imposed fiscal discipline, will increase markedly in that time frame. One does not need to be a fiscal alarmist to see 2020 as an appropriate rough deadline for bringing Japan back into primary fiscal balance.[16] This is in fact the basis for the fiscal reduction plans proposed by the Japanese government.

Moving toward Solutions

This section will map out the contours of necessary measures from an economic perspective; the following section considers the political side. At a basic level, it is easy to understand how to balance a budget that has gone into deep deficit. The government must cut spending, raise revenue, or both, in order to narrow and eventually eliminate the gap. Revenue growth can result from tax hikes, more rapid economic growth, or inflation. These parameters must form the basis of any plan to attack the deficit.

It is evident that Japanese people do not like taxes. In fact, over time, the consistent reaction of Japanese voters to proposals to raise consumption taxes has been overwhelmingly negative, as seen in 1989, 1998, and 2010. Thus, politicians have typically focused their rhetoric on cutting spending.[17] Unfortunately, cutting government spending is an exceedingly difficult task in Japan. One key reason for this is structural. Over the last 40 to 50 years, Japan has moved from a position of fiscal flexibility to fiscal rigidity. By far, the largest categories of Japanese central government general account spending are social security (national pensions and health), which accounts for nearly 30 percent of expenditure; debt service, which accounts for around 22 percent; and transfers to local government, which account for 19 percent. This leaves only about 30 percent of spending in the discretionary category.[18] "Discretionary" spending includes all defense, education, tax-funded public works, and other government functions; not only is the elimination of much of that spending not feasible, but also the amount has been essentially flat in

---

16 The primary balance excludes interest payments on government debt.

17 Prominent examples include Yasuhiro Nakasone, Ryūtarō Hashimoto, and Jun'ichirō Koizumi.

18 See chapter 4 of "Statistical Handbook of Japan 2011," Statistical Research and Training Institute.

nominal terms over the last decade. It is simply not possible to go from a bond-dependency ratio of around 50 percent to a balanced budget by concentrating on cutting solely discretionary spending. Meanwhile, debt service rises each year as the amount of outstanding bonds grows due to deficit spending, and the aging of society and the growing expense of health care compound the problem. Local government transfers can be squeezed a little, but the lack of revenue options for most local governments means that potential reductions are limited in scale. Clearly, Japan's fiscal deficits cannot be reversed by spending cuts alone, although addressing the costs of national pensions and health care must be part of the solution. (Social security spending is revisited below, following an overview of revenues, as national pensions and health insurance should, at least in principle, be managed on an actuarial basis).

The revenue side, in contrast, provides some grounds for optimism. In comparison with other developed economies, residents of Japan are not heavily taxed. Japan's national burden ratio (taxes plus social security premiums relative to GDP) is below 30 percent, lower than nearly all developed OECD countries other than the United States and South Korea. Looking at the situation of households, income tax and consumption taxes in particular are low and many Japanese households pay no income tax at all. Similarly, while the corporate tax rate is quite high at around 41 percent, most firms pay nowhere near that amount—in fact, most pay no taxes at all.[19] The surprisingly low incidence of corporate tax payment is partly due to lack of profitability for many firms due to the effects of two decades of weak economic growth, but it can also be attributed to tax loopholes (e.g., investment depreciation rules) and plain old tax evasion. Reform of all these forms of taxation will be necessary to address issues of both revenue enhancement and fairness. Nonetheless, every type of reform bears the potential for adverse effects on the economy as a whole or on specific taxpayers, which is where the political problems lie.

The consumption tax is a good place to start in this regard. One reason, of course, is that former Prime Minister Kan made it front and

---

19 "National Tax Agency Report 2008," National Tax Agency, August 2008, http://www.nta.go.jp/foreign_language/Report_pdf/2008e.pdf.

center in Japanese political discourse on deficits in 2010 and Prime Minister Yoshihiko Noda has followed his lead. But the issue is much more long-lived than that—Kan tried to raise this unpopular tax in 2010 for the same reason that Takeshita forced it through in 1988 and Hashimoto raised it in 1997. The consumption tax has long been recognized by tax authorities as having three key virtues as a revenue stream.[20] First, it is easy to collect, which is important in a system in which tax evasion by companies and self-employed individuals is rampant. Second, it is a much less volatile revenue source than corporate taxes, which track profits rather than sales. Third, and perhaps most relevant to Japan's current situation, it is one of the few taxes that has uniform effects on people who work versus people who do not—in other words, it is tailor-made to maintain equitability and a consistent revenue base in an aging society.

That said, there are also significant concerns about raising revenues through a consumption tax. Leaving aside the resentments of tax-evading small-business owners, there are two key concerns. The first is equity. While it is true that working and non-working people are treated equally by a consumption tax, such taxation is regressive in the sense that poorer households spend a greater share of their income and wealth in the form of consumption than do better-off households. This means that they are effectively taxed at higher rates. Second, some economists have expressed concern that raising the consumption tax rate will further suppress Japan's already-low consumption rate, and thus damage economic growth.[21] They point to the 1997 recession that was brought on, at least partly, by the Hashimoto consumption tax hike and warn that Japan cannot afford to repeat the mistake.

These are real concerns, but the negative effects do not have to be as bad as has been suggested. In terms of the regressiveness issue, households face a combination of consumption and income taxes. Lower-income families pay very little in income tax (often none at all), so a

---

20 As Kato notes in *The Problem of Bureaucratic Rationality: Tax Politics in Japan*, this understanding has been basic to Ministry of Finance planning regarding the consumption tax going back to the 1970s.

21 See, e.g., Richard Katz, "The Wrong Tax for Japan," *Wall Street Journal*, December 29, 2011, http://online.wsj.com/article/SB10001424052970204720204577125943307956180.html.

Japan in Crisis

modest consumption tax hike is not necessarily problematic from the perspective of equity. The effect on demand is potentially a more serious problem. Current proposals seek to reduce the impact by phasing in the increase in increments, which will provide an incentive to purchase long-lived goods toward the end of each period to avoid the next year's consumption tax. Arguably, there is also a potential benefit in the form of counteracting deflationary tendencies. However, it is likely that raising the consumption tax rate will have a negative impact on consumption. The basic argument in favor of a consumption tax hike should be made on the basis of a recognition that there are trade-offs, and that a slight negative impact on equity and consumption is outweighed by greater consistency of tax collection, intergenerational fairness, and the need to avert a fiscal crisis.

In terms of income tax, the problem arises mostly from the perpetuation of high deductions that were originally put in place for the purposes of stimulating the economy, but also from the fact that deflation makes for "reverse bracket creep." Japan's income tax structure is actually quite progressive, even without the current level of deductions, so there is room for modest increases in revenue by reducing automatic deductions and lowering tax bracket thresholds without having very negative effects on lower-income households.

Corporate tax is potentially the most complicated aspect of tax reform, despite the typical focus on consumption tax. One of the main challenges of corporate tax policy is rampant evasion of taxes through outright evasion, or creative use of accounting rules. Meanwhile, Japan's high effective corporate tax rate provides an incentive for Japanese firms to shift as much of their taxable income outside the country as possible via offshoring or transfer pricing. There actually appears to be a high degree of consensus on what to do in this case—proposals from Keidanren as well as DPJ and LDP politicians have consistently called for a reduction in the tax rate combined with a reduction in deductions and improved enforcement.

Reform of other general revenue sources (e.g., inheritance or wealth tax) could contribute to better incentives at the micro level, but are too small to make a significant difference in terms of the overall fiscal situation. It is also unlikely that they would spur much economic growth, so they remain peripheral to the main conversation.

While General Account tax revenue improvement will be an important part of how Japan gets its fiscal house in order, all the talk of the politics of the consumption tax has the effect of diverting focus from the central problem of Japanese fiscal sustainability: social security spending. Japan, like most advanced economies, has had a modified pay-as-you-go (i.e., partially funded) national pension system.[22] Initially, this meant that the bulk of workers' premiums went to retirees, with the remainder being invested through the national pension trust fund, which was meant to buffer the system when retiree benefits came to exceed worker premiums. However, the system ran low on money too quickly because premiums and payments were not actuarially based (despite periodic recalculations, such as in 1997). Instead of facing the problem head on by reducing benefits, raising premiums, and/or raising the retirement age, the authorities have instead acted to conceal the shortfall by subsidizing the system from the General Account budget. By 2010, over 20 percent of pension payments came from general account subsidies. In principle, this means general tax revenue, but, in practice, it is more accurate to think of it as borrowed money, given that over half of general account spending in 2011 was borrowed. The same story has played out in terms of health insurance, which is actually further into the red than national pensions. To get a handle on national pensions and health care, which are after all the largest and most rapidly growing part of the national budget, a serious effort needs to be made to better match premiums with benefits. Given the expansion of the senior citizen population, this is an urgent task. Unfortunately, political party manifestos have focused on the politically charged issue of pension records rather than sustainability.

So far, this section has discussed revenue growth in the form of raising or reforming taxes. An alternative is to stimulate more rapid economic growth, which would lead naturally to higher revenue growth. Unfortunately, this is not realistic as a means of restoring fiscal health

---

22 For a clear description of the system, see Hiromitsu Ishi, *Making Fiscal Policy in Japan* (Oxford: Oxford University Press, 2000), chapter 10.

in the medium term. Even if supply-side policies were able to increase Japanese growth by one percent per year—the likely maximum increase in potential growth given Japan's declining labor force and its high level of technological development—it would not come close to bringing the budget into balance. In any event, there is no magic formula that could guarantee such growth. The only feasible solution is to plan for responsible revenue increases and spending restrictions (probably not actual spending cuts, given societal needs and wants), while seeking to improve incentives at the margins.

Difficult Politics

There are, in the end, not really any practical alternatives to a balanced, gradual effort based on restraining spending growth while raising revenues by reducing deductions in income and corporate taxes (while lowering the corporate tax rate) and raising the consumption tax rate. The good news is that this is the basis for all the serious plans that have been put forward over the last decade; moreover, polls after the tsunami suggest that Japanese people may be willing to accept higher consumption taxes in order to help reconstruct the Tohoku region.

There are, however, major barriers to fiscal consolidation. One is economic. As noted, Japan's economy has been highly dependent on government consumption and investment over the last two decades, and weak demand is currently compounded by the fact that the country is just emerging from a cyclical downturn and the effects of an unprecedented natural disaster. Obviously, now does not seem to be the time to cut spending and raise taxes. However, weak domestic private demand is nothing new, as Japan has repeatedly held off on long-term changes in order to address short-term economic weakness. Sooner or later, the long-term consequences of repeated short-term decisions will arrive. Holding spending steady while allowing tax revenues to rise due to strong economic growth was a viable means of addressing yawning deficits in the 1980s, but slow potential growth now means that it will not work in the 2010s. The best approach economically is one that begins relatively slowly, but creates a clear plan for medium-term deficit reduction by phasing in revenue increases with readjustment of social security programs. This is not to say that there will be no pain involved—there will be plenty of pain to go around. Debt is, after all, the result of intertemporal spending decisions that prioritized past consumption over future consumption; the logic of Japan's fiscal situation, as laid out above, is that the future has arrived.

As severe as the economic trade-offs may be, the greater problems are political. There are three dimensions of the political challenge. The first is universal: there are no winners from deficit reduction in the short run. In principal, wage earners will benefit from an expanded tax base and younger generations will benefit in the long run from fiscal adjustment, but the short-term truth is that most taxpayers will face higher taxes and/or social security premiums, while not seeing increases in benefits or services. With even the bond markets showing no sign of alarm, voting for fiscal consolidation means supporting short-term costs that are certain in nature in exchange for uncertain long-term benefits.

The second dimension is intergenerational. In Japan, as in other democracies, older citizens vote at higher rates than younger citizens. Japan has an over-65 population of over 22 percent (about 30 percent of the electorate) and growing. In addition, older citizens have a higher propensity to vote. Adding in the cohort aged between 60 and 65 raises the number of elderly voters to 37 percent of eligible voters and 41 percent of actual votes as of the 2009 general election.[23] This issue is compounded in Japan's case by the problem of malapportionment of seats in the Lower House of the Diet. While observers have long decried the excess representation of rural districts at the expense of urban ones, it should also be noted that the population of rural Japan is much older than that of urban Japan.[24] Given the resistance to changes in social security and the consumption tax on the part of voters who are retired or are approaching retirement, these numbers make support of such policy proposals less and less attractive for politicians and parties.

As significant as these challenges are, the most serious problem,

---

23 "Association for Fair Elections," accessed February 2, 2012, http://www.akaruisenkyo.or.jp/070variou s/071various/379.

24 Yasuo Takao, "Aging and Political Participation in Japan: The Dankai Generation in a Political Swing," *Asian Survey* 49, no. 5 (September/October 2009): 860.

however, is the Japanese political system itself. As we have seen, restoring Japan's fiscal health will require a combination of consumption tax increases, reductions in pension and health benefits, and raising health premiums and pension contributions in ways that make actuarial sense. But Japanese are not eager to pay more taxes while getting fewer benefits. This is a situation that cannot be resolved without political leadership. However, the Japanese political system has developed in such a way that exercising political leadership is extraordinarily difficult. This is true not only of party and legislative politics, but also throughout the policymaking system.

My argument is that Japanese politics and policymaking are pervaded by innumerable veto points.[25] In other words, there are too many individuals, groups, and institutions that can effectively stop a policy change that they consider painful or unfair. This is perhaps most evident today in Japan's divided legislature (popularized as the "nejire kokkai" or "twisted Diet") in which minority party control of the Upper House gives it formal veto power over the prime minister's legislative proposals, but there are many more effective veto points throughout the system. The DPJ itself is functionally a coalition among a variety of groups with varying personal loyalties and policy preferences. Although its factional system is much less rigid and formalized than that of the LDP in its heyday, DPJ members' policy preferences are much more widely scattered across the ideological spectrum—leaving aside the internal frictions over defense issues, DPJ economic philosophies range from neoliberal to democratic socialist. The lack of strong intra-party mechanisms and the ever-present threat of party defection make attempts at assertive leadership a lonely and frustrating (not to mention short-lived) venture. The decision to include small minority parties in the current coalition has only multiplied veto points. A similar story, of course, was true of the

---

25 For the general theory, see George Tsebelis, *Veto Players: How Political Institutions Work* (Princeton: Princeton University Press, 2002). The concept has not been widely used in a rigorous manner in the study of Japanese politics, with a few exceptions such as Margarita Estevez-Abe, *Welfare and Capitalism in Postwar Japan: Party, Bureaucracy, and Business* (Cambridge: Cambridge University Press, 2008). J. Mark Ramseyer and Frances Rosenbluth, in *Japan's Political Marketplace* (Cambridge: Harvard University Press, 1993), used principal-agent analysis to suggest that veto points were not a problem in Japanese politics, a point of view that was controversial even then, in the context of long-term LDP dominance.

three brief LDP governments that preceded the DPJ victory in 2009.

The problem of political leadership has been compounded by the weakening of the bureaucracy since the mid-1990s. While it was never exactly true that the bureaucrats "ruled" while the politicians "reigned," for most of Japan's postwar history, bureaucrats generated policy proposals that politicians either accepted or amended.[26] Widespread dissatisfaction with post-bubble economic performance and various scandals involving bureaucrats in the 1990s helped to cement the principle of political leadership, as seen for example in the major administrative reforms mandated under Prime Minister Ryûtarô Hashimoto that significantly increased the power of the Cabinet Office (formerly the Prime Minister's Office).[27] Meanwhile, the advent of coalition governments and eventually alternation of power further weakened the agenda-setting role of bureaucrats, who increasingly shifted to a more passive stance so as not to alienate their potential future bosses in opposition parties. Despite their repeated assertions of the principle of political leadership, parties still have not developed sufficient alternative sources of policymaking expertise to effectively work around the bureaucrats; the result has been that bureaucratic resistance to a cabinet's preferences can stall new policies indefinitely, or at least until the current one-year prime minister loses his job. The new configuration of bureaucrat-politician relations thus encourages policy stalemate rather than more effective democratic control.

The profusion of veto points is, finally, also manifested in the various "subgovernments" found in virtually every policy area. In political science jargon, a subgovernment is composed of all of the actors that are consistently included in policymaking in a given area.[28] For example, in agricultural policy, this includes not only politicians from rural areas and officials of the Ministry of Agriculture, but also farmers' cooperatives and a variety of quasi-governmental organizations that are involved in the sector. Subgovernments around the world act as protectors of

---

26 The "rule" versus "reign" distinction was made by Chalmers Johnson, *MITI and the Japanese Miracle* (Stanford: Stanford University Press, 1982), 154 and 316.

27 Tomohito Shinoda, *Leading Japan: The Role of the Prime Minister* (Santa Barbara: Praeger, 2000).

28 The concept is roughly equivalent to the popular term "yuchaku."

vested interests; political leadership requires the ability and willingness to force them to accept change. But in Japan, most key actors have de facto veto rights in their own sectors. Thus, the only effective way to enforce change has been to compensate those who lose because of a policy change.[29] This worked fine in the days of Kakuei Tanaka and his LDP successors in the 1970s and 1980s, but not in a low-growth environment, where compensation to one group creates visible losers elsewhere and thus, potentially, gridlock. There is probably no issue-area where there are more losers to be found from a potential policy change than in the fiscal challenges Japan now faces. Is it any wonder that changes are small and hard to come by, despite widespread elite consensus on the parameters of a medium-term consolidation package?

Prospects for Leadership

So far, this paper has painted a mostly bleak picture. Although it has presented some good news—Japan is not facing a fiscal crisis for some time to come, there is plenty of potential to expand government revenues, and the problem can be addressed through a suite of incremental policy shifts rather than requiring sudden and drastic austerity measures—the political obstacles are daunting indeed.

One point that seems undeniable is that effective medium-term action on the debt will require a medium-term plan that commits the incumbent and subsequent administrations to a clear course of action. Relying on annual tax hikes that require annual reaffirmation will quickly lead to the breakdown of mutual commitment. Only a clear strategy of lock-in can solve the time-inconsistency and coordination problems facing Japanese politicians and leaders.

Crafting such a plan and getting it passed in the Diet will require decisive leadership. The key question is where that leadership will come from in the seemingly rudderless Japanese political system. It is not sufficient simply to deride the individual ineffectualness of leaders like Aso and Hashimoto, who often managed to appear bizarrely detached from

---

29 This was the central insight of Kent Calder's classic *Crisis and Compensation* (Princeton: Princeton University Press, 1988). See T.J. Pempel, *Regime Shift* (Ithaca: Cornell University Press, 1998), and Ulrike Schaede and William Grimes, *Japan's Managed Globalization* (Armonk: M.E. Sharpe, 2002), for how the principle has broken down in a low-growth environment.

the sentiments of the voters or even their own party members. Even leaders with decisive personalities have been thwarted repeatedly in the "twisted Diet" with regard to key policy initiatives (regardless of whether those initiatives were wise or unwise). Fiscal consolidation looks particularly difficult, as there is something for everyone to hate and little for anyone to like in the policies that it will require. Bold steps will invite attack from inside of the prime minister's own party, as well as the opposition-controlled Upper House, whose only concrete aim appears to be forcing a premature Lower House election. Even the most momentous event of 2011, the Great Tohoku Earthquake and tsunami, which offered an opportunity and incentive for effective political cooperation, did not have that galvanizing effect at the political level.

The Koizumi administration offers some insights into what can work in Japan's political system. Admittedly, part of Koizumi's legislative effectiveness had to do with the fact that his coalition was able to control both houses of the Diet, a condition that is unlikely to arise again until 2013 (and even that is far from certain). Nonetheless, several elements of Koizumi's style of governance offer lessons for the Noda cabinet. First, Koizumi was able to enforce discipline within the LDP by a combination of personal popularity among voters and a willingness to punish defectors. While there were many opponents of such signature policies as postal reform, deregulation, and reduction of public works spending, they knew that defying Koizumi openly would subject them to the risk of party censure or loss of election support.

No DPJ leader, with the exception of the controversial Ichirô Ozawa, has shown the ability to instill fear in the hearts of party members, and Prime Minister Noda appears to be no exception. Noda or a successor prime minister could, however, borrow a page from Koizumi's playbook by creating a clear platform, and then daring intra-party opponents to resist by threatening to call a Lower House election if they do not support him.

Getting the reflexively obstructionist LDP to go along with the legislative agenda will be harder, and success is by no means assured. That said, there are three potential scenarios that could surmount the gridlock:

1. In the face of Upper House rejection, the DPJ administration could dissolve the Lower House and bring its platform to the voters. If the voters support the DPJ, it could resolve the problem of the twisted Diet, most likely by weakening the bonds between the LDP and Komeito, attracting some LDP defectors concerned about their electoral prospects in the 2013 election, or by creating a wedge between the LDP's Upper House and Lower House leadership.
2. Alternatively, dissolution of the Lower House could lead to a victory for the LDP coalition, which would automatically resolve the problem of the twisted Diet, at least for the time being. Since the LDP's plans for fiscal consolidation are essentially the same as the DPJ's, serious action on averting a fiscal crisis could be achieved.
3. A third possibility would not require dissolution of the Lower House. In this scenario, the LDP might allow a viable DPJ five-year fiscal consolidation plan to pass the Upper House, on the expectation that it would be so unpopular among voters that it would guarantee LDP victory in the next election, while also saving it from the need to put through an unpopular austerity plan of its own.

None of these scenarios is a comfortable one for elected politicians. But Japan's dysfunctional political system leaves few options for a leader to effect unpopular policies through normal channels. Also, given the rapid turnover of prime ministers over the last 20 years, no national leader can reasonably expect a lengthy term of office anyway. Prime Minister Noda has, at least, said that he is willing to sacrifice his own career to pursue policies for the good of the country. He now has the opportunity to take that chance. If he does not, perhaps his successor will, but the clock is ticking.

References

"Association for Fair Elections." Accessed February 2, 2012. http://www.akaruisenkyo.or.jp/070 various/071various/379.

Calder, Kent. *Crisis and Compensation*. Princeton: Princeton University Press, 1988.

Estevez-Abe, Margarita. *Welfare and Capitalism in Postwar Japan: Party, Bureaucracy, and Business*. Cambridge: Cambridge University Press, 2008.

"Final Report of the 2011 Symposium on Building the Financial System of the Twenty-First Century: An Agenda for Japan and the United States." Harvard Law School Program on International Financial Services, November 4–6, 2011.

Grimes, William W. *Unmaking the Japanese Miracle: Macroeconomic Politics 1985-2000*. Ithaca: Cornell University Press, 2001.

Groendahl, Boris. "Banks Cut Loans to France and Italy, Pile into Bunds, Treasuries, BIS Says." *Bloomberg*, January 26, 2012. http://www.bloomberg.com/news/2012-01-26/banks-cut-loans-to-france-and-italy-pile-into-bunds-treasuries-bis-says.html.

International Monetary Fund. "Japan Sustainability Report 2011." Accessed May 18, 2012. http://www.imf.org/external/np/country/2011/mapjapanpdf.pdf.

———. "Tensions from the Two-Speed Recovery: Unemployment, Commodities, and Capital Flows." *World Economic Outlook*, April 2011. http://www.imf.org/external/pubs/ft/weo/2011/01/pdf/text.pdf.

Ishi, Hiromitsu. *Making Fiscal Policy in Japan*. Oxford: Oxford University Press, 2000.

Johnson, Chalmers. *MITI and the Japanese Miracle*. Stanford: Stanford University Press, 1982.

Kato, Junko. *The Problem of Bureaucratic Rationality: Tax Politics in Japan*. Princeton: Princeton University Press, 1994.

Katz, Richard. "The Wrong Tax for Japan." *Wall Street Journal*, December 29, 2011. http://online.wsj.com/article/SB10001424052970204720204577125943307956180.html.

Maier, Charles S. "The Politics of Productivity: Foundations of American International Economic Policy after World War II." *International Organization* 31, no. 4 (Autumn 1977).

National Tax Agency. "National Tax Agency Report 2008." August 2008. http://www.nta.go.jp/foreign_language/Report_pdf/2008e.pdf.

Pempel, T. J. *Regime Shift*. Ithaca: Cornell University Press, 1998.

Posen, Adam. *Restoring Japan's Economic Growth.* Washington, DC: Peterson Institute of International Economics, 1998.

Ramseyer, J. Mark, and Frances Rosenbluth. *Japan's Political Marketplace*. Cambridge: Harvard University Press, 1993.

Schaede, Ulrike, and William Grimes. *Japan's Managed Globalization*. Armonk: M.E. Sharpe, 2002.

Shinoda, Tomohito. *Leading Japan: The Role of the Prime Minister*. Santa Barbara: Praeger,

2000.

Statistical Research and Training Institute. "Statistical Handbook of Japan 2011." Statistics Bureau, Ministry of Internal Affairs and Communications. Accessed May 18, 2012. http://
www.stat.go.jp/english/data/handbook/index.htm.

———. "Statistical Yearbook of Japan 2011." Statistics Bureau, Ministry of Internal Affairs and
Communications, Japan. Accessed May 18, 2012. http://www.stat.go.jp/english/data/
nenkan/index.htm.

Takao, Yasuo. "Aging and Political Participation in Japan: The Dankai Generation in a Political
Swing." *Asian Survey 49*, no. 5 (September/October 2009).

Tsebelis, George. *Veto Players: How Political Institutions Work.* Princeton: Princeton University
Press, 2002.

PART 3

HURDLING POLITICAL OBSTACLES

CHAPTER 04

GOVERNANCE CRISIS IN JAPAN: RETURN TO THE BASIC BUILDING BLOCKS OF DEMOCRACY

Tetsundo Iwakuni

●

Tetsundo Iwakuni is a prominent Japanese politician who served as the Mayor of Izumo City and a member of the House of Representatives in the Diet. Mr. Iwakuni was a Visiting Professor at various American and Asian institutions, including the University of Virginia, Nankai University, and Dongseo University. After an extensive career in international finance with Nikko Securities, Morgan Stanley, and Merrill Lynch, he served as the Vice President and Director-General of the International Department of the Democratic Party of Japan, and served as an Advisor to the Policy Research Council of the Liberal Democratic Party. He received his LL.B. from the University of Tokyo.

What will it take to overcome the present governance crisis in Japan, so devastatingly highlighted by the Fukushima nuclear disaster? The entire world watched in horror as survivors of the tsunami huddled together, desperately searched for their loved ones, and patiently waited for information and direction from the government. The entire world also watched in disbelief as the Japanese government dragged its feet, whether in gathering the necessary information to take decisive action, in issuing an evacuation notice, in mobilizing the Self-Defense Forces, or in asking for vital international assistance.

This paralysis, lack of transparency, and passing of blame are not, however, the attributes of the current ruling party, the Democratic Party of Japan (DPJ), alone. Even 20 years ago, Japan's corrupt practices and lack of transparency fell under the scrutiny of international media. The opposition parties at that time laid much of the blame on the Liberal Democratic Party (LDP), and vowed to effectuate political, economic, and social reform once they gained control. And yet here we are, decades later, still suffering from the same issues as before, despite the historic transition in the ruling political party.

In short, this "governance crisis" has been developing for many years now—the confusion brought on by a lack of leadership, lack of established procedures, lack of planning, and lack of information, together with a general ethos of self-preservation and finger-pointing, have in fact become an entrenched mode of governance in Japan. And were it not for the high degree of attention focused on Japan's political leadership following the devastating earthquake and tsunami of March 11, 2011, this inertia would likely have continued. There is a Buddhist saying: "from great evil arises great good." Let us hope that we can learn from the recent bitter experiences so that we may transform them into a springboard for change.

If there is to be any hope of lasting change in Japan's mode of governance, we must look beyond the present state of crisis not only to reflect on the health of our democratic institutions and processes, but also to rethink the very foundations of Japanese democracy. While there are countless issues to be addressed, my presentation here centers around the essential question of accountability.

As an insider for over 20 years, in both local and national politics, I hope to share some insight into the various functions of government, or should I say the dysfunctions of the branches of government. The first is the lack of leadership displayed by the legislators who are so busy jockeying for power that they have forgotten their real mission: to serve the people. What is more, instead of demonstrating initiative in response to the needs of the voters, they have become mere puppets of the bureaucrats, who are not accountable to the Japanese public. One must also inquire whether the vote of no confidence continues to be a viable tool in democratic governance in Japan. Another major problem is the unconstitutional disparity in the weight of votes among the various electoral districts and the weakness of the judiciary in enforcing key decisions addressing the issue. The last area of concern is the lack of transparency, as symbolized by missing public records.

These issues, combined, have led to a serious deterioration in citizen confidence and trust. Each of these issues certainly raises questions as to the legality of the procedures in place. Unless we tackle them, we could face an unprecedented challenge to the legitimacy and credibility of the Japanese government in the eyes of its citizens. As trust erodes and apathy spreads, the citizens disengage—and a country loses the very heart of its democratic system.

The Leadership Vacuum

Almost two years since the greatest natural calamity to hit the Japanese archipelago in the postwar era, here are the facts: three thousand hospitals—the equivalent of 80 percent of all the hospitals in the three affected prefectures of Fukushima, Miyagi, and Iwate—were either completely or half destroyed, and 2,000 medical clinics and dentists were affected. Although months have passed, with full reconstruction constantly delayed, people still do not have full access to medical facilities.

Likewise, 547 nursing homes were damaged and 1,000 people are still displaced, unable to return. Although the applications have actually increased since the disaster, the total number of such facilities, unable or unwilling to reopen, has decreased, and we have a situation where the most vulnerable in our society, in need of long-term and disability care, find themselves in a "refugee" situation.

In addition, there are conflicting reports as to who decided what specific measures should be taken in the midst of the power plant crisis. Minute by minute, hour by hour, in those first few crucial days after the tsunami, faced with the very real threat of a potentially deadly nuclear meltdown, important decisions had to be taken by the top leadership. In fact, immediately after the earthquake struck, the minister in charge of the nuclear power industry requested that the prime minister declare a state of nuclear emergency. But this was delayed by several crucial hours, as Prime Minister Kan was unavailable, having decided to give priority to a joint meeting of his coalition partners, which shows the lack of awareness of the urgency of the situation and relevant responsibilities.

Legally speaking, of course, the Fukushima Nuclear Plant is the responsibility of TEPCO. But nuclear power plants also fall under the tutelage of the Nuclear Safety Agency, which reports to the Prime Minister's Office, while the industry itself is overseen by the Ministry of Industry and Technology.[1]

The situation was exacerbated because the preset rules in the hierarchy of reporting and decision making were either ignored or rendered useless during the crisis. In fact, the decision making and reporting flow should have been from the Fukushima plant to the TEPCO headquarters in Tokyo. TEPCO was supposed to report to the NSC, from which it was supposed to receive guidance and instructions. Instead of adopting a proactive stance in gathering information, the NSC simply contented itself with requesting timely information that its staff received on cell phones, not even bothering to send any of its personnel to the TEPCO headquarters less than a kilometer away, which was connected, in real-time, to the control room at the Daiichi plant. Its passive and nonchalant attitude in gathering relevant information and reporting it, as it was supposed to, to the Nuclear Disaster Task Force headquarters headed by the prime minister, meant that Kan became frustrated, de-

---

1 The administrative supervision of the nuclear energy industry falls upon the Nuclear and Industrial Safety Agency (NISA), within the Ministry of Economy, Trade and Industry (METI), whose mission is to regulate the industry and nuclear reactors. The role of the Nuclear Safety Commission (NSC), established within the Cabinet Office, on the other hand, is to inform and advise the prime minister and top officials, and of course, to act as a check to NISA.

cided to take things into his own hands, and took key decisions arbitrarily without consulting all the parties involved, thus creating greater confusion overall.

Reports later revealed that his insistence on having details reported to him personally, and that he was to have the final say, also may have served to delay certain key decisions. There was a lot at stake in this crisis: not just the future of TEPCO and its top management, of officials in the NISA or the NSC, of the cabinet members involved, but the future of the nuclear energy industry as a whole. For this reason, there continue to be conflicting accounts and much dissimulation as to the decision-making process. The whole truth may not come out for years, if ever at all.

The situation was symptomatic of something else, revealing the Achilles' heel of Japanese government: the complete ineptitude in crisis planning and management. Last, but not least, the belief—at various levels—that it was acceptable to conceal vital information from the upper echelons or, in the case of the government, from its people, was nothing short of an act of betrayal. Even when TEPCO's top management tried to get the most accurate information possible from the plant managers and workers on the ground, it did not necessarily mean that this information was fully revealed, in a timely manner, to the Japanese people.

More than a year on since the disaster, has the situation improved significantly? There are 330,000 people still living in temporary housing, and thousands had to leave behind their ancestral homes, their fields, their pets, and their livestock in the close perimeter of the Fukushima Daiichi Nuclear Power Plant. Some people found themselves spending their year-end holiday season inside gymnasiums, and a large percentage of people still had not found permanent employment, adding to the sense of depression and despair.

What is more deplorable is that although the government took "immediate measures" to remedy the situation by calling for a new administrative structure to ensure a "speedy" rebuilding process, it has taken almost one year for it to come into effect. Even though the idea of establishing a Reconstruction Agency was first suggested as far back as March

2011 and was generally supported by other political parties, it took until the end of the year for the special bill to pass the Diet, and another two months until it was to see the light of day. To be fair, disagreements with the other parties slowed down the process. The bill finally passed the Upper House of the Diet in December 2011, but it was not until February 10, 2012, just barely in time for the one-year anniversary of the tragedy, that the Reconstruction Agency finally launched its activities.[2]

As such, the governmental response following the disaster has been sorely inadequate. That the DPJ administration has taken almost a year to set up this new agency to tackle reconstruction demonstrates a blatant lack of urgency in responding to the needs of the citizens. This contrasts starkly with the situation in 1923, immediately after the Great Kanto Earthquake, which killed more than 160,000 people. Back then, a Tokyo Reconstruction Agency was established less than one month after the disaster, and disbanded five months later after having accomplished its mission.[3]

In short, this disaster was symbolic of a fundamental flaw in Japanese governance: the flaunting of authority without assumption of responsibility. There was clear confusion at the top leadership level. Who was really in charge of making the various decisions regarding the power plant, now that it had become an issue of national, if not international, security? This diffuse, obscure decision making process serves its purpose well when those involved do not want to take any direct responsibility for decisions that are made. What Japan needs instead are politicians who have the courage to assume responsibility, who understand that they are accountable to the citizens.

Japan: A Country Where the Prime Minister Is Not a "Leader," but a "Reader"

We have too often seen many familiar scenes on the NHK television channel of the live broadcasts of the Japanese parliamentary sessions.

---

2 Tatsuo Hirano was officially named to the new post as head of the Reconstruction Agency. The agency itself has a 10-year mandate until March 2021, with bureaus in the three prefectures of Iwate, Miyagi, and Fukushima and "branches" in key areas and major cities within the five affected prefectures.

3 "Tohoku Will Just Have to Wait," *Nikkei Weekly*, November 7, 2011, audio podcast, http://www.teamm2.co.jp/nikkei/tnw-listening/2011/11/tohoku-will-just-have-to-wait.

Unlike the lively, witty debate we witness in the UK Houses of Parliament between the ruling government and the opposing bench, the only real "exchange" takes place not in the plenary sessions, but in the various committee meetings, such as those of the Budget Committee on which I sat for most of my parliamentary career. From my own experience, I can assure you that, most unfortunately, the repartee between the government and the opposition can be quite tedious compared to the vivid exchanges in the United Kingdom, since in Japan, where "form" and "façade" are important, everything has to be carefully orchestrated beforehand.

Obviously, such committee meetings provide the only opportunity for the members of the opposition to directly put questions to the prime minister. My colleagues and I maximized such opportunities to ask incisive questions, seeking to get the head of the government to make clear revelations or decisions, and speak the truth to the Japanese people.

Some impromptu questions from the committee members require the prime minister to answer without notes, and even then, he usually confers with aides who provide him with clues. However, generally, the questions are supposed to be submitted a day in advance, and the answers are also prepared beforehand—not by the prime minister, nor by his aides, but by the civil servants working for the various ministries involved. When he is called upon by the committee chairman, he will raise his hand, get up from his chair to go to the podium with his notes in hand, and start reading the written text, word for word, often with no emotion whatsoever, like a bad actor reading his script for the first time. So the prime minister, supposedly a "leader," is basically only just a "reader," reading out loud the answers provided by bureaucrats.

That the prime minister, theoretically the highest elected official in the land, should provide answers given to him by government employees who have never had to run for office, have never been subjected to public scrutiny, and who, in the eyes of the public, remain anonymous and behind the scenes, is akin to the ministry bureaucrats being in the driver's seat, with the prime minister sitting next to them and the Japanese people as simple passengers in the back being taken for a ride by people who have not been vetted or authorized to run the machine.

The power and influence wielded by the government ministries in Japan is not recent news. It is a well-known fact that the career-track public servants are often top graduates of the most prestigious universities. As with other countries, such as France, the senior civil servants hail from some of the most elite schools, which develop closely tied networks. Obviously some ministries have always been more powerful than others, with the former Ministry of International Trade and Industry or the Ministry of Finance in their heyday at the center of the Japanese economic "miracle." Such ministries were to lose their privileged positions when the DPJ, in coming to power, pledged to turn the situation upside down, declaring that the country would be "run by politicians" and no longer by the bureaucrats.

However, it was yet again the case of the "revolving door" of Japanese politics. A new prime minister names mostly a new set of ministers who sit at the head of ministries with which they are more often than not unfamiliar, whereas seasoned bureaucrats and civil servants know that, before too long, their new "boss" will soon leave. This gives bureaucrats no real incentive to develop a working relationship with the ministers or the vice-ministers, as they know they will remain there working on the various issues long after the current "boss" has been replaced by yet another. Thus, despite the change in government, the members of the cabinet who are questioned during the committee sessions of the Diet still rely on the ministry bureaucrats to provide them with the answers. This is unfortunately a far cry from the "politician-led government" (seiji-shudô) so touted by the DPJ when it came to power. As with previous governments before it, it fell victim to the same phenomenon. Their power and influence may have diminished somewhat in recent years, but it remains a fact that bureaucrats—who have not been selected by the people, who are not accountable to the people—play a large role in the actual policymaking of the government.

One convincing explanation for the current weakness in Japanese leadership is that it is rooted in a bicameral structure with a relatively powerful Upper House stipulated in the Japanese Constitution when we have nejire genshô, as Jun Saito aptly points out in his paper in this edited volume.[4] Indeed, wherever and whenever the executive and the legislative are dominated by the same party, it is always easier for the executive to pass its bills through parliament. At the same time, the institutional architecture established in postwar Japan can serve to prevent abuses of power.[5] Especially in a country such as Japan, where the people are reluctant to openly voice differing opinions, where there is much less dissent, and where political culture contrasts with some other developed, more mature, democracies, the present bicameral system provides one way of structurally "building in" another possible "checks and balances" measure.[6] If the chambers were to be controlled by opposing parties, this would increase chances for true debate and demands for accountability within the walls of the Diet, instead of having the Upper House merely rubber-stamping bills. Given the paucity of direct debate of the nature that one often witnesses in Westminster, one could argue that the current bicameral system, even if controlled by opposing sets of parties that can contribute to executive instability, is perhaps the "lesser of two evils," since it serves as an additional, structural layer of scrutiny of the government.

The Defunct Vote of No Confidence

The vote of no confidence is often regarded as an indispensable "checks and balances" tool in a parliamentary system, and has been successfully utilized several times by opposition parties to either force new elections or to pressure the prime minister to resign. However, there is a discernible growth in skepticism as to its continued viability as an effective safeguard mechanism.

The motion of no confidence brought against Prime Minister Kan in June 2011 was justifiable, and perhaps inevitable, given the lack of leadership, of direction, and of information at such a critical time. So

---

4 Literally, "distorted phenomenon," a term used when the two chambers are ruled by an opposing set of parties, usually when the majority in the Upper House hails from the opposition parties.

5 In some presidential systems, the voters have been known to elect a president from one party, and deliberately give a legislative majority to an opposing party as a way to ensure that the president is not given completely free rein.

6 One could point, for example, to images in France of young teenagers and other youth who naturally demonstrate in the streets of Paris regarding school or university reforms, or publicly celebrate French presidential elections.

how is it that Prime Minister Kan was able to survive this no-confidence vote? It is regrettable to have to note that a major contributing factor was nothing more than the desire for self-preservation among the DPJ members. If faced with another election in this negative climate of distrust toward the DPJ, its representatives, particularly its junior members, knew that they faced an uphill battle. Rather than represent the true interests of the Japanese people, these politicians chose to protect their own interests. As such, there were no defecting votes and the LDP opposition party was unable to garner the votes necessary to support its motion of no confidence.

It should certainly come as no surprise to anyone that the world of politics is a murky world of compromises, behind-the-scenes negotiations, and an "ends justify the means" mentality. However, the DPJ explicitly states in its mission statement: "we stand for those who have been excluded by the structure of vested interests, those who work hard and pay taxes, and for people who strive for independence despite difficult circumstances. In other words, we represent citizens, taxpayers, and consumers." And yet, at a critical time when the Japanese citizens were demanding a change, the DPJ abandoned its own philosophical foundation by protecting the interests of politicians over those of citizens, and by voting against the motion of no confidence. This display of cowardice was a betrayal of the Japanese populace.

"I don't care who serves as Prime Minister, I just don't want them to keep changing one after another. It gets in the way of reconstruction."[7] These words, uttered by a fisherman to a Nikkei reporter, sum up popular sentiment toward political leadership. But they also succinctly grasp the reality of Japanese politics, and the deep-rooted alienation, apathy, and disappointment of the citizens toward the state of political affairs in Japan.

In the last 25 years, we have had no fewer than 18 prime ministers. In fact, we have as many as 12 ex-prime ministers still alive and well. We might say that Japan is a good country if you want to become a prime minister, as we seem to get a new one almost every year. The candidate

---

7 Quoted in an editorial by Katsuji Nakazawa, *Nihon Keizai Shimbun*, October 2, 2011.

for prime minister is designated by a vote in both houses of parliament, and then formally appointed to the position by the Emperor. However, the procedure is largely symbolic, since the nomination for this post is often predetermined by back-room deals within the ruling party or coalition.

Within the last few years, we have seen the transition occurring from one DPJ prime minister to the next, from Hatoyama to Kan, and most recently to Noda. It seems that each time a prime minister exhausts his goodwill and reaches the end of a steady decline in the public opinion polls, the party inserts another, until he too exhausts his goodwill, and then another. The system as it stands offers little transparency, not to mention a lack of accountability to constituent voters.

As such, one possible way to inject greater accountability among elected officials is to set aside the current procedure by which party leaders are selected exclusively by the party's politicians. Theoretically, the selection is also open to its registered party supporters as well. However, this procedure has often been bypassed and, over time, the exclusion of citizen-voter members has come to be accepted as the norm.

Perhaps it is time to reactivate this procedure, especially when the transition from one prime minister to another occurs without a general election. We should have a system where the party members—that is, the citizen-voters who are members of the party—have a direct say in who leads their party, rather than have this be a "negotiated deal" solely among the politicians. As the party leader is essentially put forth as the prime ministerial candidate, this would allow voters to express their approval or disapproval in a more direct manner, and to hold their elected officials more accountable. The details for such a reform have yet to be worked out, but, for example, it could be mandated that the party leaders of the major parties be elected by, say, at least one million citizen-voter party members. This would allow party leaders—i.e., potential prime ministers—to enjoy a firmer basis of power, independent of the party politicians and internal rivalry. Indeed, this would be one way of partly offsetting the weakness of the executive when the lower and upper chambers are controlled by opposing parties, by endowing the prime minister with increased moral authority rooted in the general public.

In addition to ensuring that citizens have a greater voice, we must also ensure that they have an equal voice. Despite the 1994 electoral system reforms, and some effort to correct the most glaring cases of disparity in the voter-to-representative ratios, malapportionment continues to be an issue. As such, the Supreme Court has handed down a series of decisions holding that such a disparity violates the constitutional right to an equal vote, the most recent decision being handed down in March 2011.

The Unequal Right to Vote

The equal right of all citizens to vote, regardless of race, faith, gender, or social status, is guaranteed by Article 14 of the Japanese Constitution. Nevertheless, there continue to be inequalities in the value of each individual vote depending on the electoral district. In those electoral districts with a relatively smaller population and fewer eligible voters per number of seats, it is obvious that the individual vote carries more weight.

As a result, cases have been brought before the local district courts challenging the electoral districts and the disparity in the weight carried by each vote, some of which have been heard by the Japanese Supreme Court. The first such cases brought before the Supreme Court for elections to the Upper House date back to 1962 and 1971. The ruling, issued two to three years later, declared that the voter-to-representative ratios of 4.09 and 5.08 for those elections were indeed constitutional. To date, there have been 10 cases regarding the Lower House elections, and 12 regarding elections for the House of Councillors.[8]

Since then, the Japanese Supreme Court has handed down a total of five decisions that raise a red flag for Lower House elections, and one for the Upper House.[9]

The first ruling on the unconstitutionality of such voter-to-representative ratio disparity from among electoral districts came in 1976.

---

8 Rulings were handed down by the Supreme Court on the following dates: April 14, 1976; November 7, 1983; July 17, 1985; October 21, 1988; January 20, 1993; June 8, 1995; November 10, 1999; December 18, 2001; June 13, 2007; and March 23, 2011; Rulings for these cases were handed down in February 1964, April 1974, April 1983, March 1986, September 1987, October 1988, September 1996, September 1988, September 2000, January 2004, October 2006, and September 2009.

9 For the 1992 elections, a ruling was handed down in 1996.

The Supreme Court ruled that the maximum gap in the value of individual votes of 4.99 was unconstitutional, just as it did in the rulings handed down in 1985 (maximum disparity of 4.40). Subsequently, the Court rendered judgments that the disparity ratios of 3.94 (1983), 3.18 (1993), and 2.30 (2011) represented a "situation of unconstitutionality."

The most recent decision, handed down in March 2011, was more a ruling on the electoral system. The Court determined that the current electoral system, which allocates one extra seat to each of the prefectures, fundamentally distorts the fair distribution of seats according to voter population, even though the disparity of 2.30 was relatively low. For this reason, this particular system, although considered a necessary measure more than 10 years ago to alleviate the drastic effects of the transition to the single-seat electorate system, was deemed by the judges to have lost its rationale today, and the Court has called for this system to be abolished.

In sum, we recognize an overall trend in the Supreme Court decisions, since the level of "unacceptable disparity" has fallen from 4.99 in 1976 to 3.18 in 1993. However, this level falls as low as 2.30 in the most recent case precisely because the electoral system, deemed to be the root cause of this inequality, was not corrected even though over 10 years had passed since the new electoral system had gone into effect. The judiciary is therefore playing a more assertive role in recognizing inequalities in the value of an individual vote. This is essential if citizens are to feel that their single vote truly carries weight in influencing the outcome of elections, thereby stemming political disillusionment.

While these rulings are significant, it is unfortunate that the Supreme Court has left the practical issue of enforcement to the Diet, although it is not surprising that legislators find it difficult to address this issue. Consequently, the rulings have often served as no more than a verbal warning, an advisory opinion as to the unconstitutionality of the present electoral district apportionment system.[10]

Thus, it is clear that the Diet has at times completely ignored the rulings, even if it might have been for practical purposes, such as upcoming elections. There are no excuses, however, for the feeble efforts in remedying the situation, as was the case after the 1985 ruling. Even if the Diet was able to avoid other outright "unconstitutional" judgments, these were avoided only by last-minute measures that we can only define as makeshift.

In fact, Noda finds himself in an unprecedented and incongruous situation. He certainly wields the legal prerogative to dissolve the Diet, but runs the serious risk of having the next elections declared unconstitutional—even null and void—unless measures to resolve the issue are taken beforehand, resulting in a de facto and de jure power vacuum.

How else can we remedy the situation? Of course, the clearest solution would be to stipulate that the entire Japanese archipelago be a single electoral district with proportional representation, as in the case of Israel or the Netherlands.

We could use other methods of allocating seats. The current Japanese system uses the Hare method (the largest remainder method), in order to allocate seats proportionally. Even should we use other formulas or methods, such as the d'Hondt formula, in all elections, there is no doubt that, given the fundamental rules that (1) there be 300 constituencies, and (2) an electoral district must not cover two prefectural or city governments, and given the fact that there is a wide gap between the

---

10 Regarding the ruling of unconstitutionality handed down in 1976, the Diet had taken preemptive steps in 1975 by increasing the number of seats, thereby decreasing the disparity to 2.92. For this reason, it did not take special measures after the ruling. Despite the decision of an "unconstitutional situation" by the Supreme Court in November 1983, the Diet did not take any countermeasures because it was already aware that elections were imminent. Within a year of the ruling of outright unconstitutionality, in July 1985, the Diet took temporary corrective action by increasing eight seats and decreasing seven, thereby reducing the disparity to 2.99. At the same time, the Lower House, recognizing that these were stop-gap measures, voted on a resolution to fundamentally review the electoral districts and allocations for public office, once the 1985 Census was published. Its failure to carry out its resolution meant that elections were held in 1991 without the complete overhaul of the electoral system. Therefore, the 1991 elections and the voter disparity ended up being brought before the Supreme Court. In December 1992, just weeks before the decision of an "unconstitutional situation" was expected, the Diet passed a bill amending the Law on Elections of Public Office, which brought the disparity ratio lower, to 2.77. No special measures were thus taken after the Court ruling of 1993, but in 1994, the entire electoral map and system was drastically changed from the former, multiple-seat system to the single-seat constituency system.

most populous cities and those prefectures with the lowest population, it may well be difficult to bring the inequality level to below 2.0.[11]

Other than the inequality in the value of single votes, one must also take into account the increased number of "wasted votes" in the current single-seat constituency system. Whoever wins by just a single vote ahead of another will win, even if the losing opponent had garnered almost as many votes. The votes of people who voted for the losing candidate are simply wasted, and not reflected in any way. Although the current system calls for a combination of the proportional representation blocks with the single-seat electorates, the greater the weight of seats allocated by single-seat constituencies as opposed to the proportional representation blocks, the greater the risk of distorting and burying the full expression of the people. A return to multi-seat constituencies would be one way of ensuring fewer wasted votes, allowing a fairer input by the people in the political arena.

Finally, the judicial branch could be given greater powers. Unlike the situation in the United States, where the courts can issue concrete corrective orders, it is obvious that the decisions of the Japanese Supreme Court themselves carry little weight. Despite the nominal existence of the three branches of government, it would seem that the judiciary in Japan is in a much weaker position, unable to adequately fulfill its role of "checks and balances" in the Japanese political system.

Naturally, the redrawing of electoral boundaries or the reallocation of the number of seats per electoral district is a highly sensitive issue that inevitably implicates the legislators' bases of support. In fact, their instinct for self-preservation makes it almost impossible to expect the Diet members to fulfill the task in a completely impartial manner with the citizens' rights as the highest prerogative. In addition, because of certain rules in drawing up the electoral system, it is, of course, unrealistic to realize absolute parity of individual votes.

However, there is nothing more fundamental to a democracy than the right to an equal vote. That such disparities continue to this day is unacceptable, as many citizen groups have been quick to point out. It is

---

11 It allocates seats using the "highest averages" method for party-list proportional representation.

Japan in Crisis

high time for the government to take the lead in safeguarding this key constitutional right.

In sum, we have a leadership vacuum where everyone wants a position but no responsibility. We have powerful bureaucrats with little or no accountability to the Japanese voters. We have a judiciary whose fundamental rulings go unheeded by legislators. All of this combined has resulted in increasing distrust and apathy among the populace. And if the citizens disengage, we risk losing the very heart, the most fundamental building block, of a democratic system. As such, our reform efforts must consist of a multifaceted approach that not only strengthens the functions of the government, but also rebuilds the trust of Japanese citizens.

Increasing Disengagement of the Citizenry

Let us reflect on trends in voter turnout—an indication of actual participation in the political process. The latest figures for the 2009 legislative elections show that the voter turnout for the single-seat constituencies throughout Japan ranges from 65 percent in Chiba to 78 percent in Shimane—an average of 69.28 percent for all of Japan. This was a slight increase from the national average of 67.51 percent in the previous elections of 2005.[12] These levels may seem quite respectable. However, since the postwar peaks ranging between 74.04 percent (1949) and the all-time high of 76.99 percent reached in 1958, the voter turnout in multi-seat and single-seat constituencies has fluctuated until they reached the all-time lows of 59.7 percent and 59.9 percent in the 1996 and 2003 national legislative elections, respectively, reflecting a general downward trend and increasing disaffection of the Japanese people.[13]

In fact, in the first elections held after the earthquake—elections

---

12 According to statistics on Voting Results on the official website of the Ministry of Internal Affairs and Communications.

13 When compared with other countries, the voter turnout in Japan (62 percent) for the 2000 elections, for example, is above that in the United States (52 percent), but below those in the United Kingdom (71 percent), Russia (69 percent), Canada (63 percent), Denmark (89 percent), or Germany (82 percent) for the 1998 elections. Voter turnout for Japan's legislative elections, even though generally decreasing, has consistently been about 10 percent higher than for US presidential elections, which have ranged from 61.99 percent in 1964 to 47.2 percent in 1996. See Sean Richey's paper, "Voter Turnout in Japan and the US."

for local assemblies and some governorships involving 41 out of 47 prefectures—the figures for the first round indicate that the voter turnout fell below 50 percent for the first time since the end of World War II.[14] This has been the general trend, as we saw from the figures for national elections, but 50 percent is a momentous threshold.

On a similar note, media polls have indicated that the Japanese people's trust in their politicians has fallen in the past to as low as 15 percent. People ranked their trust in doctors at 81 percent, teachers at 58 percent, whereas the politicians ranked below fortune-tellers, who came in at 20 percent. This is no doubt a fair assessment of how the people perceive the ability, or inability, of politicians in helping them to cope with their future. In 2010, after the transition in power to the DPJ, some newspapers reported that approximately 80 percent of those polled distrusted politics. It requires little effort to imagine how these figures stand today, after months of dysfunctional politics following the tsunami and nuclear crises.

A November 2011 Yomiuri Shimbun poll indicates that 76 percent of people interviewed believe that recent Japanese politics has been "degraded." Most alarming, however, is that the percentage of those who believe that their individual vote is not actually reflected in politics reached an all-time high of 81 percent, which shows that this voter alienation has increased from 67 percent recorded in the previous poll under the LDP coalition government conducted in February 2008.[15] Even though the long-awaited change in government from an LDP-centered coalition to an opposition administration was considered to be the answer to Japan's political woes, we see that, a few years into the DPJ government, the people are disappointed in their new government and even more disillusioned than ever.[16]

The most revealing element of the overall distrust of the Japanese people in their leaders is no doubt expressed in an opinion poll conduct-

---

14 The first round of local elections was held on April 10, 2011. No national-level elections have yet been held since March 2011.

15 *Yomiuri Shimbun*, November 24, 2011.

16 Ibid. Of the respondents, 45 percent declared that politicians are not viewing things from the perspective of the people, 42 percent consider decisions in policymaking to be too slow, and 88 percent believe that the policymaking by the current DPJ government is "not going well."

Japan in Crisis

ed in January 2012 by Nippon Television Network. Asked whether they were satisfied with the declaration by the government that the workers had finally achieved the cold shutdown of the Fukushima Daiichi Nuclear Power Plant in December and, therefore, that the accident itself was finally under control, only 6.6 percent replied that they accepted the statement, whereas an overwhelming 85.7 percent replied that they were not convinced. Answering a question about the level of trust and communication in their leaders, 85 percent said that Prime Minister Noda's explanations to the people were insufficient.

Murky "Transparency"

Foreign governments, based on their own data gathering and analysis, had already determined that populations were at risk, and had put entire airplanes at the disposal of their expatriates to leave Japan. Foreign companies had done the same for their staff, with airlines rerouting or cancelling flights altogether. Foreign news agencies, such as the BBC or CNN, were broadcasting more up-to-date information about the actual state of the nuclear reactors, the level of radioactivity, and the areas exposed to possible radiation according to the direction of winds, than the indigenous news stations, including the national television company, NHK. I was not alone, I am sure, in having received the latest information from family and friends overseas because in the Kanto area surrounding Tokyo, where I lived, no alarms were initially given, not even to stay inside and protect oneself from the possible airborne radiation.

In the meantime, the local Japanese population was left to fend for itself—unable to leave, unable to travel, being deprived of both information and basic necessities. Only later were the Japanese told that, in fact, the foreign governments had been right all along: there was a danger of radiation, and this danger was especially serious for young children, with dire consequences. It is a tragedy that we will not know the full measure of their exposure, and of the subsequent effects on their health, for years to come.

It would seem that governments and institutions overseas had better analyses and predictions of the direction of the winds carrying radioactive pollution than the government and institutions within Japan. It came to light later that the Japanese administration was unaware of the existence of such measuring instruments, much less of their use. In addition, the Asahi Shimbun has disclosed that NISA, on March 12, the day after the earthquake hit, had submitted a report raising the possibility of widespread radioactivity if the pressure venting at the nuclear reactor was not conducted successfully within 10 hours. The document raising the possibility of deadly radiation exposure within a few kilometers from the plant was faxed to the NSC at 2:00 p.m. In the end, TEPCO was successful in venting the pressure, but only after many failed attempts. The inhabitants in the immediate radius of the plant were not warned of this potentially deadly risk, nor were preparations made in the event of an evacuation until much later.[17]

Thus, even when vital information was made available, it failed to be analyzed and maximized with the sense of urgency necessary to protect the local inhabitants as much as possible. This lack of governance and lack of accountability can literally spell disaster not only for the Japanese people, but also for the neighboring countries. After all, radiation does not stop at national boundaries.

The government declared that it was reflecting on its past mistakes and would be more responsive. The lesson, it would seem, was unfortunately lost on the prime minister and his team because new revelations have come to light about their utter lack of responsibility in the entire 10 months after the Fukushima crisis: no minutes of any of the 23 committee meetings held from March to December 2011 by the government's Fukushima Nuclear Emergency Headquarters were ever made, much less kept.[18] This could be passed off as neglect, as several emergency headquarters at the prefectural level also admitted sparse record

---

17 Toshihiro Okuyama, "NISA Warned of Deadly Radiation at Fukushima Reactors," *Asahi Shimbun*, September 13, 2011, http://www.asahi.com/english/TKY20110913. In another revelation, it came to light that the United States had provided Japan with briefings on emergency plans for nuclear plant accidents or failures back in 2006 and 2008, which could have been critical in those first few days of the crisis. Instead of passing this information on to the power companies, or to other nuclear safety structures, NISA dismissed the likelihood of a total power failure or any such critical situation, and considered the information to be of no use. The head of the US Nuclear Regulatory Commission has declared that he believed the emergency procedures it had developed could definitely have been applied to the Fukushima incident.

18 Technically speaking, the Nuclear and Industrial Safety Agency within METI served as the secretariat for the task force.

keeping in the first few days of the crisis, when the local government employees had their hands full with dealing with the physical disaster. However, these missing minutes were already recognized back in May, when the chief cabinet secretary promised during a press conference that the situation would be remedied immediately. No corrective action has been taken, sparking rumors that this could be a deliberate cover-up, especially when politicians' futures are at stake.[19]

What the Japanese found even more appalling was that this was not the only emergency-related headquarters set up in the aftermath of the Great East Japan Earthquake that failed to keep records of its meetings. It has just come to light that of the 15 such task forces, no less than 10 have failed to keep any minutes at all, of which five have neglected to prepare either minutes or even broad outlines of subjects that were discussed.[20]

Moreover, what could be put down simply to the fault of the ruling party actually seems to be a systemic defect within the Japanese governance system as a whole: the newly named minister of reconstruction just announced to the public that no records existed for the previous two large-scale disasters, in the Kobe-Osaka area and in Niigata. In his words, not to keep records was just a "general custom" (kanshû) fol-

---

19 "Genpatsu jiko taiô, gijiroku nashi—seifu taisaku honbu, ninnshikigo mo hôchi" [No minutes of meetings after the nuclear accident—Government crisis task force takes no remedial action even after realization], *Asahi Shimbun*, January 24, 2012, http:www.asahi.com/politics/update/0124/TKY201201240551. Despite realizing the lack of any records in May 2011, it was not until the NHK requested disclosure of official information in November 2011 that the government publicly stated that "the minutes have still not been reconstituted" and apologized for the delay.

20 "Independent Commission: Prime Minister Kan and His Team's Reaction to the Nuclear Crisis Marked by 'Erratic and Stop-Gap Crisis Management,'" *Asahi Shimbun*, February 29, 2012; "Kanryô fushin de shikisha chôyô: Kan-shi no kosei seifu ryômen ni—Genpatsu Minkan Jikochô" [Distrust in bureaucrats leads to outside experts: Mr. Kan's personality reflects both negative and positive aspects according to the Independent Commission on the Nuclear Plant], *Yomiuri Shimbun*, February 28, 2012. The findings of the Independent Investigation Commission on the Fukushima Daiichi Nuclear Accident (Minkan Jikochô), made public on February 27, 2012, and as reported in *Yomiuri Shimbun* on February 28, 2012, provide additional insight into the true state of crisis management and capability for planning within the Japanese government. The partial findings were also reported in other major media sources, including the NHK evening news on February 27, 2012, and Asahi Shimbun on February 29, 2012. In response to huge public interest, the 400-page document was later published in book form. For the initial press release, and the six-page summary from *Sankei Shimbun*, see http://rebuildjpn.org.wp/wp-content/uploads/2012/02/34fc7150633ba79554f4c9c9d29885a.pdf; also see http://sankei.jp.msn.com/science/news/120228/scn12022800250001-n1.htm.

lowed by the government.[21]

This definitely constitutes a violation of the Law for Management of Official Documents that was enacted in April 2011. The law was specifically passed after strong insistence from the DPJ when it was in the opposition, accusing the government of concealing important information from the public. At the time, the national pension plan records of thousands of citizens had "disappeared." Even if the law allows for minutes to be prepared after the fact, at this point people will have to rely on vague memories and incomplete notes of who said what and when. There is a risk not only of completely concealing the truth, protecting Prime Minister Kan and those cabinet members who attended, but also that there will be a "re-creation of history."

In sharp contrast, the US Nuclear Regulatory Commission (NRC) recently disclosed 3,200 pages of internal records of teleconferences held in the immediate aftermath of March 11, 2011.[22] The minutes, generated from automatic recordings of teleconferences, along with 40,000 pages from former meetings, can even be consulted online. The contents reveal that whereas the Japanese government was still in denial about the degree of the disaster, including the remote possibility of a meltdown, the NRC as early as March 12 foresaw the need to evacuate a radius of 80 kilometers in the worst-case scenario. This was when the Japanese government was still denying exposure of reactor rods, ignoring radiation measurements far higher than the norm, and considering an evacuation limited to a three-kilometer radius.

Granted, other countries, including the United States, are not without their serious shortcomings in the face of disasters, while European countries are facing a debacle with serious implications for the world financial order. But the first and fundamental step in demanding accountability of leaders and bureaucrats in a modern democracy is public disclosure. This naturally presupposes that official documents actually exist, and that they are not destroyed. The frivolous attitude towards

---

21 "Gijiroku 'Hanshin' ikô nashi, jishin/funsai nado 8 kaigi" [No minutes exist since the Great Osaka-Kobe Earthquake, including 8 earthquake and volcanic eruption emergency committees], *Yomiuri Shimbun*, January 31, 2012, http://www.yomiuri.co.jp/politics/news/20120131OYT1T00685.htm.

22 "Bei: Nihon makase muri" [US: Impossible to leave things to Japan], *Yomiuri Shimbun*, February 28, 2012.

Japan in Crisis

the most basic responsibility for any administration, to keep records of key meetings and decisions, only underscores the lack of transparency—some say intentional cover-up—across all administrations and government institutions.

Given such lack of transparency, the trends toward lower voter turnout and increased distrust in politicians come as no surprise. One might expect that such feelings of disillusionment and disenfranchisement would cause citizens to become completely disengaged from civil and political life. And yet, there are positive signs of quite the reverse.

Fueling the Momentum for Change
The broken promises, the lack of transparency, and the utter ineffectiveness of the government in dealing with the Fukushima crisis have, ironically, served as a catalyst for increased citizen activism. Outraged by the inadequate safety measures taken by the nuclear industry, people in social categories who had never been involved in public demonstrations before were making their demands heard by the authorities. Some of these anti-nuclear demonstrations, with reports of 17,500 people attending, are not only taking place within Tokyo. Sit-ins were organized for days on end in front of the TEPCO headquarters as people demanded accurate information. Activists and senior citizens alike are now showing increased awareness of the dangers that nuclear power plants represent, and have been more proactive in demanding that government committees reviewing stress tests conducted on various nuclear plants throughout Japan not be held behind closed doors.

We also witnessed an outpouring of public support, as people, young and old, took time off work or studies and rode overnight buses to disaster areas, eager to do whatever they could do to help for the day, and returned home by another overnight bus. Such "volunteer trips" were organized in response to growing demand from ordinary citizens who were willing to pay the round-trip bus fare to do such work as raking the farms of mud and soil from the sea, discarding the debris, and cleaning out people's homes or farms. Many doctors and health care personnel also travelled to shelters in the disaster zones to offer whatever medical and psychological support they could as many people, especially the elderly, began to get sick and became bedridden.

Young mothers, and even experts appointed by the Cabinet, were demanding that the government show proof that the radiation levels were low enough to be considered "safe." The government claimed that their criteria posed no problems. One dissenting expert from the advisory panel presented his disagreements and his resignation publicly at an emotional conference, in which he declared with tears in his eyes that he could not allow the children to be exposed to such high levels of radiation. Nevertheless, the government continued to assert that it was right. In the end, however, the government brought down its assessment of the radiation levels below what was previously considered "acceptable"—a victory for civil society. But this also added further proof of the government's duplicitous ways in placing higher priority on its reputation and authority than on the lives and well-being of its people.

Such demands, and there are many other examples from socioeconomic groups and classes who had previously refrained from voicing their dissent or dissatisfaction, give us grounds for hope: they reveal that Japanese civil society is maturing to the point where it can demand accountability from the country's leaders. This is especially true when we take into account the cultural tendency of the Japanese to not speak out in public, on their personal feelings or otherwise. The traditional "virtues" according to Japanese culture of not expressing oneself in public, of placing higher priority on ensuring "harmony" within the social group or of "not making waves" have long hindered the spirit of democracy and civic action, which are indispensable to ensuring that a democratic process, and democratic structures, actually function. It is difficult to say whether these civic actions and this awareness will translate into higher voter turnout, as they are aversely motivated by greater disillusion in politics. Nevertheless, it remains a fact that the Fukushima plant crisis, the governance crisis that ensued, and the outrage and disbelief towards the leaders have thrust the people into action. Let us hope this will motivate the Japanese people to break through their traditional shell, so as to establish a new norm of being more assertive in their rights and responsibilities as citizens in a democratic state. In the future, it should not require such threatening situations for Japanese citizens to step up their involvement.

Conclusion

Looking at some of the common measures of democratic states, Japan is known to rate quite respectably among stable democracies in terms of its democratic principles, structures, and processes. However, we have identified dysfunctions which in effect underline Japan's crisis in governance. Even though they are by no means exhaustive, it is nevertheless my hope that the points raised give some sense of the extent of analysis and reform that must be effected without delay.

As is often the case, a crisis reveals many inefficiencies and weaknesses in the government, but at the same time, it serves as a catalyst for reform. What has especially become apparent through the Fukushima nuclear crisis is the degree to which Japanese politicians have come to disregard some fundamental procedures established to safeguard our democratic system. As a result, the distrust and disillusionment of the people have reached such levels that they are finally motivated to develop increased awareness and take action across social groups in a way Japan has perhaps never witnessed.

In this age of Occupy Wall Street, or, as in Europe, the "altermondialistes," we see a growing movement of people opposing multinationals and global capitalism and wishing for an alternative way of ensuring economic development. They have chosen a form some call "street democracy," of expressing themselves directly, such as through demonstrations and sit-ins. Because such forms of political and social action are through alternative channels rather than through the election process, we may have to consider whether the representative democracy model itself is not going through a crisis all over the world. The numbers of the population who deliberately or otherwise are not participating in politics, or whose voices fail to be represented by the elected officials, are rising. As Pierre Rosanvallon, a French political scientist and specialist of the French Revolution, suggested by the title of his book *Contre-démocratie* (roughly translated as *Counter Democracy*), perhaps it is important to find a way to take these levels of protest into account, and to organize such expressions of distrust in such a way as to supplement, not supplant, the official processes.

Time will tell whether, in the case of Japan, the nascent citizen awareness and growing disaffection of authorities will translate into long-term momentum and increased mobilization in politics or be expressed through alternative forms. In any case, since Japan is a younger democracy than countries such as France or the United States, we should let the representative democracy model be given the opportunity to mature and run its course.

Finally, a governance crisis in a single country can often take on the magnitude of developing into an international crisis, threatening the safety of its neighbors, when nuclear power is concerned. After all, radioactive clouds recognize no boundaries and cannot be contained within national or even regional frontiers. Japan, as with any nation with nuclear power plant installations on its soil, therefore has a grave responsibility toward the international community to correct the situation.

But here too, an optimist will point out that there was one positive angle to the near meltdown of the Fukushima power plant. It brought to light the fact that other developed countries are facing the problem of aging nuclear power plants, with the reality that even with the most advanced industrial skills, there is no way to tell whether the recycling of nuclear waste is truly foolproof and safe for our future generations. Approximately 70 percent of the respondents in the same January 2012 Nippon TV Network survey supported the statement made in December 2011 by the Japanese government that all nuclear power plants that have been in use for over 40 years will be decommissioned. Developments over the past year show that "Fukushima" has taken on a universal meaning in Europe, stirring civil society in countries as far away as Italy or Germany to demand that their governments review or completely abandon nuclear energy, and even forcing the French government to consider the shutdown of a nuclear plant. Thus, in the area of nuclear energy policy, it has forced governments to be more accountable to their citizens and more sensitive to the human life factor instead of merely economic costs.

In the final analysis, one can, and should, always remain optimistic. Although the Japanese people have sometimes been characterized as passive bystanders, with each crisis they are becoming more disillusioned and frustrated. At the same time, they are also becoming more aware and knowledgeable. As a former politician, it may be strange for me to say that in my view, it is the citizens, not the politicians, who hold the key to reform. It is my greatest wish to see the citizens channel their anger and frustration in a positive manner toward immediate and lasting reform. And it is time that the politicians themselves change, really listen to the voice of the people, and have the wisdom and integrity to put the citizens' interests above their own. The current situation, therefore, presents a perfect opportunity to reevaluate and revitalize some of the structures and mechanisms in place to ensure that Japan enjoys a vibrant and flourishing democracy.

References

Asahi Shimbun. "Genpatsu jiko taiô, gijiroku nashi—seifu taisaku honbu, ninnshikigo mo hôchi" [No minutes of meetings after the nuclear accident—Government crisis task force takes no remedial action even after realization]. January 24, 2012. http:www.asahi.com/politics/update/0124/TKY201201240551.

————. "Independent Commission: Prime Minister Kan and His Team's Reaction to the Nuclear Crisis Marked by 'Erratic and Stop-Gap Crisis Management.'" February 29, 2012.

Nakazawa, Katsuji. *Nihon Keizai Shimbun,* October 2, 2011.

Nikkei Weekly. "Tohoku Will Just Have to Wait." November 7, 2011. Audio podcast. http://www.teamm2.co.jp/nikkei/tnw-listening/2011/11/tohoku-will-just-have-to-wait.

Okuyama, Toshihiro. "NISA Warned of Deadly Radiation at Fukushima Reactors." *Asahi Shimbun.* September 13, 2011. http://www.asahi.com/english/TKY20110913.

Yomiuri Shimbun. "Bei: Nihon makase muri" [US: Impossible to leave things to Japan]. February 28, 2012.

————. "Gijiroku 'Hanshin' ikô nashi, jishin/funsai nado 8 kaigi" [No minutes exist since the Great Osaka-Kobe Earthquake, including 8 earthquake and volcanic eruption emergency committees]. January 31, 2012. http://www.yomiuri.co.jp/politics/news/20120131OYT1T00685.htm.

————. "Kanryô fushin de shikisha chôyô: Kan-shi no kosei seifu ryômen ni—Genpatsu Minkan Jikochô" [Distrust in bureaucrats leads to outside experts: Mr. Kan's personality reflects both negative and positive aspects according to the Independent Commission on the Nuclear Plant]. February 28, 2012.

————. November 24, 2011.

CHAPTER 05

THE GHOST OF THE SECOND REPUBLIC?
THE STRUCTURAL WEAKNESS
OF PARLIAMENTARY BICAMERALISM IN JAPAN

Jun Saito

I, the author, acknowledge the helpful suggestions by Yuki Asaba. All remaining errors are my own.

●

Jun Saito is an Assistant Professor in the Department of Political Science at Yale University. Dr. Saito previously taught at Wesleyan University and Franklin and Marshall College. He was once a member of the Japanese House of Representatives between 2002 and 2003. His research focuses on the institutional determinants of representation and redistribution, in particular how choices of constitutional structures and electoral institutions translate into redistributive consequences. His recent publications include, *Jiminto Choki Seiken no Seijikeizaigaku* [The Political Economy of the LDP Regime] (Tokyo: Keiso Shobo, 2010) and "Cultivating Rice and Votes: Electoral Origins of Agricultural Protectionism in Japan" (*Journal of East Asian Studies*, 2010, Co-author with Yusaku Horiuchi). He earned his Ph.D. in Political Science from Yale University, M.A. in International Relations and B.A. in International Securities from Sophia University.

In an important sense, Japan's current political crises accompanied by the bicameral division of the legislature (nejire genshō) evoke old memories of unstable governance during Japan's early postwar years and the short-lived democratic regime in South Korea known as the Second Republic (1960–1961). Constitutions that combine parliamentalism and bicameralism fail to operate properly when the majority partisan control of the two chambers is divided and the room for coalitional engineering is limited.

Unlike presidential systems where the chief executive officer of the government is elected independently for a fixed term in office, parliamentary systems that have the majority of the lower chamber select the prime minister. In bicameral parliaments, an upper house majority opposition, if any, can veto whatever policy is proposed by the cabinet unless the preferences of the opposition are accommodated by the cabinet's bills and budgets. In many cases, upper house opposition parties' partisan agendas are orthogonal to policy per se, and even accommodating opposition parties' policy preferences does not salvage the incumbent government from political instability. Serious standoffs between the lower and upper chambers simply destabilize the constitutional regime by having cabinets swayed one after another. If the upper house majority opposition can successfully make the incumbent cabinet suffer from reputational damage, cohesion within the lower house majority coalition is lost and the prime minister may eventually be forced to resign out of the party's collective electoral concern. This is the functional equivalent to impeachment in presidential systems, which would usually require a super-majority in legislatures. The institutional hurdle for removing the cabinet is thus lower in parliamentary systems with bicameral legislatures.

What is worse, once the majority control over the two chambers is split in a parliamentary system, especially in the recent Japanese contexts, agents within the political system incorporate the expectation that the current government's tenure is an ephemeral one. The incumbent prime minister faces insurmountable governance issues under this condition, as bureaucratic sabotage makes it difficult to carry out policies that work counter to the bureaucrats' parochial self-interest. In the most serious case, the dysfunction of the constitutional regime puts an end to a democratic polity itself.

While weak executive leadership seems to be a chronic symptom that defines Japanese politics, the empirical record suggests that Japanese politics in the recent decades did not necessarily always suffer from weak executives. In fact, it exhibits wild oscillation of political leadership capabilities from weak to strong. For instance, during Prime Minister Junichiro Koizumi's tenure, observers of Japanese politics were tempted to conclude that Japan had made a successful transition to the Westminster-type majoritarian parliamentary democracy. The electoral reform of 1994 had reshaped the incentive structures operating over members of the ostensibly stronger House of Representatives. Koizumi's leadership within the Liberal Democratic Party (LDP) was unprecedentedly more cohesive, and it seemed as if Japanese politics was transforming itself as was predicted by neo-institutionalist scholars of political science.

However, as Koizumi stepped down as prime minister and then the LDP-Komei coalition led by his successor Shinzo Abe suffered an Upper House electoral loss against the Democratic Party of Japan (DPJ) then headed by Ichiro Ozawa, Japanese politics changed its course by heading in erratic directions. Since September 2006, when Prime Minister Koizumi effectively abdicated the premiership in favor of Abe, Japan has seen six prime ministers come and go.[1] After the DPJ-led coalition replaced the LDP government in 2009, the DPJ as a party in power has had serious intra-party governance issues. Amidst the government handling of the March 11 earthquake and tsunami accompanied by the TEPCO nuclear power plant accidents, intra-party opposition factions urged the opposition parties to submit the vote of a non-confidence motion, which was almost about to pass had Naoto Kan's predecessor Yukio Hatoyama joined forces against Kan.

---

1 In no other advanced industrial democracies have prime ministers been replaced so frequently as in Japan in recent years. Empirical evidence suggests that cabinets in early postwar Finland were short-lived, with five prime ministers being replaced over a five-year time span in the 1950s. Aside from this example, the average duration of prime ministers' tenure is the shortest in Japan among OECD economies. See Benjamin Nyblade, "Shushō no kenryoku kyōka to tanmei seiken" [Presidentialization of prime ministers and short-lived cabinets], in *Seito seiji no konmei* to seiken kōtai [Partisan politics in turmoil and the regime change], ed. Nobuhiro Hiwatari and Jun Saito (Tokyo: Tokyo Daigaku Shuppankai, 2011), chapter 11.

Is it simply the case that Japan needs a strong charismatic leader like Koizumi to have its government organs function properly? Or is it because of the weakness of the DPJ as a party in government? In this paper, I argue that the Constitution of Japan, which combines a parliamentary leadership structure and bicameral legislature, is at the heart of the dysfunction of Japanese politics in the recent years. When the lower and the upper chambers are controlled by the same set of political parties that share collective electoral fates, as was the case during Prime Minister Koizumi's tenure, the government leadership undergirded by the Lower House electoral institutions, centered around single-member districts (SMDs), let the Japanese polity function as a normal majoritarian system. When the two chambers are controlled by different sets of political parties, the constitutional design failure is so detrimental to the executive leadership that prime ministers have had serious difficulty controlling their political rivals within their own parties, needless to mention the bureaucracy. This stark contrast was a forgotten feature of the Japanese political institutions, especially during the period of the LDP dominance from 1955 until the late 1980s, when the House of Councillors (Sangiin) was ridiculed as a mere carbon copy of the House of Representatives (Shugiin).

In order to show that the constitutional design failure is the key environmental parameter that set the stage for the current political crisis, this paper is organized in the following manner. The next section discusses the institutional foundations of the Japanese bicameral Constitution and examines how the electoral rules and the Constitution interacted. The third section compares the Japanese postwar constitutional setting and the South Korean Second Republic. Exogenous theory of democratization suggests that democratic regimes are more likely to be sustainable when the government elites have access to monetary resources that would cement electoral support.[2] The economic parameters in South Korea in the early 1960s were not compatible with political institutions that furnished numerous veto points, and the Second Republic was

---

2 Adam Przewoski and Fernando Limongi, "Modernization: Theories and Facts," *World Politics* 49, no. 1 (1997): 155–183; Carles Boix and Susan Stokes, "Endogenous Democratization," *World Politics* 55, no. 4 (2003): 517–549.

therefore short-lived. In the Japanese case, the political instability during the early postwar decade was alleviated by the establishment of the LDP. The party channeled the fruit of economic high-speed economic growth and maintained a legislative majority in the two chambers for the next three decades, and the demography was consistent with the LDP's redistributive tactics. The fourth section provides an analysis of the current legislative stalemate and concludes the paper with a prospect for the foreseeable future. Since the current legislative stalemate is rooted in the differing level of malapportionment in the two chambers, a divided legislature is highly likely to continue into the future.

Institutional Foundations of the Japanese Constitution

In its pure form, a symmetric bicameral legislature requires a concurrent majority of the two legislative chambers whenever any bills are to be enacted. By installing an institutional check against the tyranny of majority, the concurrent majority of multiple chambers effectively stabilizes policy outcomes and thus resolves the commitment problem.[3] In other words, an extra veto point by means of an extra legislative chamber strengthens the status quo bias of the political system, and thus policy change becomes more unlikely to happen than would be the case under a unicameral system, ceteris paribus.

Historically, most bicameral legislatures have had their lower chambers represent the overall population and the upper chambers the interest of the noble class. This type of class-based bicameralism has been especially common in European countries, where the democratization of the polity in the form of expanding suffrage and equalizing political rights took place gradually in a relatively long span of time. In other cases, the upper chambers indirectly represent local governments, especially in countries with federal intergovernmental structures, as in Australia and the United States. The Japanese Upper House does not fall into either category, as its members are directly elected using a slightly different set of rules than are the case with the Lower House.

Whenever the legislative decisions between the two chambers dif-

---

3 George Tsebelis, "Decision Making in Political Systems: Veto Players in Presidentialism, Parliamentalism, Muliticameralism and Multipartism," *British Journal of Political Science* 25, no. 3 (1995): 289–326.

fer, there exist various methods of settling the dispute. In many bicameral legislatures, the authorities granted to each chamber are asymmetric, and concession by either chamber is constitutionally stipulated, as is the case with budgetary compilation in Japan, where the Upper House cannot veto the Lower House decision. In other cases, bargaining in a conference committee that consists of representatives of both chambers is a common method.[4] Actual functions of the conference committees vary across systems. The current Japanese Constitution also stipulates that a conference committee should settle the difference for non-budget bills, but, except for a few notable cases such as the electoral reform bill of 1994, the conference committee has not been capable of materializing compromise bills or enforcing its will in the chambers. As a result, disagreements between the Lower and Upper Houses simply resulted in persistence of the status quo outcome.

Most parliamentary systems with bicameral legislatures, through their long course of political development, either abolished or weakened the second chamber. Because peerage is no longer consistent with contemporary democratic norms, upper houses that represented the noble class gradually became obsolete. For instance, after the Parliamentary Act of 1911, the British House of Peers is endowed only with a delaying capacity, and legislation made by the House of Commons cannot be declined. A constitutional amendment in the 1970s transformed the formerly bicameral Swedish legislature into a unicameral entity.

When the Japanese Constitution was drafted in 1946, the House of Peers (Kizokuin) of the Meiji Constitution was replaced by the House of Councillors (Sangiin), whose members are popularly elected. Although peerage-based representation was abolished, the institutional hurdle against a constitutional revision is so high that the Constitution of Japan, promulgated in November 1946 and enacted in May 1947, has remained utterly intact in its original form.[5] The series of institutional reforms in the postwar period was a social experiment of a large magnitude actively pursued by the General Headquarters of the Oc-

---

4 George Tsebelis and Jeannette Money, *Bicameralism* (Cambridge: Cambridge University Press, 1997).

5 Although the National Diet can initiate and draft constitutional amendments, the drafts require the support of two-thirds of the members in both chambers before it is presented to citizens in a referendum.

cupation authority. The Constitution was first drafted by the Supreme Commander of Allied Powers in English before being translated into Japanese. The Constitution enfranchised women, lowered the voting age from 25 to 20, and provided for a bicameral National Diet with a prime minister elected by the Lower House.

Historical records suggest that the General Headquarters of the Supreme Commander for the Allied Powers was in favor of abolishing the House of Peers but Japanese legal scholars were in favor of retaining the second chamber. Despite the fact that a nontrivial number of parliamentary systems either weakened or removed the second chamber, the Japanese polity ended up installing a potentially powerful veto point without a concrete principle of representation.

The House of Representatives or the Lower House controls the decision to nominate the prime minister and to compile the budget. The period of the LDP's single-party dominance (1955–1993) is characterized by the single non-transferable vote (SNTV) electoral rule in the Lower House. This electoral rule is decided outside the formally stipulated Constitution, but it has important implications for the function of the legislative chambers. When the SNTV rule was in use, policy maneuvering to facilitate vote division was of prime importance for incumbent legislators to secure their reelection. Vote division is a coordination problem that any majority-seeking parties have to face under the SNTV rule. Since district magnitude roughly ranged from three to five, parties seeking a majority of seats needed to field multiple candidates in almost every district, whereas smaller parties typically fielded only one, or even zero, candidates. Since votes are not transferable among co-partisan candidates, any majority-seeking party has to field an optimal number of candidates and divide the votes optimally in order to do well collectively in an election.[6] If either candidate-fielding or vote-dividing strategy fails, candidates from the same parties may fall together. McCubbins and Rosenbluth point out that, in theory, parties can instruct their loyal

---

6 Gary W. Cox and Frances Rosenbluth, "Factional Competition for the Party Endorsement: The Case of Japan's Liberal Democratic Party," *British Journal of Political Science* 26, no. 2 (1996): 259–269; Mathew D. McCubbins and Frances Rosenbluth, "Party Provision for Personal Politics: Dividing the Vote in Japan," in *Structure and Policy in Japan and the United States*, ed. Peter F. Cowhey and Mathew D. McCubbins (Cambridge: Cambridge University Press, 1995), 91-113.

supporters on which candidates to vote for based on, for instance, tele-phone number digits.[7] However, they argue that this type of method is hard to enforce and monitor. If candidates are to differentiate among themselves on the basis of broad policy appeals, the party platform as a collective good is very likely to deteriorate. Instead, the LDP candidates were assigned policy niches to obtain assignments on intra-party policy affairs research councils. This property-right system provided credibility with regard to carrying out policy benefits and ultimately helped LDP incumbents maintain its local electoral machines. Factions were orga-nized so that their members could be mutually supported in terms of allocating campaign resources and career promotions.

From the point of view of a party leader, government spending has to be geographically divisible so that party leaders can adjust to district-specific electoral climates. To put it quite simply, we can imagine it as a system wherein the party uses pork barrel projects to buy off votes. In a single-member district election, like the systems in the United States or the United Kingdom, the marginal utility of buying additional votes collapses after getting a 50 percent vote share. This does not hold true in Japan's SNTV multimember-district elections. Depending on the ini-tial endowment of LDP supporters, the party may need to buy off 80 percent of the votes in some districts (e.g., rural districts where the LDP fields four candidates against the district magnitude of four), but only 20 percent in others (e.g., urban districts where the LDP fields only one candidate). Any macroeconomic policy that has a uniform effect throughout the nation does not necessarily translate into a collective vic-tory for the LDP in an SNTV multimember-district system.

Japan's Upper House has veto power only over non-budget bills. What this means is that the Japanese Upper House is not as powerful as the US Senate, but more powerful than those in most other parlia-mentary democracies. Throughout the entire postwar period, electoral rule of the Upper House has been a combination of prefectural and nationwide districts, with half of their members elected in each elec-tion. This means that voters have had two votes to cast in each Upper

---

7 Ibid.

House election. Each of the 47 prefectures constitutes electoral districts in the prefectural portion, and the district magnitude ranges from one to four, of which 26 were single-member districts as of 1992. Until the 1980 election, the nationwide portion was a single-district SNTV, of which the district magnitude was 50. In 1983, this was replaced by a nationwide closed-list proportional representation (PR) system, a d'Hondt divisor, and again in 2001 by an open-list system.

Given the smaller district magnitudes in the local districts, national partisan swings were stronger than was the case with the Lower House. However, the more powerful Lower House wielded greater influence on the party system. For the purpose of maintaining their local electoral machines, the opposition parties tended to field candidates, even when they knew that their candidate would never win. The LDP continuously took advantage of the opposition's collective action problem, but when the national swing was large enough, and when the opposition cooperated successfully, elections resulted in a landslide. The LDP lost its majority in the Upper House in the 1989 election, after the introduction of the unpopular sales tax early that year. Losing control of the majority in the Upper House, however, did not necessarily mean that the opposition camp on the whole became a coherent unit of veto players in the Upper House. Rather, the LDP cabinets negotiated strategic policy pacts with ideologically adjacent parties, like the Democratic Socialist Party and the Clean Government Party, whenever necessary.

The nationwide SNTV, which was in use until 1980, was notorious for its excessively personalized and costly election campaigns.[8] The district magnitude was too large for the same vote division strategy, which was used in the Lower House, to work effectively. The winning strategy on the party side was to recruit well-known personalities and people with organizational support, and thus the effect of geographic divisibility was weakened. It is hardly surprising that the introduction of a nationwide closed-list PR in 1983 promoted the centralization of the Upper House with clear partisan lines. National swings were therefore magnified. Voters, on the other hand, continuously split their tickets in

8 Bradley M. Richardson, "A Japanese House of Councillors Election: Support Mobilization and Political Recruitment," *Modern Asian Studies* 1, no. 4 (1967): 385–402.

favor of their local LDP candidates and non-LDP alternatives in PR. Facing weakened electoral performances in the nationwide closed-list PR, the LDP-Komei coalition replaced it with an open-list PR in 2001, in order to identify which organization contributed votes to these parties.

Comparison of Parliamentary Bicameralism in Japan and South Korea
In the Australian Constitutional Crisis of 1975, when the divided control of the House of Commons and the Senate resulted in a continued legislative gridlock, the governor general dissolved both chambers and called a double election. When constitutional procedures for breaking the stalemate are absent, there must be creative political maneuvering to break it, such as reshuffling of the governing coalition or legislators' switching of political parties, that effectively changes the political landscape of either of the chambers. Otherwise, the end result is incessant impeachment of the cabinet by the upper house majority opposition. However, frequent reshuffling of governing coalitions without electoral consent by the voters poses a serious democratic accountability challenge. Rampant switching of political parties among legislators also results in lost credibility of the political parties and the policies they commit.

In the most extreme case of dysfunction of the government, stability of the polity itself is lost, as was evidenced by the collapse of the South Korean Second Republic in 1961. In this important historical case, the constitutional design failure was accompanied by scarcity of budgetary resources available for redistributive measures to buy off domestic electoral support that would have cemented the bicameral split. Korean military elites waged a preemptive coup against the ostensibly ungovernable parliamentary regime amidst mounting Cold War tension.

The South Korean Second Republic is more remembered as an ephemeral experience of democracy than as a case of failed constitutional design with an excessive number of veto points. In particular, Han provides a reminiscent view of the Second Republic as a noteworthy experiment of democracy.[9] Following the April 19 Revolution of

---

9 Sung-ju Han, *The Failure of Democracy in South Korea* (Berkeley: University of California Press, 1974).

1960, which was a mass protest movement that toppled the autocratic First Republic, a parliamentary constitution combined with a bicameral legislature was installed on June 15 in the same year. As the autocratic rule by Rhee Syngman attracted severe criticism at the time, the new constitution laid out an elaborate set of veto points or a mechanism of checks and balances against possible emergence of a similarly behaving autocrat. The president, who was stipulated as a more ceremonial head of the state, was indirectly elected by members of the two chambers.

The Second Republic was eventually overturned by the military elites in May of the following year. In the conventional interpretation, it was the series of rapidly spawning political liberalization and labor movements that staged the establishment of the South Korean Second Republic and indirectly put an end to itself by the May 16 coup. It is reported that more than 2,000 labor protests took place during the Second Republic period, and the weakness and instability of the regime is often attributed to developments in the societal side. On the other hand, while the installment of the parliamentary institution was intended to curb the emergence of a despotic leader, individual political actors' responses were also, at least in part, a result of the political institutional structures that embedded numerous veto points.[10] Incumbent legislators frequently switched parties, and coalition building was a complicated process. Given this institutional gridlock, social movements demanding immediate redistribution were mounting amidst economic stagnation. Since the North Korean threat was also prevalent, the military waged a preemptive attack to break the stalemate. The first democratic policy on South Korea's soil was thus terminated.

Seen from a comparative standpoint, the Second Republic sheds light on some of the important predictions provided by the theory of democracy and its survival in the contemporary literature. Since the 1950s, scholars have observed a cross-national positive correlation be-

---

10 Won-Taek Kang, "Je 2 gonghwaguk naegakjeui buranjeonge daehan jeongchijedojeok pyeongga" [Revisiting the fall of the Second Republic in South Korea: An institutional approach], *Hanguk Jeong-chioegyosa Nonchong* 30, no. 2 (2009): 45–70.

tween democracy in political regimes and economic affluence.[11] Scholars of democratization later realized that it is not the case that higher income causes the country to be more democratic, but rather that high-income countries are more likely to survive as democracies.[12]

In general, in order for incumbent political elites to stay in power through democratic means, they need to consolidate an electoral support basis to warrant victory. They could do so both by adjusting policy on ideological grounds and by making use of redistributive tactics usually referred to pejoratively as "pork barrel." The demand for pork barrel tactics, at least theoretically speaking, is larger when institutional hurdles for coalition building are higher. For instance, in comparing US state budgets, Heller empirically shows that bicameral states tend to run larger budgetary deficits.

The lesson of the Second Republic was that an institutional configuration that is unlikely to operate properly even in economically affluent societies was installed in South Korea in the 1960s, which had been impoverished in the aftermath of the Korean War and its devastation. In the presence of numerous veto points, it was difficult for the leaders of the Second Republic to revise the status quo policy, which had been defined under the Rhee administration. As Tsebelis points out, while veto points facilitate commitment to a policy, if the committed policy is incapable of responding to changing social demands, the regime itself can fall apart.[13] Since the polity was incapable of mounting redistributive pressures, the regime itself ended up breaking down without fully materializing policy change.

Despite the similarity of institutional configuration between the South Korean Second Republic and postwar Japan, the political development course of these two countries was starkly different. Unlike South Korea, where the democratic experiment failed in a year, Japan somehow engineered a political coalition that returned simultaneous electoral

---

11 Seymour Martin Lipset, "Some Social Requisites of Democracy: Economic Development and Political Legitimacy," *American Political Science Review* 53, no. 1 (1959): 69–105.

12 Przewoski and Limongi, "Modernization: Theories and Facts," 155–183; Boix and Stokes, "Endogenous Democratization," 517–549.

13 Tsebelis, "Decision Making in Political Systems: Veto Players in Presidentialism, Parliamentarism, Muliticameralism and Multipartism," 289–326.

majorities across the two legislative chambers. The establishment of the LDP in November 1955 was without doubt a critical juncture.[14]

In the conventional interpretation, the LDP was launched to cope with the rapidly expanding socialists' electoral support base.[15] By merging multiple existing conservative parties, the LDP could return a larger number of seats under the SNTV multimember district electoral institutions. As far as the party could cartelize the candidate nomination process, it was reasonable to expect the conservative parties to return an electoral majority in both the Lower and Upper Houses. Figure 1 shows the historical trend of the LDP's vote share in the Lower House. When the party was established, the total number of votes controlled by the LDP's predecessor parties were much larger than the majority of valid votes.

Establishing the LDP somehow enabled the political leaders to circumvent the institutional design failures by channeling the fruit of high-speed economic growth through pork barrel politics and cartelized electoral processes. Demographic parameters were also well suited to the LDP's tactics. Voters are more easily monitorable and mobilizable for electoral purposes in agrarian communities, and the LDP took advantage of the existing farm community population for electoral purposes.[16] The LDP channeled the stream of subsidies and other forms of clientelistic redistributive measures in an electorally effective manner.

As Figure 1 suggests, however, the LDP's Lower House vote share was declining steadily toward the late 1970s. The vote share for the Upper House elections shows very similar trends. This was partly because of the increasing urban population, which was less likely to be affected by the LDP's redistributive tactics. On the other hand, malapportionment or more simply inequality of the number of elected legislators per voter population in both chambers disproportionately benefited the LDP's

14 Early postwar Japanese politics exhibited similar institutional instability as was seen in the Korean Second Republic. Party swathing was rampant, and political parties were dissolved and reorganized between elections due to opportunistic interactions among the legislators of the time.

15 Junnosuke Masumi, *Gendai Nihon no seiji taisei* [Political regime in contemporary Japan] (Tokyo: Iwanami Shoten, 1969); Masaru Kohno, *Japan's Postwar Party Politics* (Princeton: Princeton University Press, 1997).

16 Jun Saito, *Jimintō chōki seiken no seiji keizai gaku: Riseki yūdō seiji no jiko mujun* [The political economy of the LDP regime] (Tokyo: Keisō Shobō, 2010).

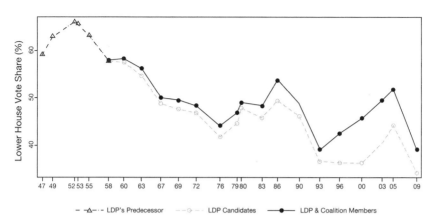

Figure 1: The LDP's Vote Share

collective electoral performance. Following the first Lower House election under the new Constitution in 1947, inequality of the values of the votes, or the population size represented by a legislator, kept growing steadily until the mid-1970s. Although the Public Offices Election Law stipulates a reapportionment of seats every five years in reflection of the latest census results, actual reallocation did not occur at least until the mid-1960s. On the other hand, high-speed growth resulted in rapid migration from rural areas into urban metropolises, exacerbating the inequality in the value of votes. Reallocation of seats under the SNTV electoral rule is only a temporary expedient, and a full-fledged disparity adjustment was not implemented until after the 1994 electoral reform.

In addition to the fact that individual incumbent legislators are unlikely to change the electoral institutions that elected themselves into the parliament, rural districts were also the cornerstones of the LDP's perverse accountability regime because rural voters were more easily monitorable and mobilizable. Since the strongholds of the LDP were disproportionately rural, the LDP was unlikely to benefit from reapportionment, which would have translated into increasing the electoral power of urban residents. Further, weak judicial independence, the LDP's power to shuffle Supreme Court justices, and the prolonged tenure of the LDP meant that the Supreme Court did not attempt to equalize the value of votes.[17] Although the *Baker v. Carr* case in the United States spawned a series of administrative suits in Japan, it was not until April 1976 that Japan's Supreme Court ruled the malapportionment of seats in the Lower House unconstitutional. Even then, the Court did not void any election results.

Figure 2 shows trends in reapportionment with the Loosemore-Hanby (LH) index.[18] The index is calculated as the sum of the absolute differences between the share of voter population size and the share of the number of seats for each of the electoral districts. If there is no inequality of voting rights or equivalently no malapportionment, it takes the value of 0, and it comes close to 100 as malapportionment increases. In general, whenever malapportionment is referred to in judicial decisions or mass media coverage, the most oft-used index is the ratio of maximum to minimum in each election. Although the LH index is not as common as the max-min ratio, it reflects the national trend of malapportionment more accurately since it equally takes malapportionment of all districts across the country into account.[19] For instance, while the ratio decreased from 5.0 to 3.5 in 1975, the LH index only decreased from 14.6 to 12.6 and reflected the reality that the electoral reform did not lead to substantial overall reduction in malapportionment. Although the 1994 electoral reform did not fully achieve the goal of the one-person-one-vote principle, it resulted in relatively large-scale reapportionment, which was unprecedented in the postwar Japanese electoral history. Accordingly, the

---

17 J. Mark Ramseyer and Frances McCall Rosenbluth, *Japan's Political Marketplace* (Cambridge: Harvard University Press, 1993); *Asahi Shimbun, Kokō no ō koku saibansho* [The court: Kingdom standing aloof] (Tokyo: Asahi Shimbun, 1994); J. Mark Ramseyer and Eric B. Rasmusen, "Why Are Japanese Judges So Conservative in Politically Charged Cases?" *American Political Science Review* 95, no. 2 (2001): 331–344.

18 The LH index is defined as $LHI = 12 \ \Sigma i \ |si/S-ni/N|$ where Si is the number of seats, and is the number of voters respectively in district i, $S = \Sigma isi$, and $N = \Sigma ini$. See Rein Taagepera and Matthew Soberg Shugart, *Seats and Votes: The Effects and Determinants of Electoral Systems* (New Haven: Yale University Press, 1989).

19 For the cross-national quantitative analysis of malapportionment using the LH index, see David Samuels and Richard Snyder, "The Value of a Vote: Malapportionment in Comparative Perspective," *British Journal of Political Science* 31, no. 3 (2001): 651–671; Burt L. Monroe, "Disproportional and Malapportionment: Measuring Inequity," *Electoral Studies* 13, no. 2 (1994): 132–149.

Japan in Crisis

LH index decreased from 13.1 in 1993 to 5.1 in 1996.[20] On the other hand, since the Upper House has not undergone significant procedures of reapportionment, malapportionment has remained a significant issue.[21]

Figure 2: Trends of Malapportionment in the Japanese Diet

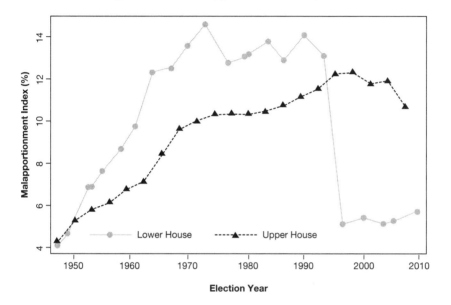

The LDP was able to make efficient use of the budgetary and regulatory favors thanks to malapportionment in both chambers that magnified rural voters. In addition to the inequality of the value of votes, the variation in the district magnitude in the electoral system also benefited the LDP toward the mid-1980s. The district magnitude varied in general from three to five in the Lower House and from one to four in the Up-

---

20 The LH index after the electoral reform is calculated in the following manner. First, the LH indexes for both SMD and PR are respectively calculated. Then, a weighted mean of these two portions are calculated by assigning weights to SMD and PR portions. For instance, the weight for SMD and PR in the 1996 election was 300/500 versus 200/500. After the 2000 election, the weights were 300/480 versus 180/480.

21 The LH index for the Upper House was also calculated in a similar fashion to the index for the post-reform Lower House. The nationwide district portion has an LH index equal to zero. Then, the LH index is weighted by the total number of district seats as opposed to the total number of seats in the Upper House.

per House. The LDP took advantage of the variance effect.[22] The party controlled most small-magnitude districts, and the opposition parties were fragmented in their urban strongholds, where the district magnitude tended to be larger. Since the LDP was on average able to return a plurality of votes in most districts, at least until the 1980s, the party could return 100 percent of available seats in districts where the district magnitude was one. On the other hand, as the LDP's electoral support base gradually shrank down to near plurality, securing seats through the variance effect became a difficult strategy. As the 1989 Upper House election results suggest, once the LDP suffered a cutback in its vote-getting performance, it recorded a miserable defeat in terms of the number of seats it won.

Fragmentation of the opposition parties due to the multimember district electoral rules for the Lower House enabled the LDP to pursue a partial coalition option when the party lost the Upper House majority in 1989. The LDP's long tenure in government and the network of local politicians and interest groups were mutually reinforcing the LDP candidates' electioneering efforts to seek seats in the parliament. It was exactly in this period, the LDP's heyday, when the Japanese Upper House was ridiculed as a mere carbon copy of the Lower House.

Another important institutional feature of the LDP's dominance between 1955 and 2009 was the party's reliance on local politicians' electoral mobilization efforts. In the Japanese Local Autonomy Law, the maximum number of municipal council members is stipulated as a non-decreasing step function, which can be well approximated by an increasing concave function. Although most of the municipal council members run for their election as nonpartisans, roughly 80 percent of them were in some way affiliated with the LDP or LDP Diet members' personal support organizations, known as kōenkai. By mobilizing these municipal council members as well as politicians at the prefectural level, the LDP somehow retained a firm grip on power. The LDP as a party and its Diet members also took advantage of the power of the purse,

---

22 Burt L. Monroe and Amanda G. Rose, "Electoral Systems and Unimagined Consequences: Partisan Effects of Districted Proportional Representation," *American Journal of Political Science* 46, no. 1 (2002): 67–89.

where the LDP Diet members described themselves as a pipeline of pork from Tokyo to their districts.[23]

Understanding the Current Stalemate

In understanding the current political stalemate in Japan, it is important to note that the institutional and demographic characteristics that bolstered the LDP's collective majority in both chambers are no longer present in the Japanese political system. For instance, the overall Japanese population is no longer so agrarian as it used to be when the LDP was established. A surge of municipal mergers toward March 2006 reduced the number of municipalities and hence municipal council members who are affiliated with the LDP. In addition, malapportionment that continuously overrepresented the LDP's support base in both chambers disappeared as a result of the 1994 electoral reform.

The 1994 Lower House electoral reform rebalanced the weights of urban and rural districts while maintaining the rural bias in the Upper House, which has led the median legislators in the two chambers to represent two different policy preferences (Figure 2). As a result of the Lower House electoral reform, the LH malapportionment index dropped from 13.1 in the 1993 general election, the last election using the SNTV rule, to 5.1 in 1996, which was the first SMD-based election. However, malapportionment in the Upper House was left largely unchanged, around 11.5 and 12.5 in the same period. Since the two chambers somehow over-represent differing constituencies, it is quite natural to expect division of the parliament.

Ironically, the 1994 Lower House electoral reform, which was intended to strengthen the majority party's leadership and efficient fusion of political authority, has ended up eroding the government leadership in the face of a bicameral division. The introduction of the SMD-based rule in the Lower House reduced the effective number of parties in the Japanese political system, and the equilibrium result is the presence of a bipartisan system in both chambers, accompanied by several small parties. While the SNTV multimember rule was in use to elect Lower

---

23 Ethan Scheiner, "Pipelines of Pork: Japanese Politics and a Model of Local Opposition Party Failure," *Comparative Political Studies* 38, no. 7 (2005): 799–823.

House members, the LDP leadership circumvented the legislative stale-mate by accommodating the preferences of the Komei Party and the Democratic Socialist Party after the LDP lost the Upper House majority in 1989. Since 2007, neither the LDP nor the DPJ government has been able to adopt this strategy, simply because the bipartisan split of the two chambers has resulted in perpetual bargaining in the form of bilateral monopoly where the room for coalitional engineering is se-verely limited. The DPJ's new government cannot get its reform agendas implemented simply because of the bicameral division accompanied by bureaucratic sabotage influenced by the shared expectation that any at-tempts to revise the status quo will be overturned. Japan's political pa-ralysis after the March 11 earthquake and the ensuing nuclear accident in TEPCO's Fukushima Daiichi plant is best understood through this institutional context.

While the political parties are perpetually confronting each other in the electoral and the legislative arenas of the political system, it ap-pears that government bureaucracy has regained autonomy from po-litical leadership. Since the newly formed DPJ government lacked the technical expertise on existing laws and budget compilation processes, the party leadership increasingly depended upon the bureaucrats for help.[24] Although the DPJ had campaigned on the basis of political lead-ership instead of bureaucratic inertia, the government bureaucracy, in particular the Ministry of Finance, has taken advantage of this symptom and started to control the agenda, which is often not compatible with the incumbent politicians' electoral agendas, such as a consumption tax increase. In general, although sometimes it may be necessary to initi-ate reforms that no elected politicians would be willing to pursue, it is highly questionable whether the current Japanese government should undertake a tax increase amidst mounting deflationary pressures and the recovery process after the disaster on March 11.

It has to be emphasized, however, that the bureaucrats' increasing clout was already observed even before the DPJ replaced the LDP after the 2009 Lower House election. Since the LDP lost the Upper House

---

24 Yukihiro Hasegawa, *Kantei haiboku* [Prime minister's defeat] (Tokyo: Kōdansha, 2010).

majority in July 2007, actors within the political system had started to incorporate legislative stalemates and hence shorter time horizons by the incumbent LDP government leadership. Prime Minister Abe resigned within two months of the July Upper House election, and was succeeded by Yasuo Fukuda and then by Taro Aso. Amidst weak political leadership, it was the bureaucrats who regained their influence in the decision-making process.[25]

Weak political leadership, which is exacerbated by the bicameral division of the legislature, had a detrimental impact on the course of the crisis response after the March 11 earthquake, tsunami, and nuclear accidents. Although swift mobilization of the Self-Defense Forces and a multinational task force aided in particular by the US military was successfully carried out in the immediate response phase, information hoarding concerning the TEPCO Fukushima Daiichi plant accidents reveals the governance and accountability issues within the Japanese political system.

Since the current legislative stalemate is institutionally rooted, it is expected that the bicameral confrontation will persist unless its causes are removed. One possibility is to abolish the Upper House, which requires a constitutional revision. Diet members' study groups are currently examining this possibility, but given the high institutional hurdle against a constitutional revision, this is a slim possibility even in the long run. Another more practical possibility is to rebalance the apportionment of seats, especially in the Upper House, which will increase the likelihood of the same party being in control of both chambers. Alternatively, the prime minister can commit to calling a Lower House election so that elections for both chambers can take place on the same day. The prime minister's prerogative to call an election is an important strategic device that is essential to his political leadership within the party; however, it is not the best political strategy for any prime minister to renounce the option of flexible Lower House election timing.

On the contrary, some of the reform plans currently under deliberation are more likely to perpetuate the bicameral standoffs. For in-

---

25 Yukihiro Hasegawa, *Kanryō tono shitō 700 nichi* [A 700 days' battle against the bureaucrats] (Tokyo: Kōdansha, 2008).

stance, the DPJ is submitting a bill that will remove the PR portion of the Lower House. Doing so will inevitably reduce the effective number of political parties in the legislature, as far as Duverger's Law generates its predicted outcome. This will reduce the likelihood of coalition reshuffling resolving the bicameral division. Rather, a serious confrontation by the two large parties, each of which controls either of the two chambers, will be institutionalized if this bill is enacted.

In conclusion, the Japanese House of Councillors is endowed with an institutionalized influence that is perhaps among the strongest in the class of existing parliamentary constitutions and therefore is essential to understanding the way Japanese politics operates. When the two chambers are under effective control by the leadership of the same political party, the Upper House is often pejoratively referred to as a carbon copy of the Lower House. However, this reflects careful engineering of intra-party politics in the way that Prime Ministers Kakuei Tanaka and Junichiro Koizumi both maintained friendly relations with the LDP's Upper House caucus. When the control over the two chambers is divided among different political parties, Japanese politics goes adrift and encounters serious accountability issues.

References

Asahi Shimbun. Kokōno ōkoku saibansho [The court: Kingdom standing aloof]. Tokyo: Asahi Shimbun, 1994.

Boix, Carles, and Susan Stokes. "Endogenous Democratization." *World Politics* 55, no. 4 (2003).

Cox, Gary W., and Frances Rosenbluth. "Factional Competition for the Party Endorsement: The Case of Japan's Liberal Democratic Party." *British Journal of Political Science* 26, no. 2 (1996).

Kang, Won-Taek. "Je 2 gonghwaguk naegakjeui buranjeonge daehan jeongchijedojeok pyeong-ga" [Revisiting the fall of the Second Republic in South Korea: An institutional approach]. *Hanguk Jeongchioegyosa Nonchong* 30, no. 2 (2009).

Kohno, Masaru. *Japan's Postwar Party Politics.* Princeton: Princeton University Press, 1997.

Lipset, Seymour Martin. "Some Social Requisites of Democracy: Economic Development and Political Legitimacy." *American Political Science Review* 53, no. 1 (1959).

Masumi, Junnosuke. *Gendai Nihon no seiji taisei* [Political regime in contemporary Japan]. Tokyo: Iwanami Shoten, 1969.

McCubbins, Mathew D., and Frances Rosenbluth. "Party Provision for Personal Politics: Dividing the Vote in Japan." In *Structure and Policy in Japan and the United States*, edited by Peter F. Cowhey and Mathew D. McCubbins. Cambridge: Cambridge University Press, 1995.

Monroe, Burt L. "Disproportional and Malapportionment: Measuring Inequity." *Electoral Studies* 13, no. 2 (1994).

Monroe, Burt L., and Amanda G. Rose. "Electoral Systems and Unimagined Consequences: Partisan Effects of Districted Proportional Representation." *American Journal of Political Science* 46, no. 1 (2002).

Nyblade, Benjamin. "Shushōno kenryoku kyōka to tanmei seiken" [Presidentialization of prime ministers and short-lived cabinets]. In *Seito seiji no konmei to seiken kōtai* [Partisan politics in turmoil and the regime change], edited by Nobuhiro Hiwatari and Jun Saito. Tokyo: Tokyo Daigaku Shuppankai, 2011.

Przewoski, Adam, and Fernando Limongi. "Modernization: Theories and Facts." *World Politics* 49, no. 1 (1997).

Ramseyer, J. Mark, and Eric B. Rasmusen. "Why Are Japanese Judges So Conservative in Politically Charged Cases?" *American Political Science Review* 95, no. 2 (2001).

Ramseyer, J. Mark, and Frances McCall Rosenbluth. *Japan's Political Marketplace.* Cambridge: Harvard University Press, 1993.

Richardson, Bradley M. "A Japanese House of Councillors Election: Support Mobilization and Political Recruitment." *Modern Asian Studies* 1, no. 4 (1967).

Samuels, David, and Richard Snyder. "The Value of a Vote: Malapportionment in Comparative

Perspective." *British Journal of Political Science* 31, no. 3 (2001).

Scheiner, Ethan. "Pipelines of Pork: Japanese Politics and a Model of Local Opposition Party Failure." *Comparative Political Studies* 38, no. 7 (2005).

Taagepera, Rein, and Matthew Soberg Shugart. *Seats and Votes: The Effects and Determinants of Electoral Systems*. New Haven: Yale University Press, 1989.

Tsebelis, George. "Decision Making in Political Systems: Veto Players in Presidentialism, Parliamentalism, Muliticameralism and Multipartism." *British Journal of Political Science* 25, no. 3 (1995).

Tsebelis, George, and Jeanntte Money. *Bicameralism*. Cambridge: Cambridge University Press, 1997.

CHAPTER 6 Kim Mikyoung
Embracing Asia: Japan's Expat Politics

PART 4

TOWARD A MULTICULTURAL SOLUTION?

CHAPTER 06

EMBRACING ASIA:
JAPAN'S EXPAT POLITICS

Kim Mikyoung

●

Kim Mikyoung is an Associate Professor at the Hiroshima Peace Institute, Hiroshima City University in Japan. Dr. Kim serves on the Governing Boards of the Association of Korean Political Studies (AKPS) and the International Political Studies Association (IPSA). She taught at Portland State University as a Fulbright Visiting Professor and served as a Public Diplomacy Specialist with the US Embassy in Seoul. She has published many articles and books on memory, human rights, and gender in Northeast Asia, including *Securitization of Human Rights: North Korean Refugees in East Asia* (Santa Barbara: ABC-CLIO, 2012) and *Northeast Asia's Difficult Past: Essays in Collective Memory* (New York: Palgrave Macmillan, 2010, Co-author with Barry Schwartz). She received her Ph.D. in Sociology from the University of Georgia, M.A. in Political Science from Kyunghee University, M.A. in Sociology and M.A. in Women's Studies from the University of Georgia, and B.A. in English Literature from Pusan National University.

Korean-Japanese under the Gaze

The island country of Japan is not escaping the whirlwind of globalization. Facing multiple challenges, Japan is trying hard to find ways to revive its fading glory. The cultural theory of "Nihonjinron"—the notion of the Japanese people as "unique" and "pure"—does not beneficially serve the needs of the fast-changing 21st century society. However, Nihonjinron's tenacity defines the tension between Japan's self-identity and its multicultural challenges. The vicissitudes of Zainichi (在日, "staying in Japan") Koreans, a most notable minority group in Japan, intersect with Japan's socio-political history. Their migration in significant numbers started during the first half of the 20th century. They began as colonial subjects, but became a stateless people upon liberation in 1945. Since then, they have been living on the margins of their host society. Having been the subjects of multiple forms of discrimination, Zainichi Koreans are now beginning to mark their place as an exemplary minority group. Two primary reasons explain these changes. First, Japan is facing an increasing economic need for more immigrant workers. The second reason is South Korea's improving stance vis-à-vis Japan. The tension between economic needs and South Korea's rising political clout, on the one hand, and cultural resistance, on the other, is dictating the dynamics of the discourse with regard to Zainichi Koreans' rights in Japan.

In 2008, Obama City went all out for the new leader of the free world, Mr. Barack Obama. Residents of the port city, in Japan's Fukui Prefecture, made great efforts in their support of Obama's presidential candidacy, from gathering signatures as a symbolic gesture to marketing his image by selling Obama fish cakes. A letter from a retired mayor of Obama City tried to give deeper significance to the coincidentally shared name by stressing the universal theme of common humanity. The historic election of Obama as the first black president of the United States and the enthusiastic reactions he generated in Japan demonstrated a glimpse of the rising awareness of multiculturalism and minority rights in the island country.

Japan is under mounting pressure to become multicultural and multiethnic. Measures to loosen up Japan's immigration policy are gaining momentum. Facing the challenges of a declining birth rate of 1.27

between 2005 and 2010 and negative growth in gross domestic product during the same period, Japan is aware of its need to address its demographic challenges in order to stay competitive in the world market. In 2000, the populations of China and India, Japan's emerging rivals and partners, were 1,261 billion and 1,014 billion, respectively. By 2050, the population of China is expected to reach 1,470 billion, and that of India is expected to reach 1,619 billion. By contrast, the population of Japan is expected to shrink from 128 million in 2005 to 94 million by 2050. The specter of a crippling labor shortage is alarming enough that the historically conservative Liberal Democratic Party has been preparing for legislation that would relax immigration policy. The ruling Democratic Party of Japan shares this concern.

Since the bursting of the economic bubble in the late 1980s and Junichiro Koizumi's reforms in the early 2000s, neoliberalism has become more prevalent in Japan, prioritizing "market forces." Communitarian practices, such as Japan's seniority system and lifetime employment, were replaced by policies fostering insecure forms of employment, such as the NEETs (Not in Employment, Education, or Training) and freetas (free arbeiters). The social fabric of Japan, supported by an affluent middle class, is on the verge of collapse. Equitable income redistribution is becoming passé. For example, the ratio of income transfers from the top quintile to the bottom quintile was 0.8, compared to the Organisation for Economic Co-operation and Development (OECD) average of 2.1 in 2008. With the rise of relative poverty, Japan's Gini coefficient has been deteriorating since 1980. According to the latest government statistics, more than 15 percent of the working population lives below the poverty line, earning less than 1.5 million yen per year. The majority of the impoverished group consists of single women and children.[1] These indicators point towards Japan losing its competitive advantage. Population decline is one of the major reasons.

Tokyo has taken various measures to deter the trend of population decline. For instance, the policy of "structural reform of family life" was

---

1 As for another socially disadvantaged group, women's suicide rate in Japan is the world's third highest, following South Korea and China. That of Japanese men ranks as the world's tenth highest. With regard to children's poverty in Japan, one out of seven underage children live in poverty.

introduced in the *2002 White Paper on the Quality of Life* (Kokumin seikatsu hakusho).[2] From the booklet distributed at various government offices, Japanese citizens learn about not only the serious implications of population decrease, but also the desirable form of a family. In the booklet, the "desirable family" is described as consisting of one Japanese male, one Japanese female, and their two children. It excludes descriptions of same-sex and interracial/ethnic marriages, let alone adoption. It purely focuses on a heterosexual marriage between Japanese. The booklet further imparts that a married couple should depend on each other, not only as equal financial contributors, but also as compatible emotional partners. The "traditional gender role within a family has to be changed in order to meet new challenges of changing times," it asserts. One man and one woman of the same ethnic background, with equal division of roles, are expected to produce two biological children. Through this pamphlet, the Japanese government is trying to dictate Japanese citizens' personal preferences by educating them about with whom they should fall in love, mate, and have children. It could be construed as an intrusive attempt to regulate people's hearts.[3] Due to aggressive public campaigns, the birth rate is on the rise, at 1.35 since 2007. The improvement, however, is far too little to remedy the current demographic imbalance. Japan is in need of higher numbers of foreign workers.

Demographics of foreign workers
As of 2005, the population of foreign residents constituted 1.57 percent (2,011,555) of the total Japanese population (127,756,815), up by 47.7 percent (649,184) from the previous decade.[4] Japan's foreign population is concentrated in the major urban industrial complexes around Tokyo, Nagoya/Toyota, and Osaka. Tokyo and Aichi (Nagoya/Toyota) Prefectures together account for 28.3 percent of the foreign population; add-

---

2 In the following year, the government introduced the Basic Law on Measures to Counter Declining Birth Rate (Shoshika shakai taisaku kihon ho), which guarantees paid maternity leave and medical coverage during pregnancy.

3 Another example of the Japanese government's efforts to regulate Japanese citizens' hearts is the newly inserted "patriotism" clause of the Constitution, added in 2007.

4 Approximately 100,000 illegal immigrants are estimated to be in Japan. See Louis D. Hayes, *Introduction to Japanese Politics*, 4th ed. (Armonk: East Gate, 2005), 152.

ing Osaka, Kanagawa, Saitama, Chiba, Shizuoka (Hamamatsu), Hyogo (Kobe), Gifu, and Ibaraki to this figure, it accounts for 70.7 percent.

Table 1: Selected Statistics on Foreign Residents (1998, 2004, 2005, 2007, 2008 in numbers)

	Status	1998	2004	2005	2007	2008
1	Total	1,512,116	1,973,747	2,011,555	2,152,974	2,217,426
2	Professor	5,374	8,153	8,406	8,436	8,333
3	Education	7,941	9,393	9,449	9,832	10,070
4	**Technician**	**15,242**	23,210	29,044	44,684	**52,273**
5	**Humanities Knowledge/ International Work**	**31,285**	47,682	55,276	61,763	**67,291**
6	Entertainment	28,871	64,742	36,376	15,728	13,031
7	**Skills**	**10,048**	13,373	15,112	21,261	**25,863**
8	Short-term Stay	59,815	72,446	68,747	49,787	40,407
9	**Study Abroad**	**59,648**	129,873	129,568	132,460	**138,514**
10	**Vocational School**	**39,691**	43,208	28,147	38,130	**138,514**
11	**Vocational Training**	**27,108**	54,317	54,107	88,086	**86,826**
12	Family Stay	65,675	81,919	86,055	98,167	107,641
13	**Specified Activities**	**19,634**	63,310	87,324	104,488	**121,863**
14	**Permanent Resident**	**93,364**	312,964	349,804	439,757	**492,056**
15	Foreign Spouse	264,844	257,292	259,656	256,980	245,497
16	Japanese Descent	211,275	250,734	265,639	268,604	258,498
17	Special Permanent Resident	533,396	465,619	451,909	430,229	420,305

Note: The bold categories increased by more than double from 1998 to 2008.
Source: Selected from Statistics on Foreign Residents [Zairyuu gaikokujin tsuke] (Heisei 13, 17, 18, 20, 21), Table 4 on "Registered Foreign Residents by Status per Administrative Unit" [Dotohuken-betsu zairyuushikaku (zairyuu mokuteki) betsu gaikokijindourokusha (tsusui)].

Skilled workers fill the labor shortage in the manufacturing sector. Student groups (e.g., study abroad, vocational training, and vocational schooling) are perceived to be a potential pool of culturally socialized future immigrants. Despite the rapid percentage increase, the number of immigrants remains relatively small when compared with other OECD countries (e.g., Britain at 4.6 percent [1999], France at 5.5 percent [1999], Germany at 9.7 percent [2002], the United States at 12.1 percent [2005], and Australia at 21.8 percent [2001]). Japan's 1.6 percent is still far below the average among the advanced economies.[5]

Koreans constitute the majority of the foreign population of Japan, at 29.8 percent according to 2005 government statistics. Other major immigrant groups include Chinese, Brazilians, Filipinos, Peruvians, and Americans. In responding to the increase in the non-Japanese population, the Ministry of Internal Affairs and Communications finally published proposals toward facilitating a society of "multicultural conviviality" in 2006.

The Japanese Immigration Control Policy has undergone gradual change since 1945. In the immediate postwar era between 1945 and 1951, immigration and emigration were strictly controlled. They remained that way until the period of rapid economic growth between 1951 and 1981. Office and factory automation systems were adopted to meet the increasing demands for labor during the period of export-oriented industrialization. There were no notable changes in the 1980s, except that a very limited number of refugees were admitted. With an emerging civil society discourse, foreigners' rights drew attention from the wider audience within Japan's society. From 1990 onwards, higher numbers of foreigners have been admitted as unskilled workers (mostly Brazilians and Peruvians of Japanese descent) and vocational trainees (mostly Chinese and Southeast Asians) while strict immigration control remains intact.

The ethnic makeup of Japanese society is already changing. For instance, the Japanese government invited 1,000 nursing students from Indonesia during 2009 and 2010 to make up for the lack of elder-care service personnel. The first batch arrived during the summer of 2009 and began Japanese language training with the help of government subsidies. In the near future, the foreign student admission quota is expected to increase from the current 130,000 to 300,000. The government also wants to pave the road for the admission of "intelligent immigrants," a desirable group, while making permanent residency permits easier to obtain by reducing the currently existing requirement of 10 years of

5 Stephen Robert Nagy, "Local Government and Multicultural Coexistence Practices in the Tokyo Metropolitan Area: Integrating a Growing Foreign Minority Population," in *Ethnic Minorities and Regional Development in Asia: Reality and Challenges*, ed. Huhua Cao (Amsterdam: Amsterdam University Press, 2009), 174.

work. However, the translation of proposals into empirical reality would be a different story. Though Japan as a country sees the necessity of having more foreigners in its territory, would the arrival of "aliens" be accepted in Japanese society?

The experience of ethnic minorities in Japan suggests that the road to multiculturalism is going to be bumpy. Accepting foreigners as a substitute for the dwindling Japanese labor force is a separate issue from acknowledging them as rightful co-inhabitants of the land. The latter is the policy domain of the government, whereas the former entails the cultural tolerance of the Japanese people. Robotic machines replaced many Japanese workers amid the economic boom of the 1960s and 1970s, but now foreigners are being tapped as a substitute for the shrinking Japanese labor pool. Without an emotive commitment by the people at a cultural level, robots and foreign workers could well be seen in the same light from economic and cultural perspectives.

Cultural resistance of Nihonjinron

The Nihonjinron "theorem" serves as an explanation for Japan's xenophobic nationalism. The theorem gained popularity in the 1980s when "the world came to see Japan" on account of its phenomenal economic growth. Japan ascended to the world's second largest economy only four decades after its unconditional surrender. The theorem arguably explicates Japan's uniqueness, for posited reasons ranging from the Japanese people's aversion to imported rice to their intellectual superiority.[6] Nihonjinron, the theory of "Japaneseness," is a genre of literature focusing on Japanese culture, people, society, history, and national interest. "Japaneseness" is analyzed by various academic fields, including sociology, anthropology, political science, archaeology, history, linguistics, and psychology. This genre of literature, including books, magazines, and daily newspapers, intends to emphasize the uniqueness of Japan and differentiate the country from the rest of the world.

As another side to the coin, Nihonjinron simultaneously serves as

---

6 The empirical evidence ranges from the unique workings of the Japanese digestive system (e.g., longer intestines than Westerners) and peace-loving attitudes (e.g., consumption of more vegetables than meat) to intellectual superiority (e.g., Japanese usage of chopsticks and the brain-stimulating visual effects of the Japanese writing system).

an effective tool in excluding foreigners from inclusion in Japan's society. As one nursing home owner told a Japanese newspaper, "I will avoid hiring the Indonesian nurses even after they pass the national qualification exams. I prefer working with young Japanese workers." The reality of an understaffed and half-idle facility apparently did not change the owner's adamant position. "Why does the government provide the Indonesians with free language training? They will go back to their country after all, and their educational subsidy comes from us, the Japanese tax payers," complained another person in a media report. Foreigners, the auxiliary labor force, are perceived to be temporary visitors, not rightful members of the society.

Japan as a nation needs foreign workers. But Japan as a society wants the least costly laborers who are as similar as possible to themselves. With the Japanese and global job markets now rapidly deteriorating, is equal protection being granted to immigrant workers? It is not likely, because debates on immigration and labor policies have proceeded with insufficient deliberation on universal human values.

Refugee politics shed a similar light on how distant Japan is from the rest of the industrialized democracies. It took 31 years before the Japanese government, a signatory to the 1951 Refugee Treaty, began cracking open its door to refugees in 1982. Japan then admitted an average of only three refugees a year between 1988 and 1997. The number increased to 20 upon the government's 1998 decision to apply a revised domestic law to international asylum seekers. As of 2002, a grand total of 284 refugees were living in Japan. The disparity with other advanced countries is glaring. Japan granted refugee status to a mere 22 cases in 2000, a year when the corresponding figures were 24,000 for the United States, 13,989 for Canada, 11,446 for Germany, and 10,185 for the United Kingdom. Japan had 216 asylum seekers in 2000, and an admission rate of about 10 percent. The figure is in drastic contrast with the 38 percent in the United States (63,650 applicants), 37 percent in Canada (37,860 applicants), 15 percent in Germany (78,760 applicants), and 11 percent in the United Kingdom (98,900 applicants).

The Japanese government cites two reasons to explain this puzzling phenomenon: geographical isolation and cultural understanding. Because Japan is an island country lacking land borders with neighbors, access to the nation for prospective refugees is limited. Or so the argument goes. Officials also assert that Japanese language skills are an important element of the refugee-screening process. However, such excuses fail to explain why only 20 Chinese (including ethnic Koreans) and 100 Burmese applied for refugee status in Japan between 1999 and 2001. During the same period, 63,000 Chinese and 110,000 Burmese sought asylum in geographically distant Western countries. They knocked on the borders of Australia and New Zealand at rates 60 times and seven times higher than in Japan, respectively. Furthermore, refugees are not likely to study a foreign language before they flee. The desperate situation propels them to leave the place of their origin. The selection criterion of linguistic proficiency poses an improbably high hurdle to the externally displaced people seeking protection through various international covenants.

The Japanese government's explanations are not convincing enough to explain why there are so few foreign workers and refugees in an otherwise ultramodern Japan: something else is going on. Japanese society avoids confronting the "something else" because to do so would cause discomfort, inconvenience, and urusa (noise)—an unwelcome assault on the aesthetic collective experience. Yet the whirlwind of globalization is forcing the Japanese modus operandi of cultural intolerance into a defensive crouch.

Foreigners in Japan are often blamed for many social woes, such as criminal activities and drug use. At the same time, violations of foreigners' human rights by Japanese are not negligible.[7] The United Nations Human Rights Report and the US Department of State Country Reports on Human Rights Practices express concerns over the "deeply rooted" racial discrimination against ethnic minorities in Japan. The controversial and discontinued fingerprinting requirement for alien registration was revived, in a different form, in November 2007. All foreigners entering Japan, with the exception of permanent residency holders, have

---

7 The Japanese universal human rights debates are almost exclusively focused on the abductees in North Korea. The Pyongyang regime violated the human rights of Japanese citizens who were forcefully taken to the socialist country. Japan, however, is silent on the protection of foreigners' rights for those living in Japan, let alone the rights of foreign victims of Japan's military conquests.

to submit index fingerprints and a photo at the Japanese port of entry. The system was resurrected in the aftermath of the September 11, 2001 terrorist attacks in the United States. Considering the fact that most terrorist attacks in Japan have been committed by Japanese (e.g., the Aum Shinrikyo sarin gas attacks in the Tokyo subway system in 1995 and the Red Army's hijacking of a Japan Airlines flight in 1970), the justifications for the requirement are very thin.

The re-emergence of nationalism in Japan, often supported by the tenacious Nihonjinron discourse, could be an outcome of globalization, where increasing numbers of migrant workers are pressuring Japan to transform into a multiethnic/multicultural environment.[8] The consecutive power changes among conservative elites add more fuel to the general socio-political trend tilting towards conservative nationalism. The Abe administration's educational reform, for instance, has introduced changes in school curricula that aim to instill patriotism among the youths. The public media has also increased the number of programs on Japan's unique culture, history, and authentic regionalism. While the civil society has embraced multicultural coexistence (tabunka kyosei), the government, business elites, and journalists tend to maintain the myth of Japan's uniqueness and homogeneity. The cultural nationalism is reflected in literature and the moral education textbooks re-enforcing the Nihonjinron ideology.

The focal points of comparison and contrast are "others," particularly from the Western countries with strong political and economic relationships with Japan. Nihonjinron has been playing a salient role in creating and sustaining Japanese identity since its encounter with the outside world. As the modernization pioneers (e.g., Fukuzawa Yukichi and Yoshida Shoin) advocated the motto of "Japanese Spirit, Western Technology" (wakon yosai), Japan has been trying hard to strike a balance between its unique identity and foreign imports. In propagating

---

8 Erich Kolig, S. M. Angeles, and Sam Wong, "Introduction: Crossroad Civilisations and Bricolage Identities," in *Identity in Crossroad Civilisations*, ed. Erich Kolig, Vivienne S. M. Angeles, and Sam Wong (Amsterdam: Amsterdam University Press, 2009), 18; Takeyuki Tsuda, "When Minorities Migrate: The Racialization of the Japanese Brazilians in Brazil and Japan," in *Asian Diasporas: New Formations, New Conceptions*, ed. Rhacel S. Parreñas and Lok C. D. Siu (Stanford: Stanford University Press, 2007), 225-251.

Japaneseness to discourse consumers, Nihonjinron serves as a major tool kit for the maintenance of national and cultural identity.[9]

> What is at issue [in the Japanese mind] is the invincible belief in that uniqueness and the claiming of uniqueness in the Nihonjinron discourse. . . . Comprehension of these unique features supposedly requires not rational or logical understanding, but an intuitive insight into Japanese culture that only natives can achieve. Thus foreigners are defined as incapable of understanding the essence of Japanese culture. This belief gives comfort to the Japanese: here is one essential "sociocultural territory" they can protect as their own. *The notion that foreigners could fully comprehend Japanese culture and therefore act and behave like any Japanese threatens their ethnic and national integrity.*[10]

In order to protect the unity of Japan along the lines of ethnic homogeneity, Nihonjinron connects the "pure-blooded" people to the land, race, culture, language, and religion of the country.[11] Japanese culture, characterized as ethnicity, artistry, citizenship, and race, leads to proprietary nationalism, since a nation consists of collective individuals.[12] In other words, it is a sentiment of "exclusive ownership" that can be exercised only by the Japanese themselves. Such proprietary nationalism indicates that "only Japanese can (or should) possess things Japanese."[13] Only those people who have Japanese blood and practice Japanese culture with native Japanese speaking ability are acknowledged as "us" vis-

9 Harumi Befu, "Symbols of Nationalism and Nihonjinron," in *Ideology and Practice in Modern Japan*, ed. Roger Goodman and Kirsten Refsing (London: Routledge, 1992), 26–46; Harumi Befu, *Hegemony of Homogeneity: An Anthropological Analysis of Nihonjinron* (Melbourne: Trans Pacific Press, 2001); Harumi Befu, "Concepts of Japan, Japanese Culture and the Japanese," in *The Cambridge Companion to Modern Japanese Culture*, ed. Yoshio Sugimoto (Cambridge: Cambridge University Press, 2009), 21–37.

10 Befu, *Hegemony of Homogeneity: An Anthropological Analysis of Nihonjinron*, 67. Italics added for emphasis.

11 Ibid.

12 Brian J. McVeigh, *Nationalisms of Japan: Managing and Mystifying Identity* (Lanham: Rowman & Littlefield Publishers, 2003), 187.

13 Ibid.

à-vis others.[14]

Zainichi Koreans live through the politics of exclusiveness framed by Nihonjinron. The colonial discourse justified the plight of the subjugated people for their passivity, submissiveness, fatalism, and self-blame.[15] According to this colonial discourse, the subjugated deserved their harsh reality for being weak, whereas the superior Japanese race prevailed over the inferior in a contemporary manifestation of Social Darwinism. Justified by their colonial legacies, Koreans have been the subjects of contempt, discrimination, and hostility, as demonstrated time and again in various opinion polls (see Tables 2 and 3).

Table 2: Do You LIKE or DISLIKE the Following Ethnic Groups? (1951)

Ethnic Group	Percentage		Frequency		Total
	Like	Dislike	Like	Dislike	
Korean	5.06	**94.94**	8	**150**	158
Chinese	22.92	77.08	22	74	96
American	**96.53**	3.47	**167**	6	173

Note: Percentage was calculated from the original frequency table.

Source: Adapted from Seiichi Izumi, "Tokyo shoshimin no iminzoku ni taisuru taido" [Average Tokyo citizen's attitude towards different ethnic groups], in Shakaiteki kincho no kenkyu *[A study on social tension], ed. Nihon Jinbun Kagakukai (Tokyo: Yuhikaku, 1951): 431.*

---

14 Japanese-Brazilians in Japan are also discriminated against for not fitting the proper stereotype of Japaneseness. Pure blood lineage does not sufficiently qualify a person to be properly Japanese. See Tsuda, "When Minorities Migrate: The Racialization of the Japanese Brazilians in Brazil and Japan," 225–251. As another example of Nihonjinron, former Prime Minister Yasuhiro Nakasone stated in September 1986 that citizens of Japan had higher average intelligence than those of the United States because Japan has no minorities: "The level of knowledge in the United States is lower than in Japan due to the considerable number of blacks, Puerto Ricans and Mexicans."

15 Teak-Lim Yoon, "Tal'shikmin yoksa'ssuki: Bi'kongshik yoksa'wa dajungjuk juchae" [Writing postcolonial histories: counter histories and multiple subjects], *Korean Cultural Anthropology* 27 (1995): 55–56.

Table 3: What Do You Think of Characters of the Following Ethnic Groups?
[(1) dishonest, (2) honest, (3) kind, (4) not kind, (5) polite/courteous, (6) rude,
(7) friendly, (8) unfriendly, (9) wicked, (10) good-natured, (11) stingy, (12) generous]

	1	2	3	4	5	6	7	8	9	10	11	12
Korean	44	1	1	9	1	15	2	6	16	0	5	1
Chinese	32	7.3	6	5	5	9	8	3	13	2.2	9	2
American	2	7.4	41	0	7	1	25	1	2	1.9	0	10

Note: Percentage was calculated and rounded from the original frequency table.
Source: Adapted from Seiichi Izumi, "Tokyo shoshimin no iminzoku ni taisuru taido" [Average Tokyo citizen's attitude towards different ethnic groups], in Shakaiteki kincho no kenkyu [A study on social
tension], ed. Nihon Jinbun Kagakukai (Tokyo: Yuhikaku, 1951): 434-35 (Table 5).

Zainichi Citizenship Rights

Rights discourse

"The politics of legal status" equates nationality with ethno-national identity and national essence. The exclusion of Koreans from Japanese citizenry is a continuation of Japan's colonial legacy. The imperial community, with the emperor as the head of state, had no place for non-Japanese people except those who were proven to be thoroughly assimilated as imperial subjects. Japan maintains a strict naturalization system that demands the highest degree of applicant assimilation into Japanese society and culture. Against the backdrop of Nihonjinron, the sovereign state of Japan exercises strict control over citizenship as a means to protect national interests and identity.

Social citizenship entails the reciprocity between rights and duties, whereas national identity constitutes the essence of citizenship. "Citizenship" is usually used interchangeably with the term "nationality," which is about one's unconditional right to enter the state's territories and the right to diplomatic protection. Today's full citizenship corresponds to nationality, and yet this has rarely been the case. In the Western experience, full citizenship was typically limited to male property owners before the introduction of universal suffrage.. In colonial empires, colonized subjects' nationality was often attributed to their "mother country," but they were not granted "full citizenship."[16] Western cultures have often given priority to civil and political rights, sometimes at the expense of economic and social rights, such as the right to work, education, health, and housing.

Japan's "politics of legal status" is an interesting contrast to Western European countries' immigration policies. Immigrant settlement led Western European countries to grant "partial" citizenship rights to resident aliens. A new group of non-citizens, "denizens," emerged for those who had permanent residence status and enjoyed extensive civil and social rights, but no electoral rights in national politics. With the increase in denizens, nationality laws have been revised, particularly in countries with the principle of jus sanguinis ("by parentage"). The changes include the establishment or broadening of the categories of second-generation immigrants who enjoy a legal claim to nationality, such as in Germany and Sweden, and greater tolerance for dual nationality, such as in Switzerland and the Netherlands. In the European context, Korean residents can be regarded as "denizens" for their partial citizenship.

Legal changes and reality
Korean migration in the late 19th century can be contextualized within regional geopolitical shifts. In the example of the Amur region in the Russian Far East, the number of settlers increased from 470 between 1891 and 1892, to 1,050 between 1892 and 1893, up to 6,300 in 1906. However, they soon became the target of migration and settlement control after Korea's annexation in 1910. The Russians feared that the settlers could be used for Japan's territorial ambitions for Russia.

The number of Korean settlers in Japan fluctuated. As Japan was garnering resources and manpower to engage in the Asia-Pacific War, the total number of settlers reached 800,000 in 1938. By the time of liberation, 2.3 million Koreans were living in Japan. Most of them returned to the Korean Peninsula, while 600,000 stayed behind. By March 1946, 546,000 applied to return to South Korea, whereas less than 10,000

---

16 Chikako Kashiwazaki, "The Politics of Legal Status: The Equation of Nationality with Ethnonational Identity," in *Koreans in Japan: Critical Voices from the Margin*, ed. Sonia Ryang (London: Routledge Curzon, 2000), 13–31.

people desired to return to North Korea.[17] The conditions of return were harsh because the Japanese government limited the total carry-out cash to 1,000 yen per person.

From 1959 until 1967, 82,000 Koreans and 6,000 Japanese (mostly wives) were repatriated to North Korea.[18] These reparations were the outcome of Tokyo's desire to remove the Korean population from its territory and Pyongyang's wish to prove itself the "true home" for the Zainichi Koreans.[19] On the other hand, South Korea and Japan normalized their relations with the signing of an agreement on the legal status of South Korean nationals in Japan in 1965. Permanent residence was granted to all those who had resided in Japan since the annexation. The Park Chung-hee regime encouraged Zainichi Koreans to reside in Japan permanently under its own anti-communist ideology, and was less concerned about their repatriation to Korea.[20] The issue of the legal status of Korean residents in Japan was settled without reaching an agreement on the permanent resident status eligibility for the grandchildren's generation during the 1961 to 1965 normalization talks. Application of the status was due in 1971, but the children born after 1971 to permanent resident parents would also be automatically granted permanent resident status. To acquire permanent resident status, applicants had to prove their South Korean nationality. It was also agreed that these stipulations were going to be reviewed in 1991 so that the status of third-generation Koreans could be settled.

During the period between 1945 and 1979, civil rights protection for non-Japanese was almost nonexistent. Foreigners were the targets of exclusion and discrimination, while also being placed under intense pressure to assimilate into Japanese society. The 1970s marked some progressive changes at the municipal levels when Japan began paying

---

17 Ninety-seven percent of Koreans in Japan came from the southern part of the peninsula.

18 Tessa Morris-Suzuki, *Exodus to North Korea: Shadows from Japan's Cold War* (Lanham: Rowman & Littlefield Publishers, 2007).

19 North Korea wanted to defeat the capitalist South in their rivalry for legitimacy. The Pyongyang regime asserted that the South was nothing more than a puppet for US imperialism, and, therefore, could not be a "true home" for the Zainichi groups.

20 Kimiko Shibata, "The South Korean Government's Position on Overseas Koreans (1961-1965)" (paper presented at the workshop on "The Japanese-South Korean Relationship," The European Institute of Japanese Studies, Stockholm, Sweden, August 21–22, 2009).

attention to social movements in the United States, such as anti-war and civil rights activism. An increasing number of municipalities in the Kansai and Kanto areas removed the nationality requirements for public office, but these remain a minority. The Ministry of Home Affairs still maintains that those who do not hold Japanese citizenship cannot be appointed to positions that involve the "execution of public power" or the "formation of the will of local municipalities." This means that non-Japanese nationals can hold only professional or clerical positions in local government that do not entail executive or managerial responsibilities. Such government policies lend justifications to private-sector discrimination against Koreans.[21] In 1979, Japan ratified the International Convention of Human Rights. The Ministries of Construction and Finance removed their nationality qualifications from Public Housing and Housing Finance Corporation law. Yet, discrimination in housing rights still remains widespread in surreptitious ways despite these legal reforms.[22]

The 1980s saw some positive changes from the perspective of equality and internationalization. In 1984, Japan ratified the Convention on the Elimination of All Forms of Discrimination against Women and Nationality. It meant citizenship could be acquired from either parent, and nationality could be chosen at the age of 22. In the following year, the Family Registration Law was revised for naturalized citizens of Korean origin, allowing them to use their original family names in the family registry. These progressive revisions of laws did not necessarily mean their actual implementation. Many reports were filed against local government offices claiming they exerted pressure against those who tried to change their Japanese names to Korean names in the family registry.[23] One notable change in the Zainichi demography is that since the late 1980s about 80 percent of Korean residents have been marrying

---

21 Yoshio Sugimoto, *An Introduction to Japanese Society*, 2nd ed. (Cambridge: Cambridge University Press, 2003), 195.

22 Ibid., 196

23 There also are many reports filed by single mothers who tried to receive government subsidies from the window clerks at local government offices. Instead of processing these lawful requests, the clerks often lectured the women on their personal life choices, such as childbirth, divorce, and employment patterns.

Japanese.

Settlement and coexistence issues have drawn more attention since 1990. For instance, in 1990 the Japanese Ministry of Justice installed a new category of permanent residents, the "general permanent residents" (ippan eijuu) under which Koreans other than South Korean passport holders could apply. The total number of foreigners under this status reached 268,000. Pro-North Korea Zainichi could enter and leave Japan using a non-Japanese passport under this policy. Furthermore, local election rights were guaranteed by the Constitution in 1995. Local public official positions were open to foreigners the following year. In the 1990s, out of 60,000 Zainichi Koreans, 25 percent were affiliated with pro-Pyongyang Chosensouren, also known as Souren, while 65 percent had pro-Seoul Mindan memberships. Around 5,000 Zainichi Koreans chose to remain stateless. In the 1970s, the number of students enrolled at Souren schools was 46,000. As of 2009, this number had decreased to 15,000. Local governments became more accommodative of the Souren graduates in their college admission policies. Before 2000, Japanese national universities did not allow applicants from the North Korean schools because their entire curriculum was conducted in the Korean language, whereas more than 50 percent of private universities permitted their applications on account of the applicants' dual language proficiency. Due to educational discrimination, the majority of Zainichi Koreans are self-employed with traditionally Korean-owned pachinko (pinball) shops.[24]

Table 4: The Industrial Distribution of Zainichi Korean Companies (Unit: number and percentage)

Classification	Total Number	Percentage
Agriculture/Mining	31	0.34
Construction	**1240**	**13.74**
Manufacturing	921	10.20
Transportation	146	1.62

24 Ju-mong Na and Young-eun Im, "Jaeil Korian kiup'eui jiyok'byol tteuksung'mit netuiwokui'kujo'ae kwanhan yonku" [A study on the regional characteristics and network structure of Zainichi Korean companies]. (paper presented at the International Studies Association of Korea, Dongguk University, Seoul, Korea, November 4, 2006).

Wholesale/Retail	794	8.79
Food/Restaurant	**1136**	**12.58**
Finances/Insurance	285	3.16
Real Estate	982	10.88
Other Services	1238	13.71
Pachinko	**1549**	**17.16**
Other Leisure	270	2.99
Professional Services	436	4.83
Total	9028	100

Source: Zainichi Chousenjinshoukourenkaigai [The Association of Korean Japanese Merchants and Industries], Douhoukeizaikenkyuu [The journal of compatriot economy] 6 (2002): 18.

Table 5 shows that Zainichi Koreans are doing better than the average Japanese in terms of occupational prestige and annual income. The Zainichi population is concentrated in the Kanto region, at 32.1 percent (16.21 percent in Tokyo); in the Kansai area, at 43.3 percent (24.43 percent in Osaka); and in Kyushuu, at 4.78 percent (3.44 percent in

Table 5: Comparative Class Positions of Majority Japanese and Zainichi Koreans

	Japanese at large	Zainichi Koreans
Class indicators	Average	Average
Educational attainment (Years of schooling)	12.35	12.01
Occupational prestige score	47.32	48.02
Annual personal income (in 10,000 Yen)	494.23	531.84
Occupational classification	Percentage	Percentage
Upper white-collar	22.4	14.2
Lower white-collar	20.2	12.4
Self-employed	23.2	52.1
Blue-collar	28.3	21.0
Agriculture	5.9	0.3
Total Percentage	100.0	100.0
Sample size	1,092	676

Source: Adapted from Myeongsu Kim and Tadashi Inazuki, "Zainichi kankokujin no shakai idou" [Social mobility of resident Koreans in Japan], in Kaisou shakai kara atarashii shimin shakai e [From stratified society to new civil society], ed. Kenji Kousaka, 181–199, vol. 6, SSM 95a (Tokyo: Daigaku Shuppankai, 2000): 189.

Fukuoka). This demonstrates a pattern of geographical concentration similar to other foreigners.

The rising tension between North Korea and Japan in the 2000s was translated into more cases of harassment and bullying against Zainichi Koreans. For example, between 2002 and 2003, about 500 attacks were reported. This led to Zainichi Koreans protesting in Tokyo in May 2007. Victims of harassment and bullying argued that the link to Pyongyang's abduction of Japanese citizens did not justify Japanese harassment of Zainichi Koreans. The cases of bullying are a reflection of traditional Japanese contempt for Koreans. These latent psychological prejudices seem to rise to the surface at the slightest appearance of provocation.

Japan's founding constitutional principles in the postwar era—pacifism, liberal democracy, and human rights—seem to exclude the rights of Zainichi. Despite their consisting of third and fourth generations of people who willingly migrated, or were forcibly taken, from the Korean Peninsula during the Japanese occupation before and during World War II, their legal status has been severely restricted in the political domain. This is in sharp contrast to the status of African Americans in the United States. The Fifteenth Amendment of the US Constitution established universal voting rights in principle, although it took the Voting Rights Act of 1965 for this key right to be fully implemented. Behind this long-fought and hard-won triumph were visionaries and activists of various races, creeds, and genders. Even though the Japanese government's immigration proposals are based on the American model, vastly different cultural norms in Japan and the United States are visible in the differing experiences of Zainichi Koreans in Japan and ethnic minorities in the United States.[25]

Conclusion: Expat Politics

Japan is currently at a crossroads. It is trying to re-establish its identity and redefine its posture in a rapidly shifting global landscape. China's rise and Japan's relative decline are at the epicenter of these changing dynamics. Japan's position vis-à-vis China in terms of military strength,

---

25 This comparative statement is not to undermine the potent racism in the United States.

economic competitiveness, and political leadership is causing much anxiety in the Japanese government. Specifically, Japan has had to tread the precarious waters between the United States, its traditional ally, and China, its emerging partner and rival. South Korea, a traditional object of Japan's contempt, is no longer dismissible. Confusion and soul-searching define the current state of affairs.

There are two defining forces whose momentum has been carried through contemporary Japanese history to the present day. First, the Meiji Restoration, Japan's response to Western encroachment, proved Japanese prowess at being an international player. Progressive visionaries such as Yoshida Shoin, Sakamoto Ryoma, and Fukuzawa Yukichi advocated that Japan emulate the more advanced West, which thereby jump-started the nation's modernization efforts. Ironically, successful modernization paved the way for the provocation of war, and eventually led to Japan's own defeat. The subsequent unconditional surrender of Japan to the allied powers in 1945 marked the second defining force in contemporary Japanese history.

Japan's postwar trajectory explains the current confusion and chaos. There is relatively wide consensus that Japan's prosperity over the past 60 years was enabled by Japan's central place in the US regional security framework. Japan's postwar economic accomplishments were fertile ground for resurrecting national pride and self-esteem. However, the majority of ordinary Japanese people nurtured mixed feelings about the awkward co-presence of the Peace Constitution and the US-Japan military alliance, which negated the very spirit and principle of the Constitution.

Things have now changed. Traditional Japanese pride and self-esteem are being overshadowed by self-doubt and a lack of specific direction. The elderly are anxious about retirement pensions, while the youth are concerned about finding employment. Rural populations are isolated and aging, and the middle-aged are worried about job security. One of the reasons behind Japan's state of hopelessness stems from policy elites' failure to preempt certain repercussions of Japan's habitual resignation to reality while being entrenched in power politics.

Japanese policy elites' dominant intellectual current has been heavily imbued with power politics. Maruyama Masao, a well-known scholar of Japanese political culture, once characterized the concept of Japanese reality as having three strong biases: it is submissive to the given, rather than rising to the challenge; it is one-dimensional, rather than multifaceted and flexible; and it is submissive to the strong and coercive against the weak. Japan's elites believe that international order is permanently predatory. Incidentally, this explains why they often come across as stolid in their recognition of Japan's tainted historical record in Asia. They blame victims' powerlessness for their unfortunate experiences, while relieving themselves from accountability for past acts of Japanese aggression.

As an extension of this lack of penitence, Japan's conservative elites consistently argue that the Peace Constitution is American-imposed and excessively apologetic. They argue that it must be amended so that Japan can become a "normal," rearmed country, which they say is only possible if Japan takes certain measures to adapt itself to the current power-centric international system. They also argue that the Peace Constitution's "excessive" human rights protections should be restricted in favor of the "national interest." Their dismissive attitude towards human rights has been translated into stringent gatekeeping. They vehemently oppose the arrival of international refugees, including North Korean escapees, into Japan's territory, and are self-absorbed when responding to Japanese abduction issues. Furthermore, this brand of politician has been largely dismissive of past atrocities committed by Japan on the Korean Peninsula, such as forcing Koreans to be laborers and "comfort women." Japanese conservative elites' particularistic perception obscures Japan's ability to regard itself in favor of universal human rights.

History suggests that human dignity is beginning to be recognized as an essential universal value. The ability to provide for basic human rights and democratic governance has become a basic norm for any state seeking legitimacy as a responsible member of the international community. The debates on historical perception between Korea and Japan are ultimately about the respect for and protection of human rights, which were violated, concealed, then ambivalently redressed by the Japanese government.

The current state of confusion and soul-searching will hopefully change Japanese power elites' perception with regard to human rights and make them recognize that other people's pains sometimes can be as hurtful as their own. This would take a healthy dosage of imaginative idealism. Such a leap in belief systems would be helpful not only in curing ubiquitous domestic woes, but also in mending fences with neighbors like Korea and China. The East Asian Community can prosper only when its members acknowledge, respect, and trust one another.

Furthermore, a breakthrough during this current state of confusion and soul-searching will only happen when ordinary Japanese people realize that it is the common citizen, not political elites, who should be in charge of Japan's future. Ownership of sovereign rights has been exercised by the peoples of South Korea, Taiwan, the Philippines, and Thailand to change the course of their respective countries. The Japanese people need to wake up to irreversible democratic trends. A starting point would be to purge, once and for all, their entrenched sense of resignation to their problematic "reality."

This paper has argued that Zainichi Korean citizenship debates should be embedded within the Korean diaspora. The debate within the diaspora is, in essence, a liberating discourse that refutes Zainichi Koreans' subordinate status in their host country, thereby denying that they should be second-class citizens because they are part of an "ethnic minority."[26] One's diasporic condition is defined by one's being situated in between one's "home" and one's host country because diasporic existence involves the simultaneous affiliation and disidentification with both places.[27]

Zainichi Koreans have an "identity bricolage" that consists of several bits and pieces that form their group and individual identity.[28] The multilayered identity of Zainichi Koreans shifts from political correctness to post-coloniality, but most of them live without a distinct Korean

---

26 Rhacel Salazar Parreñas and Lok C. D. Siu, "Introduction: Asian Diasporas—New Conceptions, New Frameworks," in *Asian Diasporas: New Formations, New Conceptions*, ed. Rhacel S. Parreñas and Lok C. D. Siu (Stanford: Stanford University Press, 2007), 1–27.

27 Ibid.

28 Kolig, Angeles, and Wong, "Introduction: Crossroad Civilisations and Bricolage Identities," 11–13.

identity in most aspects of their daily lives.[29] They do not have any particular allegiance to the motherlands of South Korea or North Korea, and do not feel particularly foreign in Japan. One element that marks their identity formation comes from their affiliation with either Mindan or Souren "expat politics." In the 1960s, for instance, the majority of them later took sides with North Korea.[30] By 1969, the Zainichi population was almost evenly divided between Souren and Mindan, but Mindan gathered more support as the South Korean economy fared better than the economy of socialist North Korea. During the 1980s, Mindan were at the forefront of civil rights movements against discrimination and the fingerprinting policies of Japan. Their activism was in synchronization with South Korea's democratization movement.[31] In the mood of détente on the Korean Peninsula, Mindan and Souren announced their decision to integrate. This quickly fell apart in 2005, with the news of Pyongyang's nuclear development programs.

The identity and status of Zainichi have been closely associated with the state of affairs on the Korean Peninsula. "Home" has still been the ground of "expat politics." By the same token, Zainichis' citizenship rights have close associations with Korea's multicultural practices. Unless Korea, the motherland, makes sincere efforts to peacefully co-exist with its own "others," Zainichis' position is bound to remain shaky. Yoo, for instance, argues that foreign workers in Korea feel discriminated against because of different modes of communication, ways of life, and work

29 Koichi Iwabuchi, "Political Correctness, Postcoloniality, and the Self-Representation of 'Koreanness' in Japan," in Koreans in Japan: Critical Voices from the Margin, ed. Sonia Ryang (London: Routledge Curzon, 2000), 55–73.

30 The progressive factions of Japan, such as the communists and socialists, were sympathetic with the plight of Zainichi Koreans in their class struggle. Back then, North Korea was better off economically, and Souren had a bigger membership than Mindan during the 1950s and 1960s.

31 Marie Söderberg, "The Struggle for a Decent Life in Japan: The Korean Minority Adapting to Changing Legal and Political Conditions" (paper presented at the workshop on "The Japanese-South Korean Relationship," The European Institute of Japanese Studies, Stockholm, Sweden, August 21–22, 2009), 5–12.

habits.[32] This rings true for the experiences of Koreans in Japan. Without an example set from "home," the voices of Zainichi are bound to be silenced.

Table 6: Complaints Filed on the Basis of Discrimination (number of cases [%])

Classification	02	03	04	05	06	07	Total	%	Closed	Pending
				Filed						
Others	25	98	117	228	117	256	841	21.0	785	56
Educational History	-	28	12	48	24	27	139	3.5	135	4
Medical History	10	16	7	21	30	31	115	2.9	110	5
Sexual Orientation	4	2	1	5	4	3	19	0.5	16	3
Criminal Record	7	3	7	23	12	17	69	1.7	65	4
Ideas	4	7	-	5	2	2	20	0.5	19	1
Skin Color	1	-	-	1	0	1	3	0.1	3	0
Ethnicity	1	-	-	1	1	4	7	0.2	6	1
Family Status	1	2	4	15	8	13	43	1.1	42	1
Pregnancy/Children	-	15	4	5	9	16	49	1.2	44	5
Marital Status	2	4	7	9	22	3	47	1.2	46	1
Appearance	2	4	6	45	10	20	87	2.2	80	7
Racial Origin	-	1	-	-	0	1	2	0.0	2	0
Country of Origin	20	19	10	19	28	37	133	3.3	119	14
Region of Origin	5	2	6	23	9	8	53	1.3	52	1
Social Status	48	75	64	297	208	117	809	20.2	793	16
Age	7	24	57	87	69	107	351	8.8	337	14
Disability	33	18	54	121	115	245	586	14.6	529	57
Religion	6	5	8	11	8	12	50	1.3	47	3
Sexual Harassment	2	1	-	62	104	163	332	8.3	296	36
Gender	11	34	25	55	44	76	245	6.1	229	16
	189	358	389	1,081	824	1,159	4,000	100	3,755	245

Source: Annual Report 2007, National Human Rights Commission of the Republic of Korea, accessed June 13, 2012, http://www.asiapacificforum.net/members/full-members/republic-of-korea/downloads/annual-reports/Annual_Report_2007.pdf.

---

32 Myung-Ki Yoo, "Jaehan woekukin nodongja'eui munhwajuk jukeung'ae kwanhan yongu" [A study on the cultural adaptation of foreign workers in Korea], *Korean Cultural Anthropology* 27 (1995): 145–81. Yoo cites the following additional reasons: (1) an authoritarian hierarchy in interpersonal relationships that places foreign workers at the bottom of the social scale; (2) contempt for manual labor, which leads one to look down on foreign workers, who are mostly in charge of the physical labor; and (3) a tendency to discriminate against people in terms of wealth and racial groups, which places foreign workers at the bottom of the scale.

Stronach explains the Japanese society as follows:

> Japanese society has always been extremely conservative in that maintaining the status quo has had greater salience than progress for progress's sake. Japanese society, forms of behavior, and institutions do not change rapidly, nor do they change without fundamental cause. Japan is the quintessential "If it ain't broke, don't fix it" society. Thus, when things are going fine, there is a strong tendency to continue the status quo. The vast majority of people in contemporary Japan are happy with the way things are right now, and the last thing they want is change.[33]

A surprising number of Japanese still cling to the founding myths of racial purity, whereas most Americans view their society's obvious multiethnic character with pride and approval. The Japanese, with strong norms of group uniformity, tend to overstate their degree of cultural homogeneity. Americans, on the other hand, tend to celebrate multiculturalism, allowing a minority candidate such as Barack Obama, with a distinctly foreign-sounding name, to reach the White House. The contrasting milieu shapes basic life opportunities for immigrants in Japan and the United States. If the American Dream is about "making it" no matter where you are from, the Japanese Dream is about "moving up" among your own kind. Economic needs and cultural paradigms change at different speeds, and Stronach's pessimism about Japanese multiculturalism remains to be proven. Japan cannot evade the winds of globalization, and its tendency towards self-absorption can no longer seem to function as a workable mode of operation.

---

33 Bruce Stronach, *Beyond the Rising Sun: Nationalism in Contemporary Japan* (Westport: Praeger Publishers, 1995), 46.

Japan in Crisis

References

Asciutti, Elena. "Asia and the Global World: Identities, Values, Rights." In *Identity in Crossroad Civilisations*, edited by Erich Kolig, Vivienne S. M. Angeles, and Sam Wong. Amsterdam: Amsterdam University Press, 2009.

Befu, Harumi. "Concepts of Japan, Japanese Culture and the Japanese." In *The Cambridge Companion to Modern Japanese Culture*, edited by Yoshio Sugimoto. Cambridge: Cambridge University Press, 2009.

———. *Hegemony of Homogeneity: An Anthropological Analysis of Nihonjinron*. Melbourne: Trans Pacific Press, 2001.

———. "Symbols of Nationalism and *Nihonjinron*." In *Ideology and Practice in Modern Japan*, edited by Roger Goodman and Kirsten Refsing. London: Routledge, 1992.

Consortium of Non-Traditional Security Studies. *NTS Alert* 1 (September 1, 2009). Compiled, published and distributed by NTS-Asia Secretariat, RSIS Centre for NTS Studies, NTU. "Dotohukenbetsu zairyuushikaku (zairyuu mokuteki) betsu gaikokijindourokusha (tsusui)" [Registered Foreign Residents by Status per Administrative Unit]. Zairyuu gaikokujin tsuke, [Statistics on Foreign Residents].

Dotohukenvetsu zairyuushikaku (zairyuu mokuteki) betsu gaikokijindourokusha (tsusui) [Registered Foreign by Status per Administrative Unit]. Zairyuu gaikokujin tsuke [Statistics on Foreign Residents].

Hatoyama, Yukio. "A New Path for Japan." *New York Times*, August 27, 2009.

Hayes, Louis D. *Introduction to Japanese Politics*. 4th ed. Armonk: East Gate, 2005.

Hillenbrand, Margaret. "Murakami Haruki in Greater China: Creative Responses and the Quest for Cosmopolitanism." *Journal of Asian Studies* 68, no. 3 (August 2009).

Iwabuchi, Koichi. "Political Correctness, Postcoloniality, and the Self-Representation of 'Koreanness' in Japan." In *Koreans in Japan: Critical Voices from the Margin*, edited by Sonia Ryang. London: Routledge Curzon, 2000.

Izumi, Seiichi. "Tokyo shoshimin no iminzoku ni taisuru taido" [Average Tokyo citizen's attitude towards different ethnic groups]. In *Shakaiteki kincho no kenkyu* [A study on social tension], edited by Nihon Jinbun Kagakukai. Tokyo: Yuhikaku, 1951.

Kashiwazaki, Chikako. "The Politics of Legal Status: The Equation of Nationality with Ethnonational Identity." In *Koreans in Japan: Critical Voices from the Margin*, edited by Sonia Ryang. London: Routledge Curzon, 2000.

Kim, Myeongsu, and Tadashi Inazuki. "Zainichi kankokujin no shakai idou" [Social mobility of resident Koreans in Japan]. In *Kaisou shakai kara atarashii shimin shakai e* [From stratified society to new civil society], edited by Kenji Kousaka, vol. 6, SSM 95a. Tokyo: Daigaku Shuppankai, 2000.

Kolig, Erich, Vivienne S. M. Angeles, and Sam Wong. "Introduction: Crossroad Civilisations and

Bricolage Identities." In *Identity in Crossroad Civilisations*, edited by Erich Kolig, Vivienne S. M. Angeles, and Sam Wong. Amsterdam: Amsterdam University Press, 2009.

Kondo, Atsushi. "Legal System for Foreign Residents in Japan: Comparison with Western Countries." Paper presented at the conference on "Gender Equality and Multicultural Conviviality in the Age of Globalization," School of Law, Tohoku University, Sendai, Miyagi Prefecture, Japan, October 15–18, 2009.

Kweon, Sug-In. "Hyunji'hwa, junghyung'hwa, jigu'hwa: Jae'maeksiko/ilbon hanin'eui Minjok'eumshik'munhwa" [Localization, typification, globalization: Ethnic food among the Koreans in Japan and Korean-Mexicans]. *Bikyomunhwa Yongu* [The journal of comparative culture] 11, no. 2 (2005).

Kwon, Hee-young. "20saegi'cho Reossia kukdong'aeseoeui hwanghwa'ron: Chosun'in iju'wa jungchak'ae daehan Reossia'in'eui taedo" [The emergence of yellow racialization discourse in the Russian far east in the early 20th century: The Russian attitudes toward migration and settlement of the Chosun population]. *Journal of Jungshin Munhwa Yongu* 29, no. 2 (2006).

Lee, Chang-hyun. "Hanil kwangae'wa nyusu bodo'eui puraeim, kurigo sangho'inshik" [News frame and social perception between Korea and Japan]. *Journal of Humanities and Social Sciences* 18 (2007).

McVeigh, Brian J. *Nationalisms of Japan: Managing and Mystifying Identity*. Lanham: Rowman & Littlefield Publishers, 2003.

Ministry of Justice Immigration Bureau. 2005.

Morris-Suzuki, Tessa. *Exodus to North Korea: Shadows from Japan's Cold War*. Lanhamk: Rowman & Littlefield Publishers, 2007.

Na, Ju-mong, and Young-eun Im. "Jaeil Korian kiup'eui jiyok'byol tteuksung'mit netuiwokui'kujo'ae kwanhan yonku" [A study on the regional characteristics and network structure of Zainichi Korean companies]. Paper presented at the International Studies Association of Korea, Dongguk University, Seoul, Korea, November 4, 2006.

Nagy, Stephen Robert. "Local Government and Multicultural Coexistence Practices in the Tokyo Metropolitan Area: Integrating a Growing Foreign Minority Population." In *Ethnic Minorities and Regional Development in Asia: Reality and Challenges*, edited by Huhua Cao. Amsterdam: Amsterdam University Press, 2009.

National Human Rights Commission of the Republic of Korea. Annual Report 2007. Accessed June 13, 2012. http://www.asiapacificforum.net/members/full-members/republic-of-korea/downloads/annual-reports/Annual_Report_2007.pdf.

Oh, Ingyu. "Toward a Post-Cold War and Post-Industrial Harmony between Japan and South Korea: Popular Culture as a New Means of Discourse between the Two Nations." Paper presented at the workshop on "The Japanese-South Korean Relationship," The European Institute of Japanese Studies, Stockholm, Sweden, August 21–22, 2009.

Parrenas, Rhacel Salazar, and Lok C. D. Siu. "Introduction: Asian Diasporas—New Conceptions, New Frameworks." In *Asian Diasporas: New Formations, New Conceptions*, edited by Rhacel S. Parrenas and Lok C. D. Siu. Stanford: Stanford University Press, 2007.

Rozman, Gilbert. "The East Asian Identity Syndrome." Paper presented at the International Convention of Asia Scholars, Daejeon, Korea, August 6, 2009.

Ryang, Sonia, ed. *Koreans in Japan: Critical Voices from the Margin*. London: Routledge, 2000.

Saaler, Sven. "Pan-Asianism in Modern Japanese History: Overcoming the Nation, Creating a Region, Forging a Nation." In *Pan-Asianism in Modern Japanese History*, edited by Sven Saaler and J. Victor Koschmann. London: Routledge, 2007.

Shibata, Kimiko. "The South Korean Government's Position on Overseas Koreans (1961-1965)." Paper presented at the workshop on "The Japanese-South Korean Relationship," The European Institute of Japanese Studies, Stockholm, Sweden, August 21–22, 2009.

Söderberg, Marie. "The Struggle for a Decent Life in Japan: The Korean Minority Adapting to Changing Legal and Political Conditions." Paper presented at the workshop on "The Japanese-South Korean Relationship," The European Institute of Japanese Studies, Stockholm, Sweden, August 21–22, 2009.

Stronach, Bruce. *Beyond the Rising Sun: Nationalism in Contemporary Japan*. Westport: Praeger Publishers, 1995.

Sugimoto, Yoshio. *An Introduction to Japanese Society*. 2nd ed. Cambridge: Cambridge University Press, 2003.

Takeuchi, Mito. "The Reinforcement of Cultural Nationalism in Japan: An Investigation of Japaneseness and 'the Notebook for the Heart.'" Paper presented at the Japan Studies Association of Canada, York University, Toronto, Ontario, Canada, August 18, 2007.

Tsuda, Takeyuki. "When Minorities Migrate: The Racialization of the Japanese Brazilians in Brazil and Japan." In *Asian Diasporas: New Formations, New Conceptions*, edited by Rhacel S. Parrenas and Lok C. D. Siu. Stanford: Stanford University Press, 2007.

Yano, Christine. "Wink on Pink: Interpreting Japanese Cute as It Grabs the Global Headlines." *Journal of Asian Studies* 68, no. 3 (August 2009).

Yoo, Myung-Ki. "Jaehan woekukin nodongja'eui munhwajuk jukeung'ae kwanhan yongu" [A study on the cultural adaptation of foreign workers in Korea]. *Korean Cultural Anthropology* 27 (1995).

Yoon, Teak-Lim. "Tal'shikmin yoksa'ssuki: Bi'kongshik yoksa'wa dajungjuk juchae" [Writing postcolonial histories: Counter histories and multiple subjects]. *Korean Cultural Anthropology* 27 (1995).

Wender, Melissa L. Lamentation as History: *Narratives by Koreans in Japan, 1965-2000*. Stanford: Stanford University Press, 2005.

Zainichi Chousenjinshoukourenkaigai [The Association of Korean Japanese Merchants and Industries]. *Douhoukeizaikenkyuu* [The journal of compatriot economy] 6 (2002).

PART 5

IMPROVING RELATIONS WITH THE ASIA-PACIFIC NEIGHBORS

CHAPTER
07

WHAT WILL IT TAKE FOR JAPAN TO RISE AGAIN? VISION, REGIONAL INITIATIVE, AND JAPAN-KOREA RELATIONS

Kazuhiko Togo

Kazuhiko Togo is a Professor and the Director of the Institute for World Affairs at Kyoto Sangyo University. Dr. Togo was Japan's Ambassador to the Netherlands, and was a Visiting Professor at numerous universities, including Temple University in Tokyo, Princeton University, Seoul National University, Leiden University, Tamakang University in Taiwan, and UC Santa Barbara. He served as the Director-General and the Chief of the Treaties Bureau for the Japanese Foreign Ministry. He was also the Director at the Institute for World Affairs in Kyoto. He received his Ph.D. from Leiden University.

In this chapter I will focus on Japan-Korea relations. But to get a full appreciation of what needs to happen in that area, it is essential to discuss two prior issues. First, how does Japan regain its sense of common national purpose—a sense that has been there at times in Japan's past but that has been lost in the last two decades? Second, if such a common national purpose can be found, can it be turned effectively into a road map for Japanese actions in its foreign policy? In this context, I then offer my thoughts on how Japan can best rise again in conjunction with its relations with its nearest neighbor, South Korea.

Recapturing Japan's National Objective

"Rich Country, Virtuous Country, and Country of Mount Fuji"
The consensus of those who gathered at this Asan Conference was that Japan has long been absent from the regional and global politico-economic scene. Clearly something went wrong in Japan and, for about two decades, this phenomenon of Japan's marginalization has been continuing.[1] Up until the end of 1989 and the end of the Cold War, which coincided with the end of the Showa Era, Japan was certainly not hidden. It was an economic giant that had risen from the ashes of World War II, and that projected its economic power even upon the United States.

But since then, something has been wrong in Japan. Examples of Japan's policy collapse include the catastrophic failure to handle the bursting of the bubble economy; Ozawa's aborted political effort to create an effective two-party system; the decline of Japan's once powerful bureaucracy due to a series of monetary scandals and policy failures; and the failure to overcome major security and diplomatic issues that were residues of the Cold War, including revision of the Japanese Constitution, relations with Russia and North Korea, and directly confronting its historical issues with China and South Korea, among others.

Such failures during the last two decades made it increasingly clear that Japanese society was permeated with a number of discords and dis-

---

1 Kazuhiko Togo, *Sengo Nihonga ushinattamono: Fukei, ningen, and kokka* [What Japan Lost after WWII: Scenery, Human Beings and State] (Tokyo: Kadokawa, 2010), 224–227.

connects. Efforts to resolve problems, such as those noted above, rarely produced cohesive policies based on national unity. The bottom line was that Japan, after it had achieved its status as an economic giant, lost its ability to reformulate a new national objective designed to reshape the country in new ways as it headed into the 21st century.

In my book *What Japan Lost after WWII: Scenery, Identity and State*, I analyzed this array of problems and the failure to establish a new direction, proposing that Japan pursue the national objective of becoming an "Open Edo."[2] I still stand by this goal, but I acknowledge that there is a need for some explanation of this term. Once an allegedly comprehensive slogan requires a detailed explanation, it loses its power. Any national objective has to be simple, transparent, and embraced with centripetal power. The conventional analysis that the Heisei period failed to produce any contending slogans for national objectives may not necessarily be right.

For example, when Kakuei Tanaka came to power in 1972, he presented a new objective of "transforming the Japanese archipelago" as a way to reconcile the contradiction between Japan's overpopulated cities and its depopulated countryside. His proposal was "to develop the regions through industrialization," transforming Japan through massive public works such as highways, bullet trains, bridges, ports, and airports.[3] But in reality Tanaka's plea for massive urbanization resulted only in further depopulation in the countryside.[4]

Prime ministers with visions based on rural life and cultural values
Masayoshi Ohira brought in a vision very different from Tanaka's. In January 1979, Ohira explained, "I wish to unite the high productivity and extensive information of urban life with the abundance of nature and intimate human relations offered by the countryside." He called this his Garden City Initiative. Unfortunately Ohira passed away in 1979 and his vision faded until its return 20 years later under the initiative of

2 Ibid.

3 Kakuei Tanaka, *Nihon retto kaizoron* [Transforming the Japanese archipelago] (Tokyo, Nikkankogyo-Shinbunsha, 1972), 78.

4 Heita Kawakatsu, Kazuhiko Togo, and Masuda Hiroya, *Tohoku kyodotai karano saisei* [Rebirth from Tohoku community] (Tokyo: Fujiwara Shoten, 2011), 24–29.

Ryutaro Hashimoto, who advanced the notion of "beautiful scenery" as the major national objective for Japan's future. In his 1998 "National Grand Design of the 21st Century," he called for the "creation of self-sustained regions and a beautiful homeland," noting that "we are going to create a new Japanese archipelago, where people of a new culture and lifestyle can live, based on the characteristics of regionally different histories and scenery." Heita Kawakatsu, an Oxford Ph.D. in economics and a well-known professor at Waseda University, was the creator of the notion of Garden Islands.

Yet by the time the program began to be implemented, Hashimoto had to resign from the post of prime minister. He was succeeded by Keizo Obuchi, who was no less imaginative regarding the creation of a new vision for Japan. In June 1999, he chose Kawakatsu to chair a committee to forge a "Beautiful Homeland and Safe Society."[5]

The report basically inherited the direction of creating a beautiful Japan embraced by nature and tradition, but directed greater attention toward the mind and spirit of individual Japanese. The notion of "Rich Country, Virtuous Country," created by Kawakatsu in 1995 after the Kansai Great Earthquake, was incorporated as the key notion of that report.[6] On January 28, 2000, Obuchi specifically stated in his national policy speech at the Diet that "the advisory board discussed from various angles under the spirit of 'Rich Country, Virtuous Country' what kind of Japan we should create in the new century."[7] At this time, "Rich Country, Virtuous Country" had almost gained the status of a national objective. Obuchi's brain coma in March 2000 and his replacement by Junichiro Koizumi ended the concept of "Rich Country, Virtuous Country" as a national objective until it was revived by Koizumi's successor, Shinzo Abe, who brought back the notion of "beautiful country" as his main motive as prime minister. His personal manifesto was published in a book entitled *Toward Beautiful Country*.

---

5 Keizo Obuchi, "21 seiki nippon no kousou," Kondankai dai-yonbun, accessed January 2, 2012, http://www.kantei.go.jp/jp/21century/990615bunka4souri.html.

6 Heita Kawakatsu, *Fukoku yutoku ron* [Theory of rich country and virtuous country] (Tokyo: Chuoukouron, 2000), 243.

7 Keizo Obuchi, "Dai147kai kokkai ni okeru: Obuchi naikaku souridaijin shiseihoushin enzetsu," accessed January 2, 2012, http://www.kantei.go.jp/jp/obutisouri/speech/2000/0128sisei.html.

When the Democratic Party of Japan (DPJ) replaced the Liberal Democratic Party (LDP) and adopted as one of its major objectives the policy of "From Concrete to Human Beings," some thought that at long last the new vision of Japan, which had begun with Ohira, was finally on a path to real policy implementation. But, again, it is not clear that the national leadership is anxious to pursue such a goal. Instead the national objective of "Rich Country, Virtuous Country" under Prime Minister Obuchi has caught the attention of Yoshinobu Ishikawa, who was governor of Shizuoka from 1993 to 2009. His slogan is "Fukoku, Yutoku, Fujinokuni," which means "Rich Country, Virtuous Country, and the Country of Mount Fuji."

Legacy of "Fukoku Yutoku"

From a historical perspective, Japan developed from the Meiji Restoration under the national objective of "Fukoku Kyohei" (Rich Country, Strong Army). There is no disagreement that Japan achieved that goal, but ultimately it completely failed as a consequence of its defeat in World War II. But then, to the amazement of all, Japan succeeded in rebounding with a new national objective of "Keizaitaikoku" (Economic Giant), although I have long maintained that we can better explain the spirit of the era as "Fukoku Heiwa" (Rich Country, Peaceful Country).

The national objective of "Fukoku Yutoku" follows logically as the next step in Japan's progression from "Fukoku Kyohei" through "Fukoku Heiwa" to "Fukoku Yutoku." By adding the new objective of virtue, "Rich Country, Virtuous Country" gains the magnetic power to address one of the fundamental weaknesses of postwar Japanese democracy. Japan developed a democracy based on a political, economic, and social system where the rights of individuals have been overly accentuated at the expense of the public good. The individual clearly belongs to a community in which all individuals must contribute and whose values should be shared. The absence of such shared values has surely contributed to the weakness in contemporary Japan, which must be more than simply "rich and peaceful."

Introducing the notion of virtue as an integral component of any new national objective can help to fill that vacuum of shared values for the society as a whole. But it also resonates with values that are universal to both Western and Eastern civilizations. Virtue is certainly an important ethical value in Greek philosophy but it is also a key concept in Confucian ethics, which requires self-restraint and compassion as the centerpiece of moral code.

By adding a third dimension, "Fujinokuni" (The Country of Mount Fuji), to his prefectural objective, Kawakatsu emphasizes the notion of "beauty." This helps make the slogan of "Fukoku Yutoku" more vivid and transparent, by acknowledging a certain global and universal commonality in aesthetics. That may also make this slogan more compelling because aesthetics may have become a lost target, particularly in the Heisei Era with its emphasis on economic dynamism. Phenomena such as "cool Japan" may have appeared to involve aesthetics and beauty but, in fact, the loss of attention to beauty was evident in the visual reality of living in Japan.

Finally, it is interesting that this objective of "Fukoku Yutoku, Fujinokuni" has been adopted by only one prefecture and has not yet crystallized as a national objective. This draws our attention to some of Japan's current political problems. Politics in Tokyo at Nagatacho and Kasumigaseki, is often trapped by inertia and paralyzed by vested interests. Some of the nation's best initiatives may now be produced by regions. This brings us to Japan's overall situation after 3/11.

3/11 and Japan's national objective

The spiritual void that many people felt during the last two decades has invigorated many Japanese intellectuals in the wake of 3/11. As many argued in the aftermath of the disaster, the time has come to pull together Japan's national strengths and concentrate our national energies on the reconstruction of Tohoku so as to make it a model for the 21st century civilization. Typically, that was my immediate response to the 3/11 disaster, and it was in that spirit that I contributed an article to the Asan Issue Brief series and co-authored a book with Governor Kawakatsu and former governor of Iwate Prefecture Hiroya Masuda titled *Tohoku kyodotai karano saisei* (Rebirth from Tohoku community).

Now that more than a year has passed since the disaster, some foundational characteristics are emerging. The responses from the Japanese people, their perseverance, their ability to endure, and the bonds among local citizens trying to stick together for the preservation and development of their communities astonished the world. Leadership emerged from a number of towns and villages symbolizing local and popular initiatives. Some efforts at the governors' level were also striking. The initial enthusiasm of Japanese all over the country who tried to help the victims with volunteer organizations was also phenomenal.

At the national governmental level, an advisory group for the prime minister was established, chaired by Makoto Iokibe, and this group formulated its vision in June, attempting to accumulate and unify the views of many opinion leaders.[8] Prime Ministers Kan and Noda may be doing their best to develop a national consensus policy on the recovery and have been adopting a series of legal decisions. After Iokibe's report was finalized, a Basic Law (June 27), a Basic Direction (July 29–August 11), a Special Zone Law (December 7), and a Law to Establish a Reconstruction Agency (December 9) were respectively adopted.[9] Budgetary support was huge, totaling 17.6145 trillion yen in three supplementary budgets adopted in April, July, and October, as well as an additional 3.7754 trillion yen in the 2012 fiscal year budget.[10] Given the enormity of the problem, the declaration on December 16 by Prime Minister Noda to freeze the nuclear reactors at Fukushima Daiichi may be the best possible policy under the given circumstances.

Nevertheless, discontent and a sense of expectations unmet were widespread. That sense was bolstered by the confusion that followed Prime Minister Kan's top-down energy policy seeking eventual complete denuclearization and his abdication in July because of his inability to bring about a consensus on that shutdown. The delay in the overall process is best symbolized by the fact that the Reconstruction Agency

8 "Fokkoku e no teigen: hisan no naka ni kibou," Higashi nippon daisinsai fukkoku kousoukaigi, accessed January 2, 2012, http://www.kantei.go.jp/jp/singi/fukkouhonbu/dai1/siryou5_1.pdf.

9 Naikakukan [Cabinet Secretariat], Nakaku kohoushitsu [Cabinet Public Relations Office], accessed Janaury 2, 2012, http://www.kantei.go.jp/fukkou/index.html.

10 "2011 nendo yosan" [Budget for F.Y. 2011], Ministry of Finance, accessed January 2, 2012. http://www.mof.go.jp/budget/budger_workflow/budget/fy2011/index.htm; "2012 nendo yosan seifuan" [Government bill for the budget for F.Y. 2012], Ministry of Finance, accessed January 2, 2012. http://www.mof.go.jp/budget/budger_workflow/budget/fy2012/seifuan24/index.htm.

was only established and began functioning on February 10, 2012.

This dysfunction at the center has been creating unfortunate backlashes in the region and among the people who suffered. The delay in supplying competent professionals who are capable of providing an overall vision for the cities, the landscape, and the country as a whole has triggered debates among varying interest groups, and these now occupy an enormous amount of time in localities. Understandably impatient people began establishing their own houses, shops, or places of work, without having achieved any consensus on how these might fit with the planning for the future. If such sprawl is the result, immediate necessity would gain preference over any adoption of a systematic future vision.

Another critical issue has been the handling of garbage. The amount of garbage has been so enormous that it hampers effective reconstruction work. Yet, the weakness and self-centered character of postwar Japanese democracy was revealed in the regional reactions to this problem. Except for Governor Ishihara in Tokyo, not a single regional government official volunteered to accept garbage from the three devastated prefectures. Governor Kawakatsu had days of strenuous talks with Shizuoka's citizens to set conditions for accepting garbage from Iwate Prefecture. He was able to achieve some consensus within the prefecture, but "experimental burning" of tiny amounts of garbage began only on February 16, 2012.[11] Kim Mikyoung's observation unfortunately gets right to the essence of the problem: "compassion is delivered with obvious constraints: moral support is offered as long as no harm is inflicted. With the clear-cut limits of safety network amid rising social isolation, the call for national unity exists mostly on the lips and purse."[12]

Recapturing Foreign Policy Initiatives
If Japan were able to achieve a national consensus on its future objective, and in so doing succeeded in stabilizing its domestic political governance, there would be a much higher chance of Japan exerting greater foreign policy initiative. In this sense, domestic efforts to establish a na-

---

11 *Shizuoka Shimbun*, February 16, 2012.

12 Mikyoung Kim, "A Cultural Critique of Ganbarism: The Fukushima Disaster Victims' Dilemma," (paper presented at the Asan Japan Conference, The Asan Institute for Policy Studies, Seoul, Korea 2011).

tional objective and agreeing on the foreign policy objective of exerting greater international leadership have to go forward in parallel with each other.

It may be axiomatic to say that the greatest political challenge Japan faces internationally is the rise of China. Conversely, how should Japan act if the rise of China is met by strong counter-pressures by the United States, which would be designed to secure its position as an Asia-Pacific power? There are several obvious issues that Japan has to face squarely in this regard. It must also deal with several emerging issues concerning its major neighbors. These include relations with China, with the United States, with Russia, and with the broad process of regional integration that is now moving forward.

The recent rise of China, in all of its economic, political, military, and cultural fronts, creates multiple reactions—awe, admiration, instability, fear, threat, and so on. Constructive cooperation is more than welcome, but China's clear indication that military force may be used to achieve the country's political objectives has caused a notable change in the minds of both policymakers and the general public, that adequate defense positioning is essential if Japan is to remain secure. One manifestation of that increased concern has been the formulation in December 2010 of the new National Defense Program Guidelines and the adoption of Japan's basic policy to strengthen maritime power and its southern defense line.

These moves seemed fully justified because of events following the September 7, 2011, collision of a Chinese fishery vessel with a Japanese Coast Guard vessel around the disputed Senkaku Islands (called the Diaoyu Islands by China). This event was indeed an important turning point in Sino-Japanese relations. The Japanese government has long adhered to Deng Xiaoping's proposal that Japan and China should set aside the issue over sovereignty of the Senkaku Islands until future generations produce better wisdom. In the past, the LDP handled a somewhat similar issue involving a Chinese landing on the Senkakus in 2004 by briefly detaining the perpetrators and then swiftly releasing them. Thus, it was a break in precedent when the DPJ government announced that Japan's reaction to the 2011 incident would be dealt with in accordance with

Japan's domestic law. Unsurprisingly, Chinese officials may well have concluded that Japan was in fact breaking away from Deng's legacy and the procedures that had grown up in response. The Chinese reaction sought to prevent Japan's seemingly new policy and it, in turn, appeared quite harsh with the arrest of four Japanese businessmen in China and the announcement that China was cutting off exports of rare-earth materials to Japan. The Kan government quickly reversed course, but its apparent subjection to Chinese pressure was not particularly attractive, even though it is clear that Japan's initial reaction had gone forward without sufficient knowledge of past history.

China's clear determination not to let Japan take any unilateral policy toward more effective governance of the islands served as a wakeup call for many Japanese people, including myself, that inadequate handling of such incidents might well lead to an actual military collision. This reminder is important as an augmentation to any diplomat's normal responsibility to make continual efforts to prevent such collisions from ever taking place. The starting point should be for Japan to become engaged in real talks with the Chinese on the matter of the ownership of the Senkaku Islands.

As Japan prepares to deal with the rise of China, the importance of the United States as Japan's ally is obvious. It is a truism to say that, at this point in history, Japan needs to strengthen the bilateral alliance with the United States. Obama's groundbreaking speech at the Australian parliament on November 17, 2011, identifying the United States as an Asia-Pacific nation adds to the importance of closer US-Japan relations. Yet, former prime minister Hatoyama's ill-prepared declaration that he intended to close the US Marine Corps base at Futenma caused a major rift in Japanese ties with the United States. Despite the clear problems posed by the base for residents of Okinawa, there is a need to stick to the Two-plus-Two agreement of 2006. It is clear that proposals to move the US Marines to Henoko are also now a non-starter and that some alternative has to be sought out. No realistic alternative has yet been found at this time.

In March 2012, Vladimir Putin returned to the office of Russian president for another six-year term. As a result, it is important for Japan to carefully examine his regional and global policies and their implications for Japan-Russia relations. The December 2011 election fiasco will almost certainly compel Putin to take a fairer, more transparent, and less autocratic domestic policy. The situation with regard to foreign policy is less clear. After being selected as the presidential candidate by his party, United Russia, in September 2011, Putin declared that his central policy would become Eurasianism, defined as the creation of a distinctive Eurasian space, different from Europe and different from Asia.

It would be constructed first of all with partners from the former Soviet republics. Its inaugurating event would be the establishment of an economic community consisting of Russia, Belorussia, and Kazakhstan as of January 1, 2012. Second, energy production remains the key economic issue and from that perspective the still relatively underexploited East Siberian and Sakhalin oil and natural gas gain critical importance. But Putin seeks to do more for the Russian economy than just energy exploitation; he seeks to create a value-added economy as well. Energy-related industries such as petrochemicals could have specific importance. Third, from this perspective of Eurasianism, the country that looms largest is China. This means that Russia has no room to antagonize China. But, in the long run, Russia also has an absolute need to not be swallowed up by China. The country that would appear to be a possible partner for Russian cooperation in dealing with China is, therefore, Japan. If the Japanese leadership is sufficiently alert to this potential, Japan-Russia relations could develop with unexpected momentum in the coming year, including achieving breakthroughs on territorial negotiations.

Finally, on matters of regional multilateralism, it is worth noting that the Asan Japan Conference was held in the wake of Noda's policy announcement that Japan would seek to join the Trans-Pacific Partnership (TPP). This may be a wise move, particularly regarding improving relations with the United States. But as a political observer who has openly welcomed the development of East Asia cooperation, including the ASEAN Plus Three (APT), and one who regrets that little has been done to strengthen regional institutions in the past decade, I believe it is necessary not only to push for the TPP but also for Japan to actively advance such East Asian regional activities as the proposed Japan-China-Korea Tripartite Free Trade Agreement, which Japan just agreed to press forward in late May 2012.[13]

Japan-Korea Relations

The broad perspective

There are strategic reasons why closer cooperation between Japan and South Korea would benefit both countries: (1) South Korea's rapid rise economically and politically combined with Japan's drift in the last 20 years has leveled many of the prior differences between the two countries, particularly in the economic arena. Professor Yoshihide Soeya's groundbreaking analysis of proposing a middle-power configuration for Japan and South Korea has increasing resonance in Japan. (2) The two countries have begun to share many of the same social problems, such as aging, emigration, and gender inequality. Also, the two have increasingly begun to share common cultural understandings and even admiration, including, for example, the wide popularity of Kanryu in Japan. (3) The two countries are juxtaposed with China, one through a common land frontier and the other through the sea. Both will clearly be directly affected by "China's rise," as well as by the rivalry and cooperation between the two giants, the United States and China. For the most fundamental issues of national security, the two countries thus have many reasons to seek areas in which to cooperate.

Positive and creative ideas for cooperation are actually numerous. For one thing, they could consider joint efforts to reduce global poverty and insecurity. Cooperation on Official Development Assistance and human security could be one realistic objective. Overcoming global problems to achieve sustainable economic development in areas such as energy, environment, global warming, and population may be another area for cooperation.

A second area for coordinated effort could involve the creation of a regional economic structure. Both South Korea and Japan have gained

---

13 Kazuhiko Togo, *Rekishito gaikou: Yasukuni, Asia, Tokyo saiban* [History and foreign policy: Yasukuni, Asia, and the Tokyo trial] (Tokyo: Kodansha, 2008), 172–182.

common benefits, and confronted common problems, with the creation of East Asia cooperative structures such as the APT or China-Japan-Korea trilateral cooperation as well as by joining wider Asia-Pacific cooperation arrangements such as Asia-Pacific Economic Cooperation or the East Asia Summit. South Korea has embarked upon a trade path that includes furthering the Korea-US Free Trade Agreement, whereas Japan seems to have opted to join the TPP. How should the two countries overcome this maze of networking and create the most effective regional economic structure? Both countries are energy poor but consume high amounts of energy. Why could they not create a more effective regional energy network? Both have a vital interest in preserving and strengthening agriculture, not only to maintain some indigenous food supply but also for the sake of maintaining national landscape and scenery. Why not compare notes and cooperate with each other in this area?

Still a third area for possible collaboration might extend to the creation of regional security architecture. Both countries are juxtaposed between a rising China, and both countries' security is dependent on the United States. The fundamental similarity in their two security conditions is startling. The Japan-Korea-US triangular cooperation is one concrete step forward.

Dealing with bilateral friction points

Despite such areas of mutually beneficial cooperation, past history still haunts the two countries. In recent years, the territorial issue around Dokdo (called Takeshima by Japan), occasionally combined with the textbook issue in Japan, has become the most critical. In the summer of 2011, the Korean Constitutional Court pronounced as unconstitutional the way that the ROK government had remained silent on the issue of "comfort women" for so long. Since then, this issue has also regained some centrality in the relationship between the two countries, as was seen on December 18, 2011, in Kyoto between Prime Minister Yoshihiko Noda and President Lee Myung-bak.

As a Japanese citizen who was born in 1945, I see several fundamental points in such historical issues. First, the nature of Japanese colonialism is a complex issue where opinions may vary depending on personal views, academic disciplines, and nationality. But there is one aspect that seems to be undeniable. The rigorous policy of Kominka (Making Imperial Citizens) adopted by Japan from around the 1930s was a policy essentially designed to "Make Koreans Japanese." For a nation proud of its ancestry, tradition, and culture, this was clearly a dagger to the heart. Korean anger could well be without limits, and as a Japanese citizen who inherited our nation's past, I simply express my apology.

What happened after Japan's defeat in August 1945 changed the situation from bad to worse. Why was Korea split in two? After all, it was Japan that started the war. If there was one country that should have been split in two as the result of the Pacific War, it should have been Japan, and not Korea, which was in fact a victim of Japanese colonization. Furthermore, Korea had to endure all of the atrocities and the tragedy of the Korean War, even though it was admittedly initiated by a fellow Korean, Kim Il-Sung. But what happened in Japan during this period? The country enjoyed its first postwar recovery under the name of the "Korean Economic Boom." Why did Korea have to suffer this tragedy when Japan was able to enjoy the fruits of prosperity?[14]

One more factor that is puzzling is the way the Japanese government cut off all postwar compensation to Korean veterans of the Japanese military if they chose to take Korean nationality, while Japanese veterans of the lost war retained their benefits. If the falling Japanese empire retained a minimum degree of pride, how could it abandon those departing Koreans who had once been loyal citizens of the empire? I simply cannot understand this matter without feeling ashamed of Japan's past decisions.

As the result of these and other factors, postwar identity in Korea was formulated by a total denial of the period under Japanese annexation. In my lectures at the university, I often ask my students: if you were a Korean, would you expect to take any other approach than total denial of your colonial past?

Serious soul-searching in Korea does not negate the fact that Japan went through its own history of soul-searching during the period

---

14 Ibid., 107–141.

of postwar reconstruction. As a result of the spiritual hollow brought about by the total defeat and foreign occupation, which Japan had never experienced in its history, total denial of Japan's past was for some time in postwar Japan the spirit of the era. Masao Maruyama, a well-known professor at Tokyo University, became its leading advocate. But the denial of the past was primarily directed at the damage caused to Japan itself rather than at the damage caused to Asia and elsewhere. Seichi Morimura (Unit 731), Katsuichi Honda (atrocities in China), Saburo Ienaga (textbook defects), as well as reports of returned soldiers from China (Chukiren) left deep imprints on public opinion about Japan's actions in Asia. At the same time, complete denial of all post-Meiji activity gradually came to be criticized as excessive and masochistic self-denial. Fusao Hayashi (Meiji born), Yukio Mishima (Taisho born), and Jun Eto (Showa born) were examples of popular writers who tried to assert some prewar Japanese honor.[15]

In 1995, Prime Minister Tomiichi Murayama issued a statement that reflected this 50-year period of postwar soul-searching. It is an unequivocal expression of apology, formulated in an unprecedentedly holistic manner: "Japan apologizes for its colonialism and aggression." One could argue that it was articulated only on behalf of those who wanted to recognize the pain caused in Asia, but nonetheless, Murayama's apology has remained alive in all cabinets succeeding Murayama's to this day. In my view, it continues to command general support among many generations of Japanese.

Koreans' unwillingness to recognize the importance of this statement, if not to accept it, is cause for sadness. But I feel humble and cannot find a better way than consolidating Japan's overall position on historical memory around the Murayama Statement. As I have stated since 2006, apology is a one-way process. One does not apologize in expectation of being pardoned. One apologizes because one acknowledges that one did something wrong.

But when it comes to reconciliation, the picture becomes very dif-

---

15 Kazuhiko Togo, "Development of Japan's Historical Memory: The San Francisco Peace Treaty and the Murayama Statement in Future Perspective," *Asian Perspective* 35, no. 3 (July September 2011): 347–350.

ferent. Reconciliation involves a two-way process. Unless the victim-side is prepared to respond to the apology expressed, there is no way for reconciliation.[16]

Shifting to the territorial issue, Dokdo has become the most volatile issue in the last five years or so of Japan-ROK relations. The essence of the issue is that for Koreans, this is more than a territorial dispute over ownership of certain islands. Instead, it is a key issue around which to discuss historical memory, pride, and identity. Dokdo formally became a part of Shimane Prefecture in 1905, five years before Japan formally annexed Korea in 1910. Koreans, however, take the Dokdo issue as a precursor to Japan's annexation of Korea. Therefore, any opinion defending Japanese ownership of Dokdo sounds to Korean ears like a justification for the Korean annexation itself. The emotional reaction from Koreans then becomes boundless. In Japan, however, that root cause of so strong an emotional reaction from Koreans is little understood.

When any action in Japan on Dokdo results in an emotional response in Korea, the Japanese government might find it difficult to act. Instead, scholars and opinion leaders in the private sector might have a useful role to play. An objective examination of historical records, as witnessed recently between some Korean and Japanese scholars, gives hope for an improved and less emotional understanding of historical facts. A forward-looking approach based on confidence-building measures, such as was discussed at the Dokdo/Takeshima/Liancourt Rocks Conference in June 2009 held by SAIS in Washington, DC. and sponsored by the Northeast Asian History Foundation, may also hold hope for the future. Japan and Korea may also learn from the rich experience accumulated in Japan-Russia negotiations to "consolidate the environment" of negotiations on sovereignty of the four Kuril Islands, such as no-visa visitations and fisheries agreements.

Another issue that surfaced after several years of relative lull is the issue of comfort women. In August 2011, the Korean Constitutional Court judged that the ROK government had not been fulfilling its duty to protect the rights of former comfort women. After three months of

16 Kazuhiko Togo, "A Moratorium on Yasukuni Visits," *Far Eastern Economic Review* 169, no. 5 (June 2006): 13–14.

quiet diplomacy, President Lee Myung-bak took this issue as the basis for a full-scale diplomatic offensive during his trip to Kyoto on December 17 and 18. In 1995, the Japanese government and people had launched the Asian Women's Fund in order to apologize and compensate to individual former comfort women from a moral and humanitarian point of view. South Korea did not accept this scheme, arguing that such a private process allowed the Japanese state to avoid taking responsibility. But the Japanese Supreme Court had ruled in April 2007 that postwar treaty obligations had resolved all possible war-related claims by individuals and, as a consequence, the Japanese government need no longer fear any further criminal indictments by Japanese courts. Why then should the Japanese government fear using budgetary money? Any moral resolution of this issue will likely require establishing some new scheme analogous to the Asian Women's Fund, which ceased to function in 2007. Only in this way might Japan be able to achieve the goals sought by the Korean government.[17]

Japanese-DPRK relations

If Japan and South Korea behave wisely and resolutely, they may be able to find a way out, even on such difficult issues as the historical and territorial problems noted above. But there is one more issue over which the significance for Japan and South Korea differs vastly and where any realistic common approach has yet to be found. This is the issue of Korean unification, and the policy to be adopted toward North Korea. For South Korea, this is about the fundamental issue of when and how Korea will regain its national identity and put an end to its tragic history, starting with Japan's annexation and leading to national division and the deadly Korean War. For Japan, how to reestablish relations with North Korea has been one of the outstanding issues that traces to World War II. The issue of unification is primarily an issue to be determined by the will of the Korean people. Realists might argue that for countries surrounding the Korean Peninsula, the current division of Korea may best serve their respective national interests, but at the same time, no country

---

17 For the activities of the Asian Women's Fund, see "Digital Museum: The Comfort Women's Issue and the Asian Women's Fund," Asian Women's Fund, accessed January 3, 2012, http://www.awf.or.jp.

would dare to appear as an obstacle should the will of the North and the South converge toward unification.

What kind of policy should Japan and South Korea take toward North Korea, bearing in mind their ultimate objective as described above? How can the two effectively coordinate their respective policies with the other essential regional powers, especially with the United States? The government of Japan has to consider whether it is in the country's long-term interest to normalize relations with North Korea before or after unification. All realists' power-based arguments probably favor normalization prior to reunification, simply because Japan might be able to strike a better bargain against a weak North than against a powerful united Korea. But such "realism" becomes totally illusionary if the Japanese government does not take into account the positions taken by South Korea and the United States. Even if the Japanese government is prepared to discard its own focus on the abduction issue, instead focusing on making a positive contribution to the Six-Party Talks, and expresses its readiness for normalization based on some "holistic approach," such as that taken by Hitoshi Tanaka between 2001 and 2002, coordination with the South and the United States still remains essential. Only in this way can Japan hope to strengthen its negotiating position vis-à-vis North Korea.

Is there such strategic calculation in the current Japanese government's policy toward North Korea? Hardly. The DPJ government reportedly contacted the North Korean government with a view to making some progress on the abduction issue in the initial months after Yukio Hatoyama became prime minister in 2009. This was carried out via two channels—one close to Hatoyama and the other close to Ichiro Ozawa—and in the last months under Prime Minister Kan in the person of Hiroshi Nakai, minister for the abduction issue in the Hatoyama cabinet. If the purpose of these contacts is merely to ensure progress on the abduction issue with an eye exclusively upon the domestic Japanese audience, and they are done with none of the strategic or holistic thinking mentioned above, then real progress in Japan-North Korea relations can hardly be expected, including with regard to the issue of abduction.

The North Korean situation was put under an entirely different light with the death of Kim Jong-Il on December 17, 2011, and its official announcement two days later. The course of events since then show that Kim Jong-Il's full power as North Korea's Supreme Leader was allegedly passed on to his third son, Kim Jong-Un, aged 29 at the time of this writing, who was officially nominated as the Supreme Commander of the Korean People's Army on December 30, 2011.[18] What kind of policy will the Japanese and South Korean governments take toward the new North Korea under Kim Jong-Un, and how will this affect Japan-South Korea relations? This is clearly an important point of analysis that goes beyond the scope of this paper.

Conclusion

This brief essay began by stating the need for an agreed-upon Japanese vision statement that can provide unity to the people and guidance to policymakers. In the wake of the 3/11 disaster, many thought such a common purpose would immediately come to the fore. Unfortunately, it did not. But my belief is that the slogan of Shizuoka Prefecture—"Rich Country, Virtuous Country, and the Country of Mount Fuji"—could well serve as such a national unifier.

Under such a banner, I believe it will be possible for Japan to regain some ability to offer foreign policy initiatives in its bilateral and regional relations. I have suggested closer ties between Japan and the United States, Russia, and South Korea as one way to ensure that the rise of China does not create regional instability and armed clashes. But it is with South Korea that Japan now has the greatest opportunity for positive cooperation going forward. Dealing with the residual issues of the past will not be easy; the issue of North Korea continues to cast a heavy shadow over their bilateral ties. But, ultimately, the two share so many common aspirations and are now at such roughly comparable states economically that the incentives for them to cooperate should far outweigh the issues that have kept them suspicious of each other for much of the postwar period.

---

18 Kim Jong-Un was reportedly born on January 8, 1983, but there are other reports that he was born either in 1984 or in 1982.

References

Asian Women's Fund. Higashi nippon daisinsai fukkoku kousoukaigi. "Fokkoku e no teigen: hisan no naka ni kibou." Accessed January 2, 2012. http://www.kantei.go.jp/jp/singi/fukkouhonbu/dai1/siryou5_1.pdf.

Higashi Nippon daisinsai fukkoku kousoukaigi. "Fokkoku e no teigen: hisan no naka ni kibou." Accessed January 2, 2012. http://www.kantei.go.jp/jp/singi/fukkouhonbu/dai1/siryou5_1.pdf.

Kawakatsu, Heita. *Binokuni Nihonwo tsukuru* [Making Japan a beautiful country]. Tokyo: Nikkan Kogyoshinbunsha, 2006.

———. *Fukoku yutooku ron* [Theory of rich country and virtuous country]. Tokyo: Chuoukouron, 2000.

Kawakatsu, Heita, Togo Kazuhiko, and Masuda Hiroya. *Tohoku kyodotai karano saisei* [Rebirth from Tohoku community]. Tokyo: Fujiwara Shoten, 2011.

Kim, Mikyoung. "A Cultural Critique of Ganbarism: The Fukushima Disaster Victims' Dilemma." Paper presented at the Asan Japan Conference, The Asan Institute for Policy Studies, Seoul, Korea, 2011.

Ministry of Finance. "2011 nendo yosan" [Budget for F.Y. 2011]. Accessed January 2, 2012. http://www.kantei.go.jp/jp/singi/fukkouhonbu/dai1/siryou5_1.pdf.

———. "2012 nendo yosan seifuan" [Government bill for the budget for F.Y. 2012]. Accessed January 2, 2012. http://www.mof.go.jp/budget/budger_workflow/budget/fy2012/seifuan24/index.htm.

Naikakukan [Cabinet Secretariat]. Nakaku kohoushitsu [Cabinet Public Relations Office]. Accessed Janaury 2, 2012. http://www.kantei.go.jp/fukkou/index.html.

Obuch, Keizo. "21 seiki nippon no kousou." Kandakai dai-yonbun. Accessed January 2, 2012. http://www.kantei.go.jp/jp/21century/990615bunka4souri.html.

———. "Dai 147kai kokkai ni okeru: Obuch naikaku souridaijin shiseihoushin enzetsu." Accessed January 2, 2012. http://www.kantei.go.jp/jp/obutisouri/speech/2000/0128sisei.html.

Shizuoka Shimbun. February 16, 2012.

Soeya, Yoshihide. *Nihonno midorupawa gaiko* [Japan's middle power diplomacy]. Tokyo: Chikuma, 2005.

Tanaka, Kakuei. *Nihon retto kaizoron* [Transforming the Japanese archipelago]. Tokyo: Nikkankogyo-Shimbunsha, 1972.

Togo, Kazuhiko. "Development of Japan's Historical Memory: The San Francisco Peace Treaty and the Murayama Statement in Future Perspective." *Asian Perspective* 35, no. 3 (July-September 2011).

———. "Japan and the New Security Structures of Asian Multilateralism." *In East Asian Multilateralism: Prospects for Regional Stability*, edited by Kent Calder and Francis Fukuyama.

Baltimore: The John Hopkins University Press, 2008.

———. "Japanese Politics, the Korean Peninsula, and China." In *Political Change in 2010-2012 and Regional Cooperation Centered on the Korean Peninsula*, edited by Gilbert Rozman. Washington, DC: Korea Economic Institute, 2012.

———. "A Moratorium on Yasukuni Visits." *Far Eastern Economic Review* 169, no. 5 (June 2006).

———. "Nikkan kagamino nakano jikoninshiki" [Japan and Korea: Self recognition in the mirror]. In *Kagamino nakano jikoninshiki: Nihonto kankokuno rekishi, bunka, mirai* [Self recognition in the mirror: history, culture, and future of Japan and Korea], edited by Kazuhiko Togo and Katsutoshi Park. Tokyo: Ochanomizu Shobo, 2012.

———. *Rekishito gaikou: Yasukuni, Asia, Tokyo saiban* [History and foreign policy: Yasukuni, Asia, and the Tokyo trial]. Tokyo: Kodansha, 2008.

———. *Sengo Nihonga ushinattamono: Fukei, ningen, and kokka* [What Japan Lost after WWII: Scenery, Human Beings and State]. Tokyo: Kadokawa, 2010.

CHAPTER 08

REGIONAL SITUATION AWARENESS AS A BASIS FOR NORTHEAST ASIAN REGIONAL COOPERATION IN DEALING WITH TRANSNATIONAL NUCLEAR DISASTERS

Kim Sok Chul

●

Kim Sok Chul is the Principal Researcher and the Director of the Emergency and Security Preparedness Department at the Korea Institute of Nuclear Safety. Since 1999, Dr. Kim has held a number of positions at the International Atomic Energy Agency, including Reactor Accident Prevention Specialist and Nuclear Security Officer. His work has focused extensively on issues of nuclear installation safety and security. He also served as the Head of the Radiological Security Department at the Korea Institute for Nuclear Safety and as the Head of the Nuclear Verification Task Force Team at the Ministry of National Defense, Korea Arms Verification Agency. He graduated from the Korea Advanced Institute of Science and Technology (KAIST).

The accident at the Fukushima Daiichi nuclear power plant highlights the urgent need for strengthening regional cooperation among the Republic of Korea (ROK), China, and Japan. From the perspective of geopolitical proximity, the nuclear safety and emergency response mechanisms of the three countries should be considered regional public goods rather than subjects of national interest.

The regional situation awareness (SA) model ensures systematic and practical responses for regional cooperation with regard to Northeast Asian nuclear emergencies, rather than simply considering nuclear emergency response as a matter for mere multilateral cooperation. The regional SA model is a theoretical model that provides a systematic link between institutional arrangements and specific and practical means of regional cooperation in responding to nuclear emergencies.

Based on Endsley's SA model, the regional SA model is a decision-making process comprised of a three-stage cognitive process, regional situation perception, comprehension prediction-decision making, and mental modeling. A regional SA model can be implemented to construct a systematic and specific Northeast Asian cooperative mechanism for managing nuclear emergencies through a regional model, which would consist of institutional arrangements and national nuclear emergency management systems, including hardware and software.

Any successful regional cooperative nuclear emergency response based on the regional SA model in the Northeast Asia region should take into account three aspects. First, the political will for the establishment and continuation of regional cooperation on nuclear emergency response should be ensured. Second, the orientation of regional cooperation with other regions, which might otherwise foster regional competition, should be set strategically. Finally, effective tripartite cooperation and a two-tiered cooperative relationship with ASEAN require specific legally binding institutional arrangements.

Background

The radiological aftermath of Chernobyl and Fukushima demonstrates that a nuclear accident anywhere constitutes an accident everywhere. This means that any nuclear accident should be immediately perceived as a global issue due to radiological dispersion via air trajectories and discharged water. Therefore, nuclear safety and emergency preparedness should not be treated as national public goods, but instead considered to be global or regional public goods. In particular, the geographical proximity of China, Japan, and Korea necessitates regional cooperation in terms of nuclear safety and nuclear disaster management.

After the 3/11 earthquake in Japan, a China-Japan-South Korea trilateral summit was held in Tokyo, Japan, on May 22 with regard to disaster management and nuclear safety. At the summit, the international community, and in particular these three countries, confirmed the need to share the lessons of the 3/11 earthquake and the need for close cooperation among the three countries in the area of disaster management. In order to do so, five cooperation principles and four cooperation strategies have been suggested in the area of disaster management. The five cooperation principles include:

1. Providing emergency rescue and aid supplies.
2. Cooperation among recipient countries for hosting emergency rescue teams and supplies.
3. Sharing experience and lessons learned from the 3/11 earthquake in Japan to apply to disaster rescue.
4. Constantly advancing existing disaster management cooperation.
5. Close cooperation through forums, including among South Korea, China, and Japan.

By these principles, the tripartite summit meeting reconfirmed the importance of strengthening nuclear safety and the necessity for transparent nuclear power plant management.

In addition to the five principles, the major cooperation strategies included hosting working-level workshops on disaster management, encouraging chief-engineer disaster management cooperation, and having professionals from all three countries participating in joint field research. Solutions for strengthening trilateral cooperation in the field of nuclear safety included improving nuclear safety, encouraging transparency in nuclear power plant management, and urging cooperation among professionals with regard to nuclear safety regulation and emergency response for nuclear power plant safety improvement against natural disasters.

The 3/11 earthquake is significant to the field of nuclear energy. South Korea, China, and Japan share the idea that nuclear energy is necessary as an alternative energy. However, safety must come first. This understanding is paramount in the field of disaster management and nuclear safety cooperation.

However, the Summit Leaders Declaration only suggests general issues with regard to cooperation among South Korea, China, and Japan. Considering the importance and the danger that the three countries' nuclear cooperation problem represents, greater effort and detailed discussions are required if we are to see results.

The Southeast Asian region in particular was known to have weak regional cooperation until the 1990s. However, the international importance and interdependence of South Korea, China, and Japan has increased. Furthermore, as the politics, economy, and safety of Southeast Asia have become global issues, the awareness of regional identity has increased. An epistemic community needs to be formed to soften the conflict of interests between the three countries and to cooperate at a regional level.

The highest purpose of nuclear safety is to protect mankind and the environment from any radiation hazard. Like any other disaster, timely and effective initial response and effective mitigation are important in disaster management with regard to nuclear power. Ensuring nuclear safety as a regional public good and acting as a regional community through a regional cooperation system are crucial. Rather than treating the regional cooperation system with regard to nuclear disaster management as a mere diplomatic mechanism, such as agreement-making, expert exchange, or training and education programs, the three countries must share in the status quo as a regional community.

This paper proposes a systematic and practical model, based on a regional SA model, for regional cooperation with regard to nuclear disaster management as a regional public good.

Asian Regional Cooperation

Examples of disaster-related multilateral cooperation in the Asian region include the Haze Technical Task Force Team's Regional Haze Action Plan from the mid-1990s, which was followed by the 2002 Agreement on Trans-boundary Haze Pollution, and the ASEAN Agreement on Disaster Management and Emergency Response at the end of 2004.

In 1977, during the Seoul Asia Nuclear Safety Consultation Summit, South Korea suggested the formation of an Asia Nuclear Safety Consultation Organization for Southeast Asian multilateral cooperation. However, most countries disagreed. Afterwards, the Forum for Nuclear Cooperation in Asia was formed by 10 member countries through changes to parts of the International Conference of Nuclear Cooperation in Asia, which was led by Japan between 1990 and 1999.

In 1972, Asian and Pacific regional members of the International Atomic Energy Agency (IAEA) formed the Regional Cooperative Agreement (RCA) for Research, Development, and Training related to Nuclear Science and Technology for Asia and the Pacific. The RCA is a government agreement with the secretariat formed under the supervision of the IAEA.

In 1996, Japan proposed the regional cooperation concept of Asiatom, which is a similar concept to Euratom, to deal with nuclear spent fuel and non-proliferation issues. The concept of Asiatom is focused on regional cooperation in Northeast Asia for enhancing nuclear safety, nuclear non-proliferation, and the establishment of a regional nuclear fuel cycle. Moreover, the concept proposed a nuclear weapons-free zone and the enhancement of collective defense for regional security. However, it failed to draw regional consensus, due to Japan-oriented policy, difficulties in directly applying the Euratom model within the Asian region, and the asymmetry of interests between South Korea, China, and Japan on the concept of collective defense.

The accident at Fukushima should lead to the formation of an epistemic community that includes the Southeast Asian countries under the premise that when it comes to nuclear safety, they are part of a common community. Several mistakes (not errors) during the consequent management at Fukushima drastically undermined global public acceptance of nuclear power. The major mistakes stemmed from delayed decisions on evaluating the consequences of the accident, the timing of early notification to neighboring countries bound by the Convention on Early Notification, and limiting international technical support from advanced countries, including the United States and France. Also, delayed information sharing and re-estimations of accident classifications led to a loss of international credibility.

The catastrophic Fukushima nuclear disaster propounded nuclear safety issues on the agenda for the second Global Nuclear Security Summit in Seoul. The grounds for this argument came from concerns that the vulnerabilities identified in Fukushima may give terrorist groups a cookbook for attacking nuclear installations. Furthermore, the IAEA has emphasized the consilience of nuclear safety, security, and safeguards, which is the so-called 3S approach. It is generally understood that nuclear safety and security at nuclear installations share the need for emergency preparedness while there are different causes that would initiate such an event, whether it be random failure or malicious intention. However, some expert groups are very reluctant to consent to this approach on the basis that nuclear safety pursues openness and transparency while nuclear security emphasizes confidentiality.

Regional Situation Awareness for Cooperative Emergency Responses during Nuclear Disasters

No generally accepted workable definition of situation awareness exists. The concept of situation awareness was introduced by a group of specialists from military and air accident investigation to identify influential factors in the cognitive performance of military or aircrews in the mid-1970s. Many scientists attempted to define situation awareness in the context of cognitive science. In this paper, my model adheres to Endsley's definition: "Situation awareness is the perception of elements in the environment within a volume of time and space, the comprehension of their meaning and the projection of their status in the near future."

In particular, securing timely and correct SA is crucial for effective disaster management with time and space constraints. Endsley presents a theoretical model of SA, reproduced here in Figure 1. Endsley's model of SA represents the interaction between human beings and the environment. The color-shaded box represents personal cognitive functions, which consists of states, three levels of situation awareness, as well as behavioral and execution capabilities (represented as "decision" and "performance of actions" boxes). This cognitive function could be influenced by two factors, namely (1) individual factors, including task, goal, and preconception, and (2) the task/system factors (top-left) comprised of system capabilities and so forth. The bottom-right box represents a mental model, which includes three categories of knowledge, namely (a) procedural knowledge, noted as "information processing mechanisms," (b) long-term memory, and (c) skills shown through "automaticity."

Figure 1 provides an overview of the major influential factors for decision-making under tactical or time-constraint conditions. As shown in Figure 1, major influential factors can be taken as characteristics of a

Figure 1: Endsley's Model of Situation Awareness

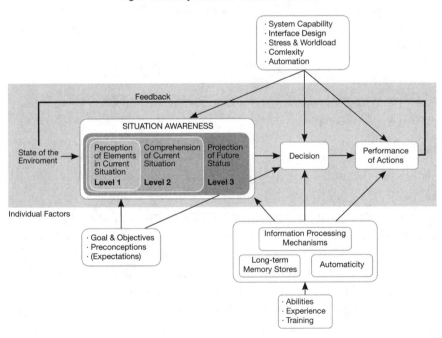

Source: "Situation Awareness," Wikipedia, http://en.wikipedia.org/wiki/Situation_awareness.

situation, situation awareness, performance goal, and information processing mechanisms.

It is generally understood that SA is the most influential factor in decision making and the selection of actions to be taken during dynamic decision processes. SA involves three levels. At level one, SA is the process of "perception of the elements in a current situation" without any specific information. At level two of SA, comprehension of the characteristics or the implications of the situation is achieved based upon specific information or knowledge. Finally, level three of SA provides a projection of the future status of the situation.

The correctness and completeness of SA is very susceptible to situation-specific information, information-processing mechanisms called "mental models," and task goals.

Endsley's SA is focused on personal cognitive processes as principal cognitive agents via the chain of perception-comprehension-projection, while the role of a group or team member is that of a messenger that transfers significant information to principal agents of cognitive functioning.

Team situation awareness is a concept of collective and dynamic team cognitive processes with shared goals and different tasks amongst the team. Remarkable research achievements on team SA have been made by Jannis Canon-Bowers, Nancy Cooke, Kim Sok Chul, and other distinguished scientists.[1]

This paper proposes the use of a regional SA model for collective and cooperative decision making or emergency responses during trans-boundary catastrophic disasters, such as the Fukushima accident, epidemic diseases, or the consequences of climate change. Efforts toward preventing and managing the consequences of trans-boundary disasters should be dealt with as sustainable global or regional public goods, not as national interests.

Figure 2 gives an example of how a regional SA model can be applied to trans-boundary disaster management in a way that incorporates

---

1 Sok Chul Kim., Soon Heung Chang, and Gyunyoung Heo, "Team Crystallization (SIO2): Dynamic Model of Team Effectiveness Evaluation under the Dynamic and Tactical Environment at Nuclear Installation," *Safety Science* 44, no. 8 (2005): 701–721; Nancy J. Cooke et al., "Measuring Team Knowledge," *Human Factors* 42, no. 1 (2000).

all elements of Endsley's model of situation awareness.

Figure 2: Proposed Regional Situation Awareness Model

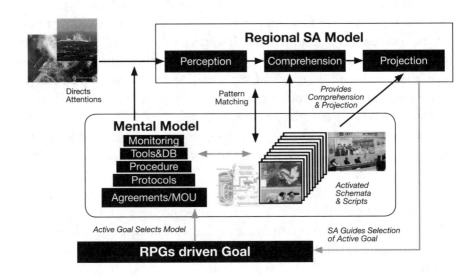

Regional situation perception
The perception phase of regional SA contains detection or identification of the possibility or occurrence of a trans-boundary disaster. Here, the situation necessitates information, knowledge, or environmental factors to be characterized as response options for disaster management.[2]

A special detection or monitoring system and an automatic early notification system can be used as tools for perception within the framework of regional SA. In the perception phase, SA should be secured without artificial polishing or transferring the situation-specific information within the region. If it is possible, on a real-time basis, to share a national environmental radiation monitoring network and safety parameters of nuclear power plants after the commencement of an accident, more prompt and effective measures for consequence management can be secured through the early perception and identification of

2 Richard W. Pew, "The State of Situation Awareness Measurement: Heading Toward the Next Century," in *Situation Awareness Analysis and Measurement*, ed. Mica R. Endsley and Daniel J. Garland (Mahwah: Lawrence Erlbaum Associates, 2000).

disaster characteristics, rather than through a diplomatic approach, such as bilateral or multilateral agreements.

Regional situation comprehension
While the situation perception phase involves data acquisition in order to begin information processing, the situation comprehension phase is about understanding and evaluating what the current situation means. The major tasks in the course of situation comprehension are to evaluate the implications of the current situation and to prepare strategies for achieving goals:

1. Identifying, monitoring, and surveillance of critical parameters necessary to evaluate the characteristics of a situation.
2. Integrating collected information.
3. Evaluating the viability of collected information.
4. Making decisions on actions to be taken.

For example, during a catastrophic nuclear accident, such as at Fukushima, the following goals for accidents in the origin country, related to situation comprehension, can be chosen:

1. Identifying root causes of the accident and estimating the magnitude of its consequences.
2. Establishing a strategic plan for restoring the plant to a stable condition at the pre-accident level.

The task goals for neighboring countries would be evaluating the domestic impact of an accident and providing technical support to an accident's origin countries for preparing mitigation strategies.

During the Fukushima accident, Korea and China experienced unnecessary social disruption, including a panic surrounding the purchase of salt in China and an uproar caused by the fear of radioactive rain due to the absence of information-sharing by Japan. Furthermore, duplicated contamination checks at international airports and seaports for passengers, baggage, and parcels originating from Japan wasted time and resources.

Regional situation projection

Correct projection of future consequences during disaster management is crucial for timely and effective decision making. Regional situation projection is the highest cognitive function of regional SA. To make a regional situation projection is to estimate future consequences of accidents or disasters and to prepare the necessary countermeasures for consequence management. In the case of nuclear disasters, based on radiological source term and meteorological data, regional situation projection provides an estimate of the magnitude of consequences in terms of the health effects on the public and the area to be affected by the accident. Sharing correct information in a timely fashion on plant characteristics, including the current status of critical safety parameters and the progression of consequences, is critical to preparing practical and viable strategies for restoring the plant status back to a stable condition.

Mental model of regional situation awareness

The mental model of regional SA can be comprised of a hardware system and a knowledge base associated with the relevant country's legal provisions, procedures, protocols, and critical information for the consequence management of a trans-boundary disaster. As shown in Figure 2, the mental model is a component of the decision-making process for consequence management. The principal agents of the mental model in regional SA can be groups of experts deployed in each country, integrated detection-monitoring-evaluation processes for consequence management, and an institutional arrangement for early notification and the provision of support for disaster management, such as bilateral or multilateral agreements.

A Regional Cooperation Model for Nuclear Disasters among China, South Korea, and Japan

Geographical proximity and the historical ties between these three countries necessitate closer regional cooperation on nuclear safety and emergency response. China, South Korea, and Japan contain 22 percent of the global population and account for 20 percent of global gross domestic product. Currently, there are 64 nuclear power plants in operation in the region, and 44 units under construction, which amounts to 20 percent and 71 percent of the total number of nuclear power plants in the world either in operation or under construction, respectively.

A regional cooperation model based on a regional SA model could be suggested as an implementation tool for the agreement reached at the tripartite summit meeting held in May 2011. The office of the tripartite secretariat was established in Seoul as a result of that tripartite summit meeting.

The tripartite secretariat could play a key role as part of the mental model within a regional SA model with a shift in this office's role from an intergovernmental office to an international organization. In particular, the installation of an operational center and special task force team within the tripartite secretariat is strongly recommended.

The mental model of regional SA would be an institutional arrangement for prompt and cooperative emergency response amongst the neighboring countries of the accident-origin country, which would include a rationale for cooperative consequence management, standardized procedures, tools, and a database pertaining to accident characteristics and radiological consequence analysis.

The following items could be considered examples for the cooperative emergency response framework:

1. Raising emergency rescue funds for cooperative consequence management.
2. Sharing information on the emergency response framework and stockpiles.
3. Visiting exchanges for emergency response exercises or drills.
4. Periodic joint tabletop exercises or communication tests.

The cooperation model associated with the regional mental model would involve an integration of technical measures for nuclear disaster management, including an earthquake monitoring network, an environmental radiation monitoring network, a safety information collection system, or an automatic notification system. Monitoring and surveillance of critical information for consequence management should be carried out by the operational center belonging to the tripartite secretariat. To give a timely analysis and evaluation of the situation, it is essential to comprehend the impact of the consequences of the accident in the neighboring country. Without a standardized methodology and evaluation criteria, it is very difficult to achieve public acceptance.

For example, China, South Korea, and Japan conducted atmospheric dispersion analyses individually but official announcements of their evaluations' results have not been made. Various rumors on airstream trajectory brought about unnecessary social disruption. A cooperation model at the projection phase may include the following activities:

1. Building a joint standing expert group on safety analysis, atmospheric dispersion analysis, and consequence management.
2. Developing a standardized evaluation methodology and database.

Conclusion

From the Fukushima accident in 2011, we have learned the valuable lesson that a nuclear accident anywhere immediately becomes a global issue, in part due to vague fears reminiscent of those with regard to nuclear weapons. There exists an urgent need for shifting paradigms in China, South Korea, and Japan to an understanding that nuclear safety and nuclear emergency management should be dealt with as regional public goods rather than national interests. Geographical proximity and active nuclear power programs in this region necessitate consolidated cooperation on nuclear safety and emergency management.

The regional SA model provides a practical and specific regional cooperation model to enhance nuclear safety and emergency management as regional public goods. For achieving practical and viable cooperation among China, South Korea, and Japan, the following three elements should be taken into account.

First, an urgent need exists to establish an epistemic community on the premise that timely and practical cooperation is inevitable for consolidating regional cooperation on nuclear safety and emergency management as regional public goods. This could, in part, be built upon the existing political willingness to continue tripartite summit meetings.

Second, positioning cooperation with other regions, including the Southeast Asian region, should be taken into account. In practice, it is very important to take into consideration the role of ASEAN, which has played a key role in establishing a cooperative program in the Asia-Pacific region.

Finally, legally binding systematic tools for practical and viable cooperation on nuclear safety and emergency management should be prepared as soon as possible.

References

Brannick, Michael T., and Carolyn W. Prince. "An Overview of Team Performance Measurement." In *Team Performance Assessment and Measurement: Theory, Method, and Applications*, edited by Michael T. Brannick, Eduardo Salas, and Carolyn W. Prince. London: Psychology Press, 1997.

Cooke, Nancy J., Eduardo Salas, Jannis A. Canon-Bowers, and Renee J. Stout. "Measuring Team Knowledge." *Human Factors* 42, no. 1 (2000).

Chun, Chaesung. "Nuclear Energy Cooperation of Northeast Asia in the 21st Century." Paper presented at the Korean Nuclear Society's Workshop for Nuclear Energy Cooperation of Northeast Asia in the 21st Century, Busan, South Korea, October 26, 2005.

Davis, Curtis W., III et al. "Enhanced Regional Situation Awareness." *Lincoln Laboratory Journal* 16, no. 2 (2007).

Endsley, Mica. R. "Theoretical Underpinnings of Situation Awareness: A Critical Review." In *Situation Awareness Analysis and Measurement*, edited by Mica R. Endsley and Daniel J. Garland. Mahwah: Lawrence Erlbaum Associates, 2000.

Hauland, Gunnar. "Measuring Team Situation Awareness in Training of En Route Air Traffic Control: Process Oriented Measures for Experimental Studies." Ph.D. dissertation, Risø National Laboratory, 2002.

Jeon, Jinho. "Post Fukushima and Korea." Current Issues and Policy 183 (2011). http://www.sejong.org/Pub_ci/PUB_CI_DATA/k2011-07_1.PDF.

Jeong, Hyung-Gon, and Yooyeon, Noh. "Results and Future Tasks of the Korea-China-Japan Summit." *KIEP World Economy Update* 11, no. 17 (2011).

Jun, Bong-Geun. "The Significance and Challenges of the 2012 Seoul Nuclear Security Summit." *International Issues & Prospects* (2011). http://www.ifans.go.kr/webmodule/htsboard/template/read/ifansread.jsp?boardid=7891&typeID=20&tableName=TYPE_LEGNAME&seqno=616257.

Kaul, Inge, et al. "How to Improve the Provision of Global Public Goods." In *Providing Global Public Goods: Managing Globalization*, edited by Inge Kaul. Oxford: Oxford University Press, 2003.

Kim, S. C., Soon Heung Chang, and Gyunyoung Heo. "Team Crystallization (SIO2): Dynamic Model of Team Effectiveness Evaluation under the Dynamic and Tactical Environment at Nuclear Installation." *Safety Science* 44, no. 8 (2005).

Kim, Young-Jae, and Seong-Whun Cheon. *An Analysis of Nuclear Cooperation Model in Northeast Asia for the 21st Century.* Daejeon: Korea Atomic Energy Research Institute, 2005.

Klein, G. "Source of Error in the Naturalistic Decision Making Tasks." In Proceedings of the Human Factors and Ergonomics Society 37th Annual Meeting. Human Factors and Ergonomics Society (1993).

Nordhouse, W. D. "Paul Samuelson and Global Public Goods: A Commemorative Essay for Paul Samuelson." In *Samuelsonian Economics*, edited by Michael Szenberg. Oxford: Oxford University Press, 2006.

Pew, Richard W. "The State of Situation Awareness Measurement: Heading Toward the Next Century." In *Situation Awareness Analysis and Measurement*, edited by Mica R. Endsley and Daniel J. Garland. Mahwah: Lawrence Erlbaum Associates, 2000.

Starter, N. B., and David D. Woods. "Situation Awareness: A Critical but Ill-Defined Phenomenon." *International Journal of Aviation Psychology 38A* (1991).

Wikipedia. "Situation Awareness." http://en.wikipedia.org/wiki/Situation_awareness.

Yang, Maeng-Ho. *A Study on the Establishment of Nuclear Cooperation Policy towards the Era of Northeast Asian Countries in the 21st Century*. Daejeon: Korea Atomic Energy Research Institute, 2006.

Yeo, Andrew. "Bilateralism, Multilateralism, and Institutional Chance in Northeast Asia's Regional Security Architecture." Catholic University of America/East Asia Institute, *EAI-Follows Program Working Paper Series* 30 (2011). http://www.eai.or.kr/data/bbs/eng_report/201104281643832.pdf.

CHAPTER 09

THE US-JAPAN ALLIANCE
AND JAPAN'S FUTURE

Michael Auslin

Michael Auslin is a Resident Scholar in Asian Studies and the Director of Japan Studies at the American Enterprise Institute (AEI). Dr. Auslin is a frequent commentator for the US and foreign media, including the *Wall Street Journal*. Prior to joining AEI, he was an Associate Professor of History and Senior Research Fellow at the MacMillan Center for International and Area Studies at Yale University. His recent publications on Asia and Japan include, *Pacific Cosmopolitans: A Cultural History of US-Japan Relations* (Cambridge: Harvard University Press, 2011) and "Security in the Indo-Pacific Commons: Toward a Regional Strategy" (AEI Press, 2010). He received his Ph.D. from the University of Illinois at Urbana-Champaign, M.A. from Indiana University at Bloomington, and B.S. and F.S. from Georgetown University.

Perhaps the key question facing the over 50-year-old US-Japan alliance is whether it still remains at the core of America's Asia strategy as well as Japan's security strategy. In other words, is the alliance still the fundamental relationship that both sides have assumed it has been for the past half a century or more? The most reasoned and prudent answer is a qualified "yes," and this essay will attempt to explain what those qualifications are.

Historical Background[1]

The template for postwar US-Japan security cooperation was determined just as Japan regained sovereignty in 1952 at the end of the seven-year US occupation. US forces would remain in Japan in large numbers on bases on the main islands and in US-controlled Okinawa, while Washington would continually express hope and support that Japanese governments would eventually rearm the country sufficiently for self-defense purposes. From the perspective of weak postwar Japanese governments, the US security presence meant that they could begin to focus on rebuilding the country's shattered economy, as well as knit together the social fabric that had been rent by the war.

The United States, for its part, developed this new relationship with Japan due to global challenges and responsibilities that it had now inherited as the only superpower, as well as the leading nation of the liberal West. The framing issue of these decades, of course, was the emergence of a global competition between the Soviet Union and the United States. Although it had been a bitter enemy for four years, Japan immediately became America's postwar strategic linchpin in the Pacific, a position to which Japan's leadership acquiesced in exchange for security guarantees and the freedom to focus its scarce resources on national rebuilding. From a strategic perspective, the US presence in Japan acted as a bulwark against Soviet expansion in Northeast Asia, and the alliance became the cornerstone of US policy in Asia. The triumph of Mao Zedong's Chi-

---

1 This chapter is an updated version of an essay written in January 2010 to commemorate the 50th anniversary of the US-Japan alliance. This section on the historical background of the alliance takes heavily from this paper: Michael Auslin, "The US-Japan Alliance: Relic of a Bygone Era?" American Enterprise Institute for Public Policy Research, *Asian Outlook* 1 (January 2010), http://www.aei.org/files/2010/01/07/The%20US-Japan%20Alliance.pdf.

nese Communist Party in 1949 and North Korea's invasion of South Korea in 1950—events that left Japan the only major non-communist country in Northeast Asia—cemented the importance to the United States of maintaining Japan as its key Pacific partner. Without Japan, Washington would not have been able to draw an iron chain across archipelagic Asia, stretching from the Aleutian Islands down through Japan to Taiwan and Southeast Asia. This chain, often portrayed graphically on maps, served to cut the Soviet Union and the PRC off from access to the Pacific and the increasingly important global commons.

By the time the United States and Japan renegotiated the security treaty in 1960, making it an alliance more between equals, Cold War crises were emerging around the world, particularly in Berlin, Cuba, and Indochina. Yet, the 1960 treaty largely followed the 1951 agreement in focusing primarily on Japan's defense and only secondarily on the issue of "international peace and security in the Far East" (as it was expressed in Article IV). The core of the 1960 alliance agreement rests in Article V, which commits both parties to "act to meet the common danger" of an armed attack against either, but with the caveat that each would so act "in accordance with its constitutional provisions and processes." This would prove to become a significant issue in alliance relations once the Cabinet Legislation Bureau determined in 1981 that Japan's postwar Constitution did not allow for the exercise of the right of collective self-defense. Despite such limitations, the Japanese decision to allow long-term US bases on its soil, and the American willingness to maintain those bases, represented a fundamentally different US presence in Asia than had been the case before World War II. The permanent US presence meant that Asia's overall development, both economic and political, and the role of Japan in promoting that development, became factors in US global strategy.

The battle over Europe may have been the centerpiece of the Cold War, but the liberal internationalist order President Harry S. Truman created, and which his successors—Dwight D. Eisenhower, John F. Kennedy, and Lyndon B. Johnson—continued, could not have succeeded without a resolute US commitment to Asia. As a base of military operations during the Korean War, Japan allowed the US Air Force and Navy to hold their presence on the war-torn peninsula and eventually struggle to a negotiated ceasefire. These events proved to Washington policymakers that if the United States wished to maintain its regional presence and not surrender to what it believed to be a united communist front between the Soviet Union and China, then Japan was the military key to holding Northeast Asia in the same way that the Philippines served to anchor the US presence in Southeast Asia.

During these decades, however, Washington's security calculations ceased to be the sole strategic rationale for the alliance with Japan. During the 1960s, Japan's economic boom commenced, and the country's real gross domestic product grew at an annual rate of 8.9 percent. While growth slowed dramatically during the 1970s due to the oil shocks, by that time, Japan had become the world's key exporter of high-tech consumer goods, steel, ships, and automobiles. In other words, Japan had become crucial to global economic growth and, increasingly, the health of the US economy. From one perspective, then, the US-Japan alliance became committed to defending Japan against any potential threat that could harm the new economic powerhouse. And with the Soviet Union attempting to spread its influence in Southeast Asia, Japan's role as a northern bulwark against communism was highlighted by its successful capitalist economy, a model that other modernizing nations, such as South Korea, Taiwan, and Singapore, were emulating.

With the collapse of the Soviet Union in 1991, the Cold War ended, and along with it, much of the preceding decades' rationale for the alliance disappeared. Under leader Deng Xiaoping, China fully embarked on a domestic-growth plan that put a premium on trade relations and economic liberalization, all of which benefited Japanese and US companies that rushed in to do business with China. While the Clinton administration saw China as a "strategic partner," believing that economic relations would be sufficient for preserving peace in Asia, security specialists increasingly saw post–Cold War stability as fragile and lacking the bonds of trust among Asian states that would allow them to solve serious disputes among themselves. Indeed, as the decade wore on, China emerged more clearly as a potential security threat when it began upgrading its military, including its strategic missile corps. In general, however, the People's Liberation Army was very underdeveloped. Even so, in 1996 China fired ballistic missiles off the coast of Taiwan in an attempt to intimidate the island's prodemocracy voters before a presidential election. In response, the United States sent two aircraft-carrier battle groups into the Taiwan Strait in a clear message to Beijing not to upset regional stability or pressure Taiwan into accommodating China.

At the same time, the Kim family regime in North Korea commenced a two-decade-long effort to develop nuclear power and eventually obtain atomic weapons. The United States was drawn further into East Asia's underlying instability, as several crises throughout the decade brought Washington and Pyongyang to the brink of a military clash, particularly in 1993. The Korean crises demonstrated to both US and Japanese officials that despite the alliance, the two countries were not realistically prepared to act together in cases of regional conflict. Due in part to this realization and to China's new power, as well as to the rape of an Okinawan schoolgirl by a group of US Marines in 1995, the two allies agreed in 1996 to reform the alliance. This culminated in the 1997 revised US-Japan Defense Guidelines. Through negotiations with the Clinton administration, the Status of Forces Agreement (SOFA) was revised, and Tokyo agreed to take greater responsibility for its own defense by playing a more active role in supporting US troops engaged in operations in areas surrounding Japan.

Events over the next years only highlighted the new challenges facing the alliance and the need for more joint cooperation. In 1998, Pyongyang launched a Taepodong ballistic missile over Japanese territory, signaling Japan's vulnerability to such weapons of mass destruction and providing further impetus for defense modernization. The Japan Defense Agency immediately began working with the US Department of Defense to upgrade Japan's missile-defense capabilities. For its part, the United States agreed not only to license Japanese production of advanced antiballistic missile systems, but also to increase the sharing of intelligence and to station more US Navy Aegis-equipped destroyers outfitted with missile defenses in Japanese waters. Yet restrictions on collective self-defense, as well as the general inviolability of Article 9 of the Japanese Constitution, continued to limit the amount of joint planning the allies could do and raised concerns in Washington that Japan would employ its military in a crisis only under narrow circumstances.

An unexpected test of the US-Japan alliance came with the September 11, 2011, terrorist attacks on the United States. Japan's new prime minister, Junichiro Koizumi, quickly moved to support President George W. Bush's war on Al Qaeda and the Taliban and later the US invasion of Iraq. Japan dispatched Self-Defense Forces (SDF)—including Air Maritime SDF—to Iraq, Afghanistan, and the Indian Ocean in a variety of support and logistical roles. This appeared to mark a decisive break from Tokyo's traditional unwillingness to become involved in global security crises. Koizumi's actions were in stark contrast with what had happened in 1991, when Japan's government, under Prime Minister Toshiki Kaifu, refused to provide support for the first Gulf War (Operation Desert Storm).

Some of the groundwork for Koizumi's new approach had been laid even before the 2000 US election, when a panel of US-Japan experts led by Richard Armitage and Joseph Nye published a report on the future of the US-Japan alliance. The panel was in close contact with Japanese counterparts and provided a road map for alliance relations that fit the preferences of Koizumi and other Liberal Democratic Party (LDP) leaders like Shinzo Abe. Still, the impetus for Koizumi's action came primarily from his own belief that Japan needed to adopt a more global role and from his political willingness to push through the Diet the various Special Measures Laws that would allow Japan to dispatch noncombatant SDF to the Middle East.

Over the next half-decade, Japan's SDF would be engaged in one operation or another, even after both Koizumi and Abe had left office. Yet Abe's sudden resignation after barely a year in office signaled the beginning of a retrenchment of Japanese security operations abroad. Abe came to power with an ambitious program for reforming Japan's national security mechanisms in ways that would allow Japan to participate even more fully with US forces and, thus, expand the scope of the alliance along the lines envisioned by the Armitage-Nye report. Among his goals were a revision of Article 9, the creation of a Japanese National Security Council, increased military budgets, and a more centralized intelligence organization. Abe's resignation and the succession of Yasuo Fukuda, a compromise LDP premier elected after Abe's departure, halted all of these plans. For the next two years, a weakened LDP had no ability or will to discuss the future of the alliance with the United States.

The Alliance under the DPJ (2009–Present)

Since coming to power in 2009, the Democratic Party of Japan (DPJ) has found itself in an increasingly difficult position vis-à-vis the United States. Responding in part to his liberal base as well as to left-wing elements in the party, Prime Minister Yukio Hatoyama began his term by reopening the question of the 2006 agreement to move US Marines from their airbase at Futenma on Okinawa to a more remote location in the northern part of the island. This push was buttressed by comments by DPJ founder Ichiro Ozawa questioning the need for the current level of US forces in Japan. In addition, the DPJ moved swiftly to take direct control of diplomatic relations with Washington, thereby cutting experienced bureaucrats out of the loop and endangering the long-standing working relations between Tokyo and Washington. These moves led to months of protracted negotiations with Washington, in which working relations became strained. In reality, both sides knew that there was no real alternative to the Futenma agreement, but national and local politics made it difficult for the DPJ to embrace the plan. Okinawans, in particular, used the DPJ's hesitancy to push strongly for the expulsion of US Marines from the island. In March 2011, the devastating Tohoku earthquake and tsunami, followed by the Fukushima nuclear crisis, served to knock the Futenma issue off the political radar, while also showing how close the two allies actually were, demonstrated best by the intensive and generous disaster relief and aid provided by American forces alongside their Japanese counterparts.

Due in part to his mishandling of the Futenma issue, Hatoyama stepped down just a year into his premiership. Since Hatoyama's resignation in 2010, and the equally failed one-year premiership of Naoto Kan, the state of the alliance and the political relationship today is best characterized as being in a "waiting period." The Futenma issue itself has been unresolved for 10 to 15 years, thus underscoring both stability in

US-Japan relations and a strong element of stagnation. This occurred in part as both countries recategorized their foreign policies and considered how they will merge to work effectively together in the 21st century.

Two particular areas mark this waiting period, both directly related to domestic politics. First is whether or not new Prime Minister Yoshihiko Noda would survive more than a year after taking power in September 2011. The issue of political longevity is important because it indicates the level of political stability in the country, and directly affects the working relationships that come from having knowledge of one's counterpart across the table. Many of those in high positions in Tokyo and Washington admit that it is very hard to get a political rhythm going when there is turnover in the leadership that results in yearly turnover in the ministries, turnover in the cabinet, and so on. Strong working relations with senior bureaucrats, while important, cannot substitute for the high-level direction of political leaders. Thus, at one level, analysts of the US-Japan relationship continue to wait to see if Prime Minister Noda will survive, and if he does, to see if he can build that type of stability in the working relationship that has been absent since Prime Minister Koizumi left office in 2006.

The second way in which the US-Japan alliance is in a waiting period is related to the US domestic situation and who will be the next president. Whether President Obama is re-elected or a Republican defeats him, there will almost certainly be a change-over in faces. It is unlikely that the current team working on Japan and Asia will carry over to a second Obama administration, and if there is a change in the administration an entirely new set of individuals will take over Asia and Japan policy at the political level. Normally, very few initiatives come out at the end of a presidential administration; rather, there is often a focus on trying to resolve outstanding problems and possibly creating some new momentum. In general, however, administrations are wary of anything new that could cause unforeseen problems, and instead reserve their energy for dealing with any crises and disasters. Often when analysts try to look at the "big picture" in foreign policy or bilateral relationships, it is easy to miss out on the realities of American political cycles.

Focusing specifically on the alliance and the broader US-Japan relationship, the state of the relationship does not look particularly weak, even if there is a lack of commitment and energy by both political leaders. For all of the problems related to Futenma, if the alliance is analyzed from its narrow definition as a specific set of security obligations, there appears to have been steady movement over the past decade or more. If one compares where the alliance is today to where it was in 1995 or even 2000, one immediately notices some dramatic developments and improvements. Perhaps most important is the burgeoning relationship in ballistic missile defense (BMD), in which Japan and the United States have conducted numerous tests together while actively fielding an increasingly capable BMD capability through Aegis ships and ground-based interceptors. Beyond this, the movement to co-locate air defense headquarters is moving forward, and during the Bush years there was regular discussion between the US Navy and the Maritime Self-Defense Forces about the Proliferation Security Initiative and rebuilding both countries' anti-submarine warfare capability.

Given that, it is legitimate to ask why the Futenma issue has taken as long as it has to be resolved, why it became such a touchstone in the way that it did, why there was such political mishandling of the issue on the part of Hatoyama, along with mixed signals from the Americans, and the like. All these questions go to the core of high-level political management of the alliance, and the answers to them may help indicate the degree to which the alliance will be able to function smoothly in the future. Most analysts believe it is fair to say that the Futenma issue has damaged the working relationship between Tokyo and Washington. At the same time, the two countries seemed to recognize the seriousness of the situation, even if they could not solve it, and both decided ultimately to act responsibly and soberly in trying to keep Futenma from poisoning the broader relationship. There was no threat to cut off relations, and senior American and Japanese officials continued to go back and forth across the Pacific regularly. The April 2012 agreement to "delink" Futenma from the move of 9,000 US Marines off Okinawa showed that the two allies could successfully move beyond such obstacles, even if it took several years to do so. While doubt still remains over whether Futenma will ever be moved to Henoko, the rest of the 2006 realignment agreement is poised to move forward.

It is particularly worth noting that the successes and troubles in the alliance discussed above are taking place in the context of the transformation of Japan's security since the end of the Cold War. These changes, related to the rise of China and the spread of weapons of mass destruction, were codified in the 2010 National Defense Program Guidelines (NDPG). Tokyo committed to a new security paradigm of "dynamic deterrence" that included a strategic focus on its southwestern islands, the East China Sea, and the broader Asian commons as areas of primary concern. The NDPG is a strategic document, as it focuses primarily on how Japan should approach its security, responsibilities, and commitments in a changing world.

Interestingly, just at the moment that Tokyo has begun to talk about shifting the Japanese strategic vision down southwest, there is the re-emergence in the northeast of Russia, which has indicated it will significantly build up its defenses on the disputed Kuril Islands and on Kamchatka. This includes installing new anti-ship missiles and air defenses and basing attack helicopters and destroyers in the region, so as to regain the geopolitical influence it had in the region during the Cold War. If Russia does rebuild its military capability in the Pacific, and if China continues to expand its navy and air force while the United States begins to deeply cut its military budget, then Tokyo will be faced with an uneasy geopolitical situation.

In some ways, such an environment would mirror what Tokugawa Japan faced in the 19th century. Back then, the Americans were encroaching from the east, over the Pacific, while the British came from the south, and the Russians from the north, causing a strategic crisis for Japan. This led to dramatic domestic changes in Japanese thinking about the world, and led directly to the political crisis that resulted in the overthrow of the Tokugawa shogunate and the triumph of the modernizing Meiji Restoration. Therefore, if today's three trends continue over time, it is not unrealistic that Japan may feel that same sense of strategic pressure.

In response to these trends, the Obama administration has made clear that it plans on "pivoting" or "rebalancing" to the Asia-Pacific region, in order to shore up America's position and better protect its interests. The president and secretaries of state and defense have repeatedly announced that the United States is a Pacific power. Some believe that there is a risk to so publically announcing that Washington will focus on Asia. While no one wants to see America turn away from Asia, the fact is that the United States will remain a global power whether it wants to or not, and will retain its global responsibilities whether it wants to or not. Therefore, every time that Washington finds itself pulled back to the Middle East, or it has to commit significant resources to a humanitarian crisis like it did in Japan in March 2011, there will be criticism that America is not upholding its primary focus on Asia.

The even larger question, however, is whether the US pivot is real or rhetorical. With at least $500 billion in defense cuts looming in the United States, there is little doubt that the American military will get smaller in coming years. If so, then is the pivot a realistic strategy or not? The Obama administration has attempted to flesh out the idea of the pivot by announcing the deployment of up to 2,500 US Marines (some of them from Okinawa) to Darwin, Australia, and the extended deployment of four new littoral combat ships to Singapore. In addition, there is speculation that the Philippines may agree to host limited US forces on a rotational basis, thereby bringing American troops back to the islands two decades after the closing of the Subic and Clark bases. However, only time will tell as to whether or not these measures are sufficient to continue securing US interests in the region as it faces an increasing number of challenges.

From this perspective, the Noda administration can develop the trends in the NDPG to synergize with US moves. As Washington seeks to expand its presence in the region, Japan can facilitate Washington's efforts by building up its defenses in the East China Sea and in cooperating more closely in confidence-building measures throughout East Asia. A more involved role will require a commitment in funds, as well as a readiness to react quickly to requests for assistance and partnership. But such willingness can help pave the road ahead for the alliance.

The Road Ahead

As the US-Japan alliance passed its half-century mark in 2010, change was accelerating throughout Asia, as well as in Japan and the United States. China's rise to economic, political, and military prominence has significantly changed conditions in Asia since the 1990s. At the same time, new governments in Tokyo and Washington have pledged dramatic breaks with the recent past and have shifted their focus to domestic issues rather than foreign ones. With the current global economic crisis and the continuing wars in the Middle East and South Asia, pressures on the alliance to define its role in the coming years have mounted.

The DPJ's rise to power seems to have fundamentally shifted Japan's political landscape. While the US administration turnover between the Democratic and Republican parties is common, the accession of an opposition party to power in Japan for the first time in over 50 years raised questions as to the future of the alliance under DPJ rule. These fears were realized, if partly, by the drop-off in relations during the Hatoyama and Kan administrations.

Of greater concern for the long-term viability of the alliance was whether Washington and Tokyo continued to share common political and security goals for maintaining East Asian stability and prosperity. One key example of this possible divergence in objectives that will remain an issue well into the future is North Korea. As the new leadership in North Korea takes power after the death of long-time dictator Kim Jong-Il, the nuclear crisis continues to drag on, only with greater uncertainty as to the stability and policies of Kim Jong-Un, the new paramount leader. The failed April launch of a "satellite," in reality a disguised ballistic missile test, underscored the degree to which the Kim regime remains committed not only to its missile and nuclear programs, but also to a destabilizing posture in the region. Thus, both Washington and Tokyo retain their focus on missile defense, which now has resulted in several successful interception tests by Japanese Maritime SDF destroyers outfitted with Aegis antimissile systems. Yet, with Tokyo beginning to reduce its commitment to future missile-defense systems and with no current political movement on negotiations with North Korea (the Six-Party Talks), it is unclear whether Washington and Tokyo share the same vision for dealing with Pyongyang. Furthermore, Japan's demand that the status of its citizens abducted by North Korea be fully resolved has also caused strains within the alliance, since the Bush administration treated such concerns as secondary to the goal of achieving North Korean denuclearization.

Considering the failure thus far to end Pyongyang's nuclear programs, US unwillingness to pressure North Korea on the abductees issue has resulted in subdued, yet real, resentment on the part of some Japanese officials. That said, Japanese support for the US-led Proliferation Security Initiative (to stop the export of illicit materials) and United Nations sanctions against North Korea have allowed the allies to work together to control the maritime domain in Northeast Asia.

Japan and the United States share the same strategic conundrum regarding China: how can each country maintain and develop economic relations with China while attempting to hedge against its growing military capabilities? Because of China's growing capability, the US Navy and the Japanese Maritime SDF are increasingly focused on threats to the Asian commons, especially the East and South China Seas. They are particularly concerned about the power of China's Navy, which now has over 60 submarines and increasing numbers of destroyers, patrol ships, Coast Guard–equivalent vessels, and the like. With China stating its plans to build several aircraft carriers, alliance military planners are questioning why Beijing is developing power-projection capabilities that could be used to deny access to US naval ships and to control strategic waterways. Similarly, the growth of the Chinese Air Force's fighter squadrons, including advanced 4.5-generation fighter planes, indicates that the United States, along with alliance partners like Japan, may not have air superiority in the case of a conflict with China (such as over the Taiwan Strait) in the future. This, combined with the expansion of China's strategic rocket forces, complicates the alliance's plans for ensuring peace and stability in Northeast Asia. Exacerbating such strategic changes is the Obama administration's decision to halt America's F-22 Raptor fleet at 187 planes and to disallow the export of variants of the Raptor, leaving Japanese planners uncertain about whether the United States will continue to maintain a credible regional force to protect Japan.

These security-related issues raise important political questions for the future of the alliance. Neither Washington nor Tokyo wants to see trade and political relations with China deteriorate, but both naturally question why Beijing continues to build such powerful military capabilities. When Japanese and US leaders inserted a clause on their interest in peaceful resolution of territorial issues in the Taiwan Strait in their 2005 Security Consultative Committee joint statement, Beijing's negative reaction led them to remove the words in subsequent official statements. Given the alliance's stated commitment to respond to "situations in areas surrounding Japan," however, concerns over Beijing's unwillingness to work more closely with regional powers on security issues have brought up the question of how the alliance can work together to shape Chinese behavior in positive ways for regional stability.

It appears the grander aspirations of the early Bush-Koizumi years to create a "global US-Japan alliance" have now been scaled back. As evidence of this, observers point to the Hatoyama administration's decision to end the Japanese Maritime SDF's eight-year Indian Ocean refueling effort in support of Operation Enduring Freedom in Afghanistan. It is perhaps more correct, however, to recognize that today each partner in the alliance has global interests that allow for opportunities of cooperation for the United States and Japan to mutually protect the other's interests. Tokyo's decision in 2009 to contribute nearly $5 billion toward reconstruction in Afghanistan is a symbol of the DPJ's attempts to play a leading role in nontraditional security operations. Similarly, the recent Japanese Maritime SDF mission off the coast of Somalia to conduct antipiracy operations is a good example of Japan rethinking its global security role. Tokyo determined that such a commitment was in Japan's national interests and dispatched two destroyers and two P-3 airborne surveillance planes to protect Japanese shipping. These ships are interacting with the US-led international Combined Task Force 151, providing information and maintaining open sea lanes. While this is not an alliance operation, Japan's SDF working in conjunction with US naval vessels indicates how political priorities the alliance partners share can be expressed in ad hoc activities in and outside of the Asia-Pacific region. Moreover, Japan recently built its first overseas base since World War II, at Djibouti, which has been viewed as a testimony to Tokyo's commitment to protect its interests while providing public good from which its partners may benefit. These initiatives by Japan may portend a relationship in which Washington cannot take Tokyo's support or participation for granted, even as both approach shared security concerns from a national perspective. Instead, both sides will have to decide the best means of interaction after each has chosen a particular policy, even over concerns that are shared.

Still, the various challenges the alliance faces in Asia should occupy the attention of strategists and operations planners and should lead to continued close cooperation and a well-articulated set of shared strategic objectives. The ballistic-missile threat from North Korea and the steady growth of Chinese missile, maritime, and air forces will only increase in coming decades. These jeopardize regional stability and can be used to target not just population centers, but also Japanese and US military forces that could be used to deter or defeat such threats. Thus, continued cooperation on ballistic-missile defense should be of the utmost priority to the alliance. Indeed, missile and air defense, along with antisubmarine warfare, should be expanded to encompass other friendly countries, such as South Korea and Australia, thereby building off current maritime-cooperation activities. Similarly, Tokyo's decision to purchase the fifth-generation F-35 will achieve the twin goals making the Air SDF more credible in dealing with both China and North Korea, while allowing Japan to join a possible airpower coalition of Asian nations flying the same planes, including South Korea, Australia, and Singapore. Working in concert, Tokyo will be able to become part of a larger community of nations committed to upholding Asian stability.

Ultimately, however, the credibility of the alliance will rest on the combination of military capability and a willingness to maintain stability in Asia utilizing the capacities that each partner possesses. In this regard, then, the Obama administration's moves to cut advanced weapons systems such as the F-22 and to scale back missile-defense plans naturally raise questions about long-term US military capabilities in the Pacific. Will the Obama administration maintain US force levels in Asia at their current strength? Most importantly, will the Noda administration reach the defense goals expressed in the NDPG?

This leads one back to consideration of the US-Japan relationship more broadly, not just the alliance. Though the alliance has undergone general positive development, the broader political and economic relationship has been far more ambiguous. Just one metric of success is tied to the question of the DPJ maturing or growing into its role as a ruling party. Its success is connected to the survival of the party after two failed premiers in a row. This naturally makes the political relationship between Tokyo and Washington more ambiguous, even as further uncertainty is introduced by Washington reassessing its policy and position in Asia. The ongoing debate in Washington over what US relations with China will be, what should they be, and what America is willing to do to bring them to that level affects Japan and other partners. Thus, the waiting period discussed above mandates that both sides pause to see how domestic politics play out in both countries before they can talk about moving into the next era of the alliance. Then, the discussions will have to center on the question of what that actually means in terms of the particular policies, the deployment position of US forces, and the type of common interests we pursue with Japan.

In this regard, the alliance must continue to rest on a basis of traditional "hard power." Clearly, the two allies should continue to research, develop, and deploy missile-defense systems on land and sea. Moreover, they must keep up their conventional forces, including advanced fighter aircraft, submarines, surface vessels, and intelligence and surveillance systems. These efforts are, and will continue to be, expensive, especially in a time of reduced budgets. However, the goal of preserving peace requires a formidable military deterrent to any country that may be considering the employment of force to obtain its objectives or to attain asymmetric advantages that can negate US and Japanese military superiority.

No matter how vigilant and capable the two countries remain, however, peace in the Asia-Pacific region cannot be upheld solely by the United States and Japan. A successful system of regional security cooperation requires the efforts of many states. Indeed, one way to maintain the alliance's importance in coming years is to create regional trilateral or quadrilateral mechanisms with the US-Japan alliance at the core. Two natural groupings would be Japan-US-South Korea and Japan-US-Australia. These countries already have limited ongoing trilateral discussions and policies, but expanding these in the areas of basic security cooperation, joint exercises, information sharing, and disaster relief, for example, can help build a community of shared interests among liberal allies in the Asia-Pacific region.

Embarking on such an approach will also help the alliance collaborate to engage China. Japan and the United States have common economic and political interests with China, and coordinating outreach could help set clear benchmarks for progress on many issues, including climate change, confidence building, and trade promotion. It does not make sense for Tokyo and Washington to always deal with Beijing independently given these common interests, although each country will follow its own policies and national goals when talking with China. Given the concerns both the United States and Japan have about China's military buildup, or the effects of Chinese industry on pollution, joint efforts to begin dialogues with China or the presentation of a shared position could be extremely useful.

It is in this trilateral US-Japan-China relationship that the economic aspect of Tokyo-Washington ties may be most important. While Japan has agreed to join negotiations over the nascent Trans-Pacific Partnership, the fact that both it and the United States are so dependent on China for trade and economic growth implies that further market liberalization and domestic reform can and should be pursued within a framework of expanding political-economic relations with China. Japan remains an economic powerhouse, with a highly skilled workforce and excellent research facilities, along with a robust industrial base. Yet it is at risk of falling behind South Korea and China if it does not invest in modernization of its industries, add more infrastructure, and increase scientific exchange with global partners.

An alliance focus on developing next-generation technology, smart grids, energy generation, and the like could bring the United States and Japan closer together. Yet it also provides a platform for embracing free trade in goods and services with China and South Korea, along with

Vietnam and India. Certainly Japan's universities remain magnets for students from Asia, and promoting joint research and more open trade both regionally and with the United States will help Japan's economy grow in the coming decades of a shrinking population and aging workforce. That, in turn, will strengthen perceptions of the leadership of the US-Japan alliance in Asia, as well as provide deeper grounds for alliance cooperation over the next generation.

Conclusion

The alliance has served as the cornerstone of Japanese defense and East Asian stability for 50 years. It has done so because of the willingness of both Japan and the United States to bear heavy burdens. Without Japanese support and bases, there would be no credible US military presence in Asia. Without the alliance, there is no assurance that the peace among the major powers in the past 50 years would have continued, or that regional powers would have been able to develop their economies to the degree that they have. For these reasons, the alliance should continue and maintain its core focus on defending Japan and maintaining stability in East Asia.

That said, the alliance has always required delicate political management by Tokyo and Washington. The two countries have often disagreed on issues of host nation support, SOFA, base location, and joint training. This is natural, and the efforts of thousands of bureaucrats over the past five decades have resulted in the continuation of a positive working relationship. Perhaps the most worrisome trend today is the slow erosion of trust between alliance managers on both sides of the Pacific and a growing sense of frustration with each other. Today, as East Asia changes dramatically—with the rise of China, the continuation of economic integration, and the potential spread of weapons of mass destruction—the Obama and Noda administrations must decide if they view the alliance as a key element in their security strategies or as an outdated relic of a bygone era.

There are great benefits to be had throughout Asia from closer economic integration, but greater dangers if old territorial or historical disputes are not resolved peacefully. If Asia is to continue to be the engine of global economic growth, then Japan's role as the leading liberal democratic nation with a civil society based on individual freedom and the rule of law is indispensable. In playing both a regional and global role, it is natural for Japan to work with the United States to promote the values and policies that have most benefited both countries. The same holds true for the United States, which will continue to be the underwriter of global and regional security for the foreseeable future. The costs and difficulties of maintaining the alliance are far outweighed by the benefits the alliance continues to bring to Japan, the United States, and Asia as a whole.

CHAPTER 10

AN ECONOMIC STEP TOWARD REVITALIZING JAPAN AND US-JAPAN TIES

T.J. Pempel

●

T.J. Pempel is the Jack M. Forcey Professor of Political Science at the University of California, Berkeley. He served as the Director of the Institute of East Asian Studies from 2002 until 2006. His research focuses on comparative politics, Japanese political economy, and Asian regional issues. His most recent publications include, *Security Cooperation in Northeast Asia* (New York: Routledge, 2012, Co-editor with Lee Chung Min) and "Soft Balancing, Hedging, and institutional Darwinism: The Economic-Security Nexus and East Asian Regionalism" (*Journal of East Asian Studies*, 2010). He received his Ph.D., M.A., and B.S. from Columbia University.

From today's vantage point, it is difficult to recall that only 20 short years ago Japan's economy was the envy of the world. Its gross national product (GNP) was soaring, its banks were among the richest in the world, Ginza coffee shops catered to Japan's nouveau riche with expensive cakes flaked with real gold, and a triumphalist business executive could declare that all Japan might need to buy from the United States were mop handles and buckets. From that self-congratulatory perch, Japan has fallen far. Once an economic wonder to be emulated, it is now an economic nightmare to be avoided.

Throughout most of the 1990s, Japan's gross domestic product (GDP) staggered along at an anemic zero to one percent. The country has seen dramatic falls in its global ranking in per capita GDP, along with its labor and capital productivity, while it has been cursed by huge and rising levels of public-sector debt, sustained deflation, rising youth unemployment, and visible homelessness in its major cities. The country that once led the world in the introduction of tantalizing consumer products now struggles to shed the label "Galapagos Tech"—an evolutionary wonder producing goods only for its isolated residents who are divorced from globalization. The global economic depression that began with the Lehman shock of 2008 sucked Japan along with most other countries into an even deeper economic eddy. Stock market indicators in 2012 were at half the level they enjoyed 12 years before and only one-quarter the level they had been at the end of the 1980s.

Equally, Japan's diplomatic relations with the United States are nowhere near as glowingly interdependent as they were in the period before the end of the Cold War. Political leaders from both capitals continue to invoke the centrality of the US-Japan security relationship, but whether one looks at the growing diplomatic and economic ties between the United States and a "rising China," the travel schedules of US officials, sour personal relations between most US and Japanese heads of state, the inability of the two countries to resolve differences over the relocation of Futenma, and the Japanese decision to pull back from the Indian Ocean ships that had supported US actions in Afghanistan, it is hard not to conclude that the bilateral relationship has surrendered a good deal of its prior centrality and mutual accommodation. Indeed, one recent report by several top US policymakers is replete with worrisome assessments that the relationship is a "rhetorical façade" and a "brittle partnership," replete with "major structural flaws," whose "foundation is weak and growing weaker."[1] Their report is congruent with a new US mood that Madsen and Samuels characterize as "strategic disappointment."[2]

There is no shortage of political and economic analysts anxious to highlight factors contributing to Japan's economic sluggishness. And the bilateral relationship is subject to, if anything, even more minute dissections of every twist and turn. This paper does not strive to engage all of the competing views that have been put forward, nor does it suggest a comprehensive miracle solution or the proverbial "silver bullet" that will revitalize Japan's economy while simultaneously reinvigorating US-Japan relations. It does, however, suggest one course of action readily available to Japan that could give a substantial upward jolt to both. I contend that Japan's economy and US-Japan relations would be substantially improved if Japan were to embrace negotiations for the Trans-Pacific Partnership (TPP) with enthusiasm.

This suggestion is made in response to four basic trends. First, East Asia, and particularly Northeast Asia, is becoming increasingly interdependent economically but in ways that have been marked by a decreased centrality for Japan, previously the centerpiece of the region's economic dynamism. Second, Japan has been sclerotic in the liberalization of its domestic economy and in joining the burgeoning wave of bilateral and multilateral free trade agreements. Third, and in part as a consequence of closer economic ties across East Asia, US markets have become less important to East Asian exporters, including Japan. Fourth, the United States and the Obama administration have recommitted the United States to multilateralism and geoeconomics as key components of America's Asia-Pacific policies, and, if Japan wishes to be part of this

---

1 Michael Finnegan, "Managing Unmet Expectations in the US-Japan Alliance," *National Bureau of Asian Research*, NBR Special Report #17 (Seattle: National Bureau of Asian Research, November 2009), http://www.nbr.org/publications/specialreport/pdf/preview/SR17_preview.pdf#xml=http://search.nbr.org/_VTI_BIN/texis.exe/webinator/search/pdfhi.txt?query=finnegan&pr=NBR&prox=page&rorder=500&rprox=500&rdfreq=500&rwfreq=500&rlead=500&rdepth=0&sufs=0&order=r&cq=&id=4ef1935417.

2 Robert Madsen and Richard J. Samuels, "Japan, LLP," *National Interest*, May/June 2010, http://nationalinterest.org/article/japan-llp-3444.

shift, it must enhance more than simply the military and defense link-ages between the two countries.

Japan has not surfed these trending waves very well. Or more ac-curately, Japan has not dealt with them in ways that have fully enhanced the economic and security benefits they offer. And as I will argue, that failure is rooted in the inability or unwillingness of Japanese politicians to break the death grip held by powerful domestic veto groups that have continually and effectively resisted political initiatives to address these trends with new policies that would negatively affect their vested interests. The Japanese political system, which has impeded efforts to adjust to the country's long-term economic slide, would benefit from a bold shock sufficiently powerful to break the stifling lock these groups now hold. Only after their resistance has been effectively defeated will Japanese politics be able to embrace economic policies that will address Japan's long-term loss of competitiveness and help restore long-term dy-namism to the country. The TPP represents one such potential jolt.

East Asian Economic Interdependence
In the last two decades, East Asia has become increasingly connected economically as a consequence of expanding cross-border trade and in-vestment, the result of which has been an explosion of regionally based multinational production facilities. In the 1970s and 1980s, Japan, rid-ing high on its combination of high educational levels, scientific and technological prowess, and sophisticated industrial facilities, was the principal engine driving enhanced East Asian economic interdepen-dence. Japanese corporations driven by economic self-interest were aided by government policies that spurred trade and foreign direct investment (FDI) across East Asia, catapulting Japan forward as the region's and the globe's most powerful economic engine. In the process, Japan jumped from producing seven percent of global GDP in 1970 to 10 percent in 1980, and then surging to nearly 18 percent at the country's peak in the early 1990s.

Asian imitators followed quickly as firms and governments, ini-tially in Taiwan, South Korea, Hong Kong, Singapore, and later across Southeast Asia and China, emulated Japan's focus on economic development rather than military prowess, including the country's explicit model of export-led growth. Cross-border investment, trade, and production soared, obfuscating the region's previously rigidly defended national borders. In particular, once China broke with Maoism and embraced its version of socialist-capitalism, it underwent 20-plus years of double-digit economic growth that, among other things, opened up extensive trade and investment opportunities for firms from Japan, South Korea, Hong Kong, and Taiwan. More recently China itself has become an important source of outgoing FDI.[3] The result was a dramatic ramping up of the global economic weight of East Asia. Between 1970 and 2009, Asia's collective share of world GDP rose from roughly 15 percent to 27 percent.

Figure 1 shows the growth in intra-East Asian regional integration through trade and investment. With particular gusto since the mid-1990s, intra-East Asian investment has taken a startlingly sharp spike upward. Today over 60 percent of investment by Asian investors remains within the region. Furthermore, by 2011, intra-East Asian trade had risen to 56 percent of its total trade, a figure close to that of the European Union. Such intra-regional trade links have been especially vigorous among Japan, China, and the ROK (Figure 2).

Yet as East Asia's regional borders became less restrictive as barriers to regional economic activity, and as the region has prospered collectively in response, Japan, the initial catalyst for the region's economic success, has become ever less the driver or the beneficiary of East Asia's enhanced regional economic strength. Much of this is the result of Japan's diminished economic weight. Between the early 1990s and today, Japan's share of global GDP shriveled to eight percent, a share almost equal to that which it had held in 1970. In the last 20 years, Japan has managed to erase virtually all of the gains in global economic weight

---

3 Asian Development Bank, "Emerging Asian Regionalism: A Partnership for Shared Prosperity" (Manila: Asian Development Bank, 2008); Ellen L. Frost, *Asia's New Regionalism* (London: Lynne Rienner, 2008); T.J. Pempel, "How Bush Bungled Asia: How Unilateralism, Militarism, and Economic Abdication Have Weakened the US across Asia," *Pacific Review* 25, no. 5 (2008): 547–600; Kishore Mahbubani, *The New Asian Hemisphere: The Irresistible Shift of Global Power to the East* (New York: Public Affairs, 2008); William H. Overholt, *Asia, America, and the Transformation of Geopolitics* (Cambridge: Cambridge University Press, 2008); World Bank, *The East Asian Miracle: Economic Growth and Public Policy* (Oxford: Oxford University Press, 1993).

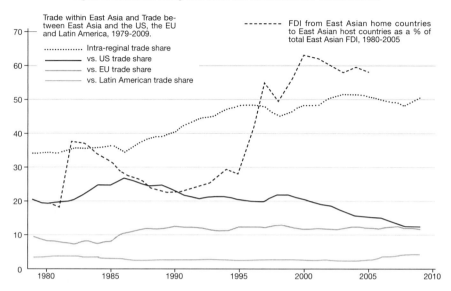

Figure 1: East Asia's Rising Star: Trade and Investment over Three Decades

Source: Avery Goldstein and Edward D. Mansfield, "Peace and Prosperity in East Asia: When Fighting Ends," Global Asia 6, no. 2 (Summer 2011): 11.

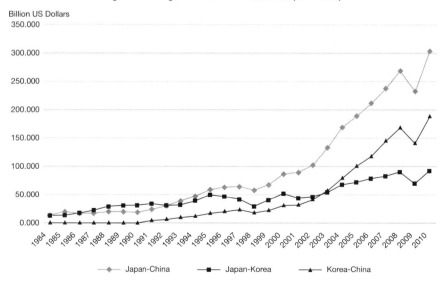

Figure 2: Intraregional Trade in Northeast Asia (1984–2010)

that it had gained between 1970 and 1990. Meanwhile, in the last 30 years, the rate of Chinese economic growth has been averaging eight percent growth in GDP per annum. The economy has increased more than tenfold during that period. In the process, China's share of world GDP rose from five percent in 2005 to 9.5 percent in 2010 and, of symbolic significance, in 2011 China replaced Japan as the world's second largest economy in nominal GDP. The result has been that China has been eclipsing Japan as the economic engine of the region. Even countries skeptical of China's long-term political goals are finding it in their self-interest to accommodate China's enhanced economic and diplomatic muscle. Such accommodation has of course also been made by the United States, as American consumers have scrambled to purchase Chinese exports and as the US Treasury Department has become in thrall to Chinese purchases of US debt instruments.

The limits of Japan's role in East Asia were most dramatically driven home by the sharply negative dismissal by the United States, the International Monetary Fund (IMF), and China of Japan's bold proposal at the G-7 IMF meetings in Hong Kong in the fall of 1997 to create an Asian Monetary Fund (AMF). Japanese officials, despite the country's own economic woes, put forward a scheme for the AMF as a 10-country fund of Asian economies (that did not include the United States) to be capitalized at $100 billion (roughly one-half to come from Japan) and that would not be constrained by strict adherence to IMF conditionality in offering aid to troubled financial systems in Asia. The United States and the IMF were livid in their opposition, and China quickly joined them to oppose any efforts at such demonstrations of "Japanese hegemony" within the region. Despite the fact that Japanese assistance eventually played a significant part in subsequently easing the worst effects of the crisis through financial help, and even though it was instrumental in the creation of the Chiang Mai Initiative, which many see as a reincarnation of the original AMF, the message was unmistakable: neither the United States nor China were prepared to accede to Japan's regional financial leadership and Japan could not by itself grab that leadership

Figure 3: Overtaking the Leader: GDP Per Person at Purchasing-Power Parity (2011 prices, $'000)

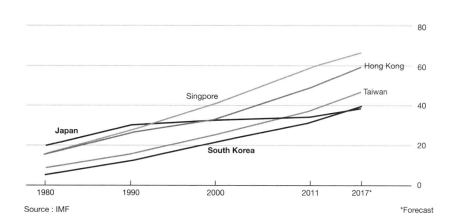

Source : IMF

*Forecast

Source: "Asian Economic Rankings: A Game of Leapfrog: South Korea May Soon Be Richer than Japan," The Economist, April 28, 2012, http://www.economist.com/node/21553498.

role.[4]

Another indication of Japan's diminished role in East Asia's regional economic integration has been the reduced centrality of Japanese capital to investment across East Asia. Japan was the largest investor by far during the 1980s (nearly a five-to-one margin over the number-two investor, the United States). During the 1990s, Japan retained the number-one position but its lead was then only 1.5 times that of the United States. And by the 2000s, Japan had fallen to the number-two slot.

Not only has China, as noted, become a center of regional production for all of East Asia and the driver of regional economic development, but also other countries have closed their once-wide economic gaps with Japan on living standards and wealth. Japan, long the economic leader in the region, has fallen behind the pack.[5] As one recent comparison of per capita GDP noted, "For years, Japan was Asia's richest and most powerful economy. It was the first Asian economy to industrialize, and the

4 T.J. Pempel, *Remapping East Asia: The Construction of a Region* (Ithaca: Cornell University Press, 2005).

5 Andrew MacIntyre and Barry Naughton, "The Decline of a Japanese-Led Model of the East Asian Economy," in *Remapping East Asia: The Construction of a Region*, ed. T.J. Pempel (Ithaca: Cornell University Press, 2005), 77–100.

emerging Asian tigers—Hong Kong, Singapore, South Korea, Taiwan and later China—merely followed in its tracks. Now, however, Japan is steadily being overtaken."[6] Data show Japanese citizens now lagging behind their richer counterparts in Singapore, Hong Kong, and Taiwan, with South Korea poised to pass Japan within five years (see Figure 3).

Complicating Japan's eroding economic centrality in East Asia is the fact that the country continues to be handicapped diplomatically by serious mistrust toward Japan within a number of other Asian countries, most notably Korea and China. Discordant historical memories, unresolved territorial issues, and concerns about real or imagined increases in Japanese nationalism feed such anxieties.

Japan's Tepid Approach to Free Trade Agreements

Japan's diminished role across the region can be traced in part to its lethargy in liberalizing its domestic market and in joining the stampede of East Asian countries to expand their trade liberalizations with one another.

As World Trade Organization (WTO) negotiations in the Doha Round have slumped, numerous East Asian countries have moved aggressively in the last decade-plus to forge a host of bilateral and minilateral free trade agreements (FTAs). Many of these are intra-Asian; others extend to embrace trade partners from around the globe. There were multiple motivations for the rapid increase in FTAs by East Asian states. As Aggarwal argues, East Asian free traders had become frustrated by the combination of slow progress in WTO meetings in Seattle and Cancun, a possible reduction in access to US markets, and the desire to develop enhanced regional trade outlets that might reduce their dependence on the US market.[7] For others, FTAs represented defensive or catch-up actions against what were perceived to be anti-Asian trade barriers erected by NAFTA and the European Union. Still further impetus arose as domestic free traders utilized FTA agreements as a crowbar with which to

---

6 "Asian Economic Rankings: A Game of Leapfrog: South Korea May Soon Be Richer than Japan," *The Economist*, April 28, 2012, http://www.economist.com/node/21553498.

7 Vinod K. Aggarwal, "Bilateral Trade Agreements in the Asia-Pacific," in *Bilateral Trade Agreements in the Asia-Pacific*, ed. Vinod K. Aggarwal and Shujiro Urata (London: Routledge, 2006), 12.

wrench open hitherto closed segments of their own domestic markets.

At the front of the pack has been South Korea, which, despite often powerful domestic opposition, has signed agreements with over a dozen countries, including two of its major industrialized trade partners, the United States and the European Union. These trade arrangements and the scheduled elimination of tariffs on Korean auto exports have already begun to allow Korean auto makers to increase production within Korea while simultaneously ramping up production at facilities in overseas operations from China to Brazil. China has also been forceful in opening its domestic markets to foreign direct investment, and to exports from Southeast Asia and Taiwan among others. Though Japan certainly has its share of domestic forces favoring FTAs, the country has been far slower and less inclusive in embracing such market-liberalizing moves.

Perhaps the sharpest contrast in the use of FTAs can be found in the different actions by China and Japan in the 2000 ASEAN Summit in Hanoi. Much to everyone's surprise, China offered to forge a China-ASEAN FTA. This proposal helped convince ASEAN members that the rise of China could potentially generate win-win economic cooperation in a market of some 1.7 billion people. Quite significantly, Chinese negotiators offered an "early harvest" of lower tariffs for agricultural goods from Southeast Asia coming into China. Because agricultural exports are so critical to the growth strategies of most countries in Southeast Asia, particularly to its newest members, the Chinese move proved particularly deft politically. In addition, it also underscored the extent to which democracies such as Japan and the United States, although much richer, were constrained from making similarly generous gestures due to the power of their domestic farm lobbies. As a case in point, Japan's Prime Minister Koizumi was caught somewhat flat-footed by the Chinese surprise and could only respond by proposing a joint discussion of a comprehensive economic partnership that did not come into play until 2007, and excluded any serious liberalization of the Japanese agricultural markets.

Japan currently has 10 FTAs (or Economic Partnership Agreements—EPAs—as Japan prefers to call them) in place, but of these one is with ASEAN as a whole and six additional bilateral arrangements are with ASEAN member states. Meanwhile, none of Japan's agreements are with any of the country's top five trade partners. Moreover, Japan cancelled negotiations that had been ongoing for an FTA with South Korea and has been loath to pursue the trilateral trade liberalization to which it was committed as a target of its Trilateral Agreement with the ROK and China. As John Ravenhill documents, only 14 percent of Japan's exports are covered by existing FTAs (or EPAs), compared to 56 percent for ASEAN, 45 percent for Hong Kong, 25 percent for China, and 28 percent for South Korea.[8]

A parallel reluctance was seen in 1998 when Japan unilaterally bucked the more multilateral Asia-Pacific Economic Cooperation (APEC) agreement, to move forward Early Voluntary Sector Liberalization (EVSL), a process by which it had initially agreed to abide.[9]

Diminished Centrality of the US Market for Japan

One of the most striking trends in Asia-Pacific and intra-East Asian trade has been the substantial decline in both East Asia's and Japan's trade dependency on the United States, as East Asian economies have become more dependent on one another. This is clear from Figure 1 as well as Figures 4 and 5. Figure 1 shows the drop in overall East Asian dependence on the US market. Figure 4 shows the specific declines in the salience of the US market for Northeast Asian exports, while Figure 5 shows the bilateral figures for Japanese trade with its Northeast Asian partners along with those involving the United States.

Japan's postwar foreign policy pivoted on close ties to the United States, both militarily and economically. Japanese defense expenditures were kept low in exchange for US security guarantees and US bases on Japanese territory. Moreover, to spur the economic recovery of its most important Cold War ally in East Asia after World War II, the United

---

8 John Ravenhill, "Extending the TPP: The Political Economy of Multilateralization in Asia" (paper presented at the Asia Pacific Trade Economists' Conference, ARTNeT, United Nations Economic and Social Commission for Asia and the Pacific, Bangkok, Thailand, November 2–3, 2009), http://www.unescap.org/tid/artnet/mtg/2-3John%20Ravenhill.pdf.

9 Ellis S. Krauss, "The United States and Japan in APEC's EVSL Negotiations: Regional Multilateralism and Trade," in *Beyond Bilateralism: U.S.-Japan Relations in the New Asia-Pacific*, ed. Ellis S. Krauss and T.J. Pempel (Stanford: Stanford University Press, 2004), 77–100.

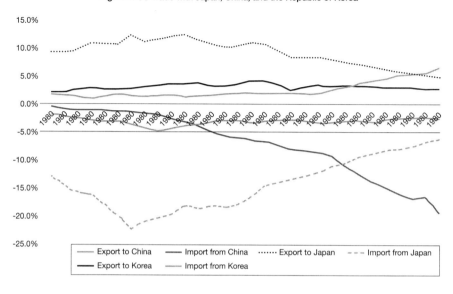

Figure 4: US Trade with Japan, China, and the Republic of Korea

Figure 5: Japanese Trade Levels 1988–2009

% of Total Trade

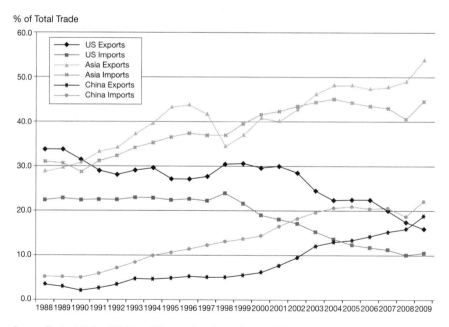

Source: Trade statistics, Ministry of Finance, http://www.jetro.go.jp/en/reports/statistics.

States opened its markets to Japanese exports without demanding recip-rocal access for American goods in Japan. The two consequently became major trading partners with one another. As late as the latter half of the 1980s, approximately 11 percent of all US exports went to Japan while 20 percent of US total imports came from Japan. For Japan, some 36 to 39 percent of its exports went to US markets while 23 percent of its total imports came from the United States. By 2010, Japan was taking only 4.8 percent of total US exports and accounted for only 4.1 per-cent of America's total exports, while the United States was taking only 16 percent of Japan's exports and only 11 percent of American imports came from Japan.

Although imports from China to Japan have skyrocketed, Japan is losing importance as a destination for imports from the rest of East Asia (Figure 5). Thus as Japan becomes less economically central to most of East Asia, and its economic dependence on the United States continues to diminish, its reliance on the Chinese market is soaring. A particularly dramatic way to appreciate that basic point is to realize that between 2000 and 2007 Japan's trade with China rose 70 percent while that with the United States dropped 36 percent.

Yet while the data show how much less significant the US-Japan trade connection has become over the last 15 years, and despite the di-minished economic centrality of the United States to Japan's economy, Japanese foreign policy has remained unshakably anchored by its close bilateral links to the United States.

America's Re-engagement with East Asia, Multilateralism, and Geoeconomics

The George W. Bush administration broke with decades of US foreign policy with its military unilateralism and its embrace of the doctrine of "preventive wars" in the Middle East and Central Asia. In an address to a joint session of Congress on September 20, 2001, President George W. Bush said, "[e]ither you are with us, or you are with the terrorists." Faced with such a dichotomous choice, but also embracing the advice of many in the Japanese Ministry of Foreign Affairs and the defense es-tablishment, Prime Minister Koizumi was quick to commit Japan to an embrace of the Bush approach in the wake of 9/11. Koizumi ended 50-plus years of Japanese security politics to send ships to the Indian Ocean in support of the war in Afghanistan and a contingent of Self-Defense Forces troops to Iraq. The Defense Agency was upgraded to a ministry, the two countries collaborated on missile defense, Japan's space program was militarized, an American nuclear carrier was based in Japan, and Japan broadened its security arena to include Taiwan at least implicitly. Japan's Coast Guard saw its budget and its mission enhanced, and Japan became the headquarters of the US Army's I Corps, thus weaving Japan more fully into US global military strategy. In the process, both North Korea and China were explicitly identified as potential threats to Japan.[10]

Satisfying as such moves were to many in both the US and Japanese military establishments, they marked a clear departure from the traditional economic role Japan had long played in Asia while simultaneously giving voice to those in the region who saw the moves as part of a rising tide of xenophobia marked by Japan's tortured self-absolution of the country's role in World War II, and to disquieting voices from Japan's always noisy nationalist and chauvinistic right.

The Obama administration moved swiftly to reverse a number of the shortcomings of the George W. Bush administration. Multilateralism, East Asia, and geoeconomics all regained the status they had lost in the tool box of American diplomatic policy during the previous administration. Within East Asia, the administration made numerous moves to create a fresh climate, to reestablish American credibility as more than just an "offshore balancer," and to demonstrate engagement with the more complex multilateral and multidimensional aspects of East Asian regional interactions. As Secretary of State Clinton put it in a 2011 article entitled "America's Pacific Century," "[t]he Asia-Pacific has become a key driver of global politics" and the United States needed to remain fully engaged with that dynamic region. Clinton articulated six key lines of action: strengthening bilateral alliances; deepening America's working

---

10 T.J. Pempel, "Japanese Strategy Under Koizumi," in *Japanese Strategy Toward Asia*, ed. Gilbert Rozman, Kazuhiko Togo, and Joseph P. Ferguson (New York: Palgrave, 2007); Pempel, "How Bush Bungled Asia: How Unilateralism, Militarism, and Economic Abdication Have Weakened the US across Asia," 547–600.

relations with emerging powers, including China; engaging with regional multilateral institutions; expanding trade and investment; forging a broad-based military presence; and advancing democracy and human rights.[11] Clinton's general message was underscored as Obama himself announced a so-called "pivot" toward Asia, which in fact represented less of a "pivot" and more of a return to a prioritization of Asia over the Middle East and South Asia.

The Obama administration has engaged more deeply with East Asian regionalism, marked by numerous top-level visits by American officials, the signing of the Treaty of Amity and Cooperation, the appointment of an American ambassador to ASEAN, and the US decision to join the East Asian Summit (EAS), capped by the attendance of President Obama at the November 2011 EAS meeting in Bali, Indonesia. The Obama administration also sought to resuscitate APEC in its November 2011 meeting in Honolulu. Such American efforts have been layered into already well-established institutional arrangements created and most heavily influenced by Asians themselves. The United States, in effect, is something of a latecomer to East Asian regional institutions, such as the EAS, and its credibility in other bodies, such as APEC, which had been allowed to languish, clearly has to be refurbished.

The areas where the United States has devoted its greatest regional multilateral efforts have been in trade, economics, and finance. Revitalization of APEC and its economic focus, the "insourcing" of manufacturing jobs to America, and renewed attention to trade balances and exchange rates have all been part of a renewed effort to rejuvenate America's economic strengths and to mobilize economics as a tool of its overall diplomacy. Anxious to reverse some of America's dwindling success in exports, as well as to offset the declining number of jobs for American workers, Obama has set a goal of doubling US exports to $3.14 trillion a year by the end of 2014. During the 2011 APEC meeting, Obama explicitly identified Asian economic ties as the key to that goal. In addition, his administration has advanced bilateral FTAs with the passage in October 2011 of the Korea-US Free Trade Agreement (KORUS), along

---

11 Hillary Clinton, "America's Pacific Century," *Foreign Policy*, November 2011, http://www.foreignpolicy. com/articles/2011/10/11/americas_pacific_century.

with bilateral FTAs with Columbia and Panama.

Critical to the combination of a "pivot" toward Asia and an enhanced focus on economics as a tool of US diplomacy, the Obama administration has taken a strong position in favor of joining and expanding the TPP. The TPP was originally a relatively minor agreement reached in 2005, brought into effect on May 26, 2006, among four relatively small economies: Brunei, Chile, New Zealand, and Singapore (the P4). The four countries that forged the original pact were joined between 2008 and 2010 by five others: Australia, Malaysia, Peru, Vietnam, and the United States. Early in 2008, the United States indicated that it would like to negotiate with the TPP on financial issues, but negotiations were not scheduled to begin until after the Obama administration took office in early 2009. But the new administration demonstrated that it was anxious to embrace the TPP, and in his first trip to Asia in November 2009, President Obama reaffirmed the US commitment to taking a full stake in the TPP. A month later, on December 14, 2009, US Trade Representative Ron Kirk notified Congress that President Obama planned to enter TPP negotiations "with the objective of shaping a high-standard, broad-based regional pact."[12] Twelve rounds of negotiations have been held as of May 2012 with the goal of forging what the negotiators call a "Twenty-first Century" trade agreement, one that systematizes trade regulation among all members and that is comprehensive in coverage of all trade-related issues, including, for example, rules of origin and labor protections, and encompassing not simply trade but the promotion of economic development and collective growth.[13] The goal is to have the basic language of the agreement hammered out by the APEC summit meeting in September 2012.

The TPP is now quite comprehensive in the goods and services it proposes to cover. Even though the current partners for the TPP represent but a small portion of total US trade (the combined TPP partners would rank number six as America's most valued trade partner), the goal

---

12 United States Office of the Trade Representative, "Trans-Pacific Partnership Announcement," news release, December 14, 2009, http://www.ustr.gov/about-us/press-office/press-releases/2009/december/trans-pacific-partnership-announcement.

13 C. L. Lim, Deborah Kay Elms, and Patrick Low, eds., *The Trans-Pacific Partnership Agreement: A Quest for a Twenty-first Century Trade Agreement* (Cambridge: Cambridge University Press, 2012).

of many participants is to put in place an agreement that can attract additional signatories and become the template for freer trade and investment across the Asia-Pacific. As Barfield and Levy noted, "An agreement with the United States, Japan, Australia, New Zealand, and Chile at its core would have the economic heft to set a new standard for Asian integration."[14] Furthermore, if the TPP remains open to new members, as expected, it could serve as the foundation for a Pacific Ocean-spanning free trade area.

As Fergusson and Vaughn noted, "[e]conomic linkages can also reinforce strategic relationships. If US trade ties were diminished as a result of being excluded, then US strategic interests and leverage could also suffer. Some view the TPP as a useful initiative that, when pursued in combination with other diplomatic initiatives, could do much to improve not only trans-Pacific trade relations but also help positively affect change in the perceptions of Asian states of the US commitment to Asia."[15]

Two decades ago, James Baker, then Secretary of State, warned it would be a strategic mistake for the United States to allow "a line to be drawn down the middle of the Pacific" with the United States on one side and the nations of Asia on the other. It was that worry that spurred US participation in APEC. The TPP and APEC are now linked in the trade and regional strategies of the Obama administration. Certainly, a successfully negotiated TPP and a reinvigorated APEC would once again give considerable momentum to pan-Pacific trade and regional institutions as a partial offset to "Asians only" bodies, such as ASEAN Plus Three and (until recently) the EAS. Clearly, the new American efforts are made in the expectation that the TPP will shape the regional economic architecture in ways that will involve comprehensive standards and in the process add to US economic leverage over developments in East Asia while of course being a plus for regional economic growth and US business interests in the process.

---

14 Claude Barfield and Philip I. Levy, "President Obama, the TPP and Leadership in Asia," *East Asia Forum*, January 26, 2010, http://www.eastasiaforum.org/2010/01/26/president-obama-the-tpp-and-u-s-leadership-in-asia.

15 Ian F. Fergusson and Bruce Vaughn, "The Trans-Pacific Partnership Agreement," Congressional Research Service R40502, June 25, 2010, http://fpc.state.gov/documents/organization/145583.pdf.

Japan's Slow Dance with the TPP

It is with such a background and logic that I believe it is in Japan's long-term self-interest, economically and diplomatically, to enter into negotiations surrounding the TPP. Joining the TPP would allow Japan to resume a position of leadership in East Asian trade arrangements and regional economics. Some of East Asia's most dynamic economies, including China, South Korea, and Indonesia, are not expected to join the TPP in the near future. Japan as a party to the TPP would hold a powerful position in bridging arrangements among these non-TPP economies and their various FTA arrangements with the standards of the TPP in ways that would also benefit Japan's development of new markets and provide it with a regional leadership role in the rising trade volume across the region.

Thus, on November 11, 2011, Prime Minister Noda announced his intention to have Japan join the ongoing TPP negotiations. Since that initial enthusiastic embrace of the TPP, and as of this writing, however, the TPP has moved quickly and it is now on its 12th round of negotiations with the stated goal of announcing a completed agreement at the November 2012 APEC meeting in Vladivostok. And yet Japan has still not moved formally to request inclusion in the negotiations. Six of the nine negotiating countries have indicated an interest in having Japan join the negotiations; the United States, Australia, and New Zealand are continuing to negotiate with Japan over how far it would be willing to go in its domestic policy shifts and in its structural reforms. It is now becoming clear that Japan will probably not be on board before negotiations are complete or nearly complete. For Japan, there would be clear advantages to being an early mover, the major advantage being the influence that an early negotiator has over the rules that are eventually set. Once the terms of the TPP are fixed, it will be up to those anxious to join to do so on a "take it or leave it" basis. Whether Japan will in fact actually participate in negotiations before they are completed appears unlikely at the present. Joining on such terms will pose an even higher hurdle for Japan to clear than having been in since late 2011 or early 2012.

Domestic politics have been the major impediment preventing

the current government from moving forward more rapidly. Essentially, Japanese politicians have been loath to enter into any agreements that would require substantial liberalization of politically powerful—if often economically marginal—sectors of its domestic economy. That means most particularly its highly protected agriculture sector and also many of its cosseted service industries. The Japanese "developmental state" that thrived from roughly the early 1950s until the late 1980s pivoted on a castle-like defense of its domestic market against inside-the-walls competition from foreign investments and imports, as well as protecting many small and medium-sized sectors from competition against larger domestic competitors. Exports abroad plus protection at home worked well as a grand economic strategy for Japan's postwar economic catch-up. And so long as the GNP expanded at rates twice those of the rest of the OECD countries, any inherent economic inefficiencies built into the system for political reasons were easily masked and budgetarily manageable. Alternatively stated, the high growth rates achieved by Japan's most dynamic sectors provided government coffers with an ever-expanding revenue stream, a portion of which could be allocated to sustain economically inefficient sectors at only marginal cost to the overall economy. But with time such sectors gained an ever more secure place at the government trough. Once Japan's economy had "caught up" to the rest of the industrialized world, such neo-mercantile protectionism became ever more economically draining to sustain. What was needed was far more domestic consumption, greater efficiency in the use of capital, and an overall Schumpeterian embrace of "creative destruction" that could catapult Japan's economy to a new plateau. Politics, however, continue to impose formidable barriers to such an economic transformation. The politically entrenched opponents of such a transformation were well positioned to prevent any such shift.

The long-term rule of the Liberal Democratic Party (LDP) rested on a politically critical but economically unwieldy array of powerful interest groups that for much of the last 20 years have had a stranglehold over economic changes that could challenge their privileged positions. Central has been the power of the agriculture and fisheries lobbies, which, under Japan's electoral system, have been able to leverage their relatively small numbers into critical electoral support. For decades, the LDP was the major beneficiary of such votes and hence most in thrall to agricultural protection. And in opposition, the Democratic Party of Japan (DPJ) initially promised a number of changes that suggested that, if allowed to govern, the party would make a dramatic break with patterns of the past, including the protection of vested interests linked to the LDP, as well as proposing that Japan develop stronger diplomatic and economic ties with East Asia, an increasingly important economic sphere for Japan through the creation of an East Asia community.[16]

Yet, ironically, the DPJ gained power in the 2009 election only by successfully appealing to and gaining substantial electoral support from the very same protectionist sectors that had previously been mainstays of the LDP's long rule. Promises designed to make the DPJ even more appealing than the LDP to agriculture were an electoral strategy engineered by Ichiro Ozawa, long an éminence grise in Japanese politics. The end result is that today both the LDP and the DPJ have been competing for the farm vote with equal gusto. Japan has thus been deprived of any political leadership with the socio-economic support needed to break with the protectionism of the past.

When Noda first began considering joining TPP negotiations, he also committed himself to coming up with measures that would revitalize Japanese agriculture and enhance its international competitiveness, much as had been done in South Korea to alleviate farmers' opposition to KOR-US. (The Korean measures had their effect, and 2011 farm exports had doubled over their level four years earlier.) Such an effort at enhancing the global competitiveness of Japanese farms would make sense. The value of the global agricultural market is expected to surpass $2 trillion by 2013.[17] However, the Japanese government, most especially the Ministry of Agriculture, Forestry and Fisheries, has been loath to embrace the possibilities for transforming Japanese agriculture from its almost exclusive focus on the domestic market and encouraging farmers to move toward enhanced global exports of more niche-oriented prod-

---

16 Democratic Party of Japan, "The Democratic Party of Japan's Platform for Government," August 18, 2009, http://www.dpj.or.jp/english/manifesto/manifesto2009.pdf.

17 "Free Trade Would Open Fertile Foreign Markets," *Nikkei Weekly*, April 30, 2012.

ucts. Japan in 2009 was the fifth largest producer of agricultural goods (behind China, the United States, India, and Brazil), but Japan's farm exports in that year were a rather miniscule $3 billion, well below South Korea's, leaving Japan with an agricultural trade deficit of nearly $50 billion.[18]

The combined LDP-DPJ approach to agricultural policy to date has remained the provision of extensive subsidies to the nation's farmers with no insistence on their becoming more internationally competitive for fear of losing a critical voting bloc. As a consequence of the importance of the rural votes to the party, internal DPJ resistance has prevented the announcement of any plans to move the Japanese agricultural sector toward greater global competitiveness, and hence to reduce the resistance to greater liberalization of agriculture within Japan.

Not surprisingly, given the reliance of many DPJ members on rural voter support, a Nikkei poll taken in November 2011 showed that 60 percent of DPJ legislators were opposed to Japan's joining the TPP. Those in favor cited the potential rise in Japan's GDP by a presumed two trillion yen ($26 billion), while opponents stressed the damage the TPP would do to the powerful agricultural bloc.[19]

Noda had originally intended to announce Japan's decision to participate in the TPP during his visit to Washington, DC, at the US-Japan summit on April 30. The announcement was to demonstrate the improved relationship within the specific area of trade and economics. It was to show the return of the two countries' ability to cooperate on issues of economic importance in the Asia-Pacific. The plan was to get approval from participating nations and for Japan to become involved in negotiations early enough to have a say in shaping the rule-making process. In fact, Noda decided to wait, fearful that developments in Japanese domestic politics just before his departure to the United States would serve as a rallying cry for TPP opponents.[20]

Most specifically, Ozawa, a staunch opponent of Japan's participa-

18 "Japan Agricultural Sector Sits on Huge Potential for Global Growth," *Nikkei Weekly*, April 16, 2012.

19 Frances McCall Rosenbluth, "Japan in 2011: Cataclysmic Crisis and Chronic Deflation," *Asian Survey* 52, no. 1 (January/February 2011): 15–27.

20 "Ozawa's Return Could Stymy Noda," *Nikkei Weekly*, April 30, 2012.

tion in the TPP, and a linchpin in the DPJ's ties to agricultural interests, had long been marginalized on the issue of the TPP as the result of a long-running court case in which he was accused of financial violations of Japan's campaign laws. It was during this marginalization that Prime Minister Noda made his announcement that Japan would seek to join the TPP negotiations. However, Ozawa's acquittal in April 2012 emboldened him and his relatively large number of followers to re-exert power within the DPJ, starting with opposition to the TPP, as well as to the consumption tax that Noda has also committed to advancing. Should Ozawa succeed in stalling the consumption tax and the TPP, the probability is of a DPJ split and an early election, one in which the divided DPJ would find it impossible to continue to govern or to continue any movement on the TPP.

Because now both the DPJ and the LDP are competing for farm votes, any negotiations between the two parties to pass the consumption tax are sure to strengthen agricultural voices should any bipartisan deals be cut. That could well mean the shelving of Japan's involvement with the TPP in return for bipartisan passage of the consumption tax. Furthermore, the devastation of Fukushima, a heavily rural segment of the country, continues to make it emotionally difficult to act in ways that could be portrayed as still a fourth blow to the region after the earthquake, tsunami, and nuclear meltdown.

Clearly Japan's relationship with the TPP is now a rapidly unfolding drama. Whether Prime Minister Noda can resuscitate Japan's plans to enter negotiations in a timely manner has become increasingly problematic, particularly with the parliamentary battle over the consumption tax still looming. If Japan fails to join the negotiations and a successful agreement is reached by the current nine negotiating countries, Japan will have lost a major opportunity to use a powerful outside weapon as a wedge with which to open stagnant sectors of the Japanese economy and simultaneously to demonstrate its ability to move in synch with the new US focus on geoeconomics. Joining the TPP after it has been negotiated might still be one way to advance on that front, but it would be far less powerful symbolically than having been in the negotiations from the beginning. But absent participation in the TPP, whether now or a year or two from now, Japan will continue to confront the same fundamental policy difficulty: how to regain some measure of its earlier economic dynamism.

The current political system now impedes that dynamism, and, until something substantial changes in the politics of Japan, Japan will continue to lose influence in the rest of the region to its more globalizing neighbors. It also runs the risk of telegraphing to its American allies that while the country may be valuable as the Pacific's most "unsinkable aircraft carrier," it has marginalized itself on the economic and financial issues that are far more likely to drive developments in Northeast Asia in the next quarter-century. Making these changes will not be easy, and political courage is surely demanded if Japan is to escape from the downward spiral in its economic strength and influence as well as in its bilateral ties to the United States.

References

Aggarwal, Vinod K. "Bilateral Trade Agreements in the Asia-Pacific." In *Bilateral Trade Agreements in the Asia-Pacific*, edited by Vinod K. Aggarwal and Shujiro Urata. London: Routledge, 2006.

Asian Development Bank. "Emerging Asian Regionalism: A Partnership for Shared Prosperity." Manila: Asian Development Bank, 2008.

Barfield, Claude, and Philip I. Levy. "President Obama, the TPP and Leadership in Asia." *East Asia Forum*, January 26, 2010. http://www.eastasiaforum.org/2010/01/26/presidentobama-the-tpp-and-u-s-leadership-in-asia.

Clinton, Hillary. "America's Pacific Century." *Foreign Policy*, November 2011. http://www.foreignpolicy.com/articles/2011/10/11/americas_pacific_century.

Democratic Party of Japan. "The Democratic Party of Japan's Platform for Government." August 18, 2009. http://www.dpj.or.jp/english/manifesto/manifesto2009.pdf.

The Economist. "Asian Economic Rankings: A Game of Leapfrog: South Korea May Soon Be Richer than Japan." April 28, 2012. http://www.economist.com/node/21553498.

Fergusson, Ian F., and Bruce Vaughn. "The Trans-Pacific Partnership Agreement." Congressional Research Service R40502. June 25, 2010. http://fpc.state.gov/documents/organization/145583.pdf.

Finnegan, Michael. "Managing Unmet Expectations in the U.S.-Japan Alliance." *National Bureau of Asian Research*, NBR Special Report #17. Seattle: National Bureau of Asian Research, November 2009. http://www.nbr.org/publications/specialreport/pdf/preview/SR17_preview.pdf#xml=http://search.nbr.org/_VTI_BIN/texis.exe/webinator/search/pdfhi.txt?query=finnegan&pr=NBR&prox=page&rorder=500&rprox=500&rdfreq=500&rwfreq=500&rlead=500&rdepth=0&sufs=0&order=r&cq=&id=4ef1935417.

Frost, Ellen L. *Asia's New Regionalism*. London: Lynne Rienner, 2008.

Goldstein, Avery, and Edward D. Mansfield, "Peace and Prosperity in East Asia: When Fighting Ends." *Global Asia* 6, no. 2 (Summer 2011).

Krauss, Ellis S. "The United States and Japan in APEC's EVSL Negotiations: Regional Multilateralism and Trade." In *Beyond Bilateralism: US-Japan Relations in the New Asia-Pacific*, edited by Ellis S. Krauss and T.J. Pempel. Stanford: Stanford University Press, 2004.

Lim, C. L., Deborah Kay Elms, and Patrick Low, eds. *The Trans-Pacific Partnership Agreement: A Quest for a Twenty-first Century Trade Agreement*. Cambridge: Cambridge University Press, 2012.

MacIntyre, Andrew, and Barry Naughton. "The Decline of a Japanese-Led Model of the East Asian Economy." In *Remapping East Asia*: The Construction of a Region, edited by T.J. Pempel. Ithaca: Cornell University Press, 2005.

MacIntrye, Andrew, T.J. Pempel, and John Ravenhill, eds. "Conclusion." In *East Asia: Coping with the Crisis*. Ithaca: Cornell University Press, 2008.

Madsen, Robert, and Richard J. Samuels. "Japan, LLP." *National Interest*, May/June 2010. http://nationalinterest.org/article/japan-llp-3444.

Mahbubani, Kishore. *The New Asian Hemisphere: The Irresistible Shift of Global Power to the East*. New York: Public Affairs, 2008.

Nikkei Weekly. "Free Trade Would Open Fertile Foreign Markets." April 30, 2012.

———. "Japan Agricultural Sector Sits on Huge Potential for Global Growth." April, 16, 2012.

———. "Ozawa's Return Could Stymy Noda." April 30, 2012: 2.

Overholt, William H. *Asia, America, and the Transformation of Geopolitics*. Cambridge: Cambridge University Press, 2008.

Pempel, T.J. "Between Pork and Productivity: The Collapse of the Liberal Democratic Party." *Journal of Japanese Studies* 36, no. 2 (Summer 2010).

———. "How Bush Bungled Asia: How Unilateralism, Militarism, and Economic Abdication Have Weakened the US across Asia." *Pacific Review* 25, no. 5 (2008).

———. *Remapping East Asia: The Construction of a Region*. Ithaca: Cornell University Press, 2005.

Ravenhill, John. "Extending the TPP: The Political Economy of Multilateralization in Asia." Paper presented at the Asia Pacific Trade Economists' Conference, ARTNeT, United Nations Economic and Social Commission for Asia and the Pacific, Bangkok, Thailand, November 2–3, 2009. http://www.unescap.org/tid/artnet/mtg/2-3John%20Ravenhill.pdf.

Rosenbluth, Frances McCall. "Japan in 2011: Cataclysmic Crisis and Chronic Deflation." *Asian Survey* 52, no. 1 (January/February 2011).

United States Office of the Trade Representative. "Trans-Pacific Partnership Announcement," news release, December 14, 2009. http://www.ustr.gov/about-us/press-office/press-releases/2009/december/trans-pacific-partnership-announcement.

World Bank. *The East Asian Miracle: Economic Growth and Public Policy*. Oxford: Oxford University Press, 1993.

2011 ASAN JAPAN CONFERENCE

Michael Auslin is the Director of Japan Studies at the American Enterprise Institute (AEI).

Bong Youngshik is a Senior Research Fellow and the Director of the Center for Foreign Policy at the Asan Institute for Policy Studies.

William W. Grimes is the Department Chair of International Relations and a Professor of International Relations and Political Science at Boston University.

Tetsundo Iwakuni is a Visiting Professor at various institutions in the US and Asia, including the University of Virginia and Nankai University.

Kim Mikyoung is an Associate Professor at the Hiroshima City University-Hiroshima Peace Institute in Japan.

Kim Sok Chul is the Principal Researcher and the Director of the Emergency and Security Preparedness Department at the Korea Institute of Nuclear Safety.

Gregory W. Noble is a Professor at the Institute of Social Science, the University of Tokyo.

Masakatsu Ota is a Senior Writer at Kyodo News and an Adjunct Fellow for the Program on Global Security and Disarmament at the University of Maryland.

T.J. Pempel is the Jack M. Forcey Professor of Political Science at the University of California, Berkeley.

Jun Saito is an Assistant Professor in the Department of Political Science at Yale University.

Kazuhiko Togo is a Professor and the Director of the Institute for World Affairs, Kyoto Sangyo University.

INDEX

Baker, James: 272
balance sheet recession: 63
Bank for International Settlements (BIS): 89
Bank of Japan: 88
"Beautiful Homeland and Safe Society" initiative: 199
bond issuance: 62
Bush, George W.
      administration (government): 248, 268-269
      Address to Congress, September 20, 2001: 268
      "military unilateralism": 268
      President: 241, 268-269

Chernobyl disaster: 219
Chiang Mai Initiative: 262
China, People's Republic of (PRC)
      Chinese Communist Party: 237
      economic growth: 252, 260, 262
      fishery vessel collision: 204
      foreign direct investment: 259-260, 265
      People's Liberation Army (PLA): 240
      rise of: 9, 20, 182, 207, 247
      Tiananmen Square massacre: 20
citizen activism: 129
Clean Government Party: 144
Clinton, Bill
      administration (government): 239-240
Clinton, Hillary: 269-270
Cold War: 20, 23
collective action dilemma: 66, 144
collective defense: 222
colonialism
      apology: 209-211
      Honda, Katsuichi (atrocities in China): 210
      Murayama Statement: 210
      Ienaga, Saburo (textbook defects): 210
      Morimura, Seichi (Unit 731): 210
Confucian ethics: 201
Convention on Early Notification: 223
Convention on the Elimination of All Forms of Discrimination against Women and National-
      ity: 179

D

debt, public sector: 10, 13, 55-56, 67, 73, 84, 257
declining birth rates: 11, 165
decline in savings rates: 55, 65
deflation: 13-15, 55, 61, 63, 65, 67, 69, 71, 73, 86, 92-93, 154, 257
Democratic Party of Japan (DPJ): 13, 35, 55, 73-76, 85, 93, 97-98, 100-101, 109, 111, 113,
      115, 117-118, 124, 128, 138-139, 154, 156, 166, 200, 204,
      213, 242, 247, 249, 275-277
Democratic Socialist Party: 144, 154
Democratization
    exogenous theory: 139
demographics of Japan
    aging population: 11, 13, 15, 183, 207, 253,
    demographic projections: 71
    dependency ratio: 58
Deng Xiaoping: 204-205, 239
Djibouti: 24, 250
Dokdo/Takeshima/Liancourt Rocks Conference, June 2009: 211
Duverger's Law: 156
"dynamic deterrence": 24, 245

E

Early Voluntary Sector Liberalization (EVSL): 266
East Asia
    cross-border cooperation: 22
    regional security: 183, 208, 222, 251, 254
    regionalism: 173, 270
East Asia Summit
    Bali, November 2011: 270
East China Sea: 24, 245-246, 248
Eastern civilization: 201
Economic Partnership Agreements (EPAs): 25, 265-266
Eisenhower, Dwight D.: 238
elections, Japan
    electoral reform, 1994: 18, 138, 141, 149-150, 153
    malapportionment: 15, 75, 96, 119, 140, 148, 150-151, 153
    "pork barrel" redistribution: 143, 147-148
    proportional representation (PR): 121-122, 144
    Public Offices Election Law: 149
    rural areas (districts): 15, 17, 18, 96, 98, 143, 149, 153
    single non-transferable vote (SNTV): 142-144, 148-149, 153
    voting: 96, 117, 142, 150, 276

Endsley, Mica R.: 219, 223-226
Eto, Jun: 210
Eurasianism: 206
Euratom: 222
European Union: 260, 264-265
Eurozone: 16, 88-89

immigration
    ethnic repatriates: 19
    vocational trainees: 19, 169
International Atomic Energy Agency (IAEA): 222-223
International Conference on Nuclear Engineering (ICONE)
    Miami, Florida, July 2006: 41
International Convention of Human Rights: 179
International Mercy Corps: 57
International Monetary Fund (IMF): 62, 73, 87, 262
Investigation Committee on the Accident at Fukushima Nuclear Power Stations of Tokyo
    Electric Power Company: 12, 36
Iokibe, Makoto: 202
Iraq
    US invasion, 2003: 241
Ishikawa, Yoshinobu: 200
Ishihara, Shintaro: 203
Iwate Prefecture: 43, 57, 110, 201, 203

Japan Atomic Energy Commission: 33
Japan-China-South Korea Trilateral Summit
    Tokyo, Japan, May 22, 2011: 220
    Summit Leaders Declaration: 221
Japan-China-South Korea Tripartite Free Trade Agreement: 207
Japan-DPRK bilateral relations
    abduction issue: 184, 213
Japan-Republic of Korea bilateral relations
    collective security: 222
    "comfort women": 184, 208, 211-212
    Cooperation on Official Development Assistance: 207
    Dokdo (Takeshima): 208, 211
    global warming cooperation: 207
    human security cooperation: 207
    textbook issue: 208
Japan-Russia bilateral relations
    Kuril Islands dispute: 211, 245
Japan-US Alliance
    ballistic missile defense (BMD): 244, 250
    military stability in East Asia: 23
    Status of Forces Agreement (SOFA): 240, 253
    US-Japan Defense Guidelines, 1997: 240

K

M

Mao Zedong: 237
Maoism: 260
Maruyama, Masao: 184, 210
Masuda, Hiroya: 201
Meiji Constitution: 141
Meiji Restoration: 183, 200, 245
Meiji Sanriku Tsunami: 43
"middle powers": 21, 207
Mindan: 180, 186
Mishima, Yukio: 210
Miyagi Prefecture: 43, 57, 110
Multiculturalism: 19, 165, 170, 188
Murayama, Tomiichi: 210

N

Nagasaki: 33-34
Nakai, Hiroshi: 213
Nakasone, Yasuhiro: 75
National Defense Program Guidelines, December 2010: 24, 204, 245
national pension: 59, 61, 71, 73, 86-88, 90-91, 94, 97, 128, 183
nationalism: 19, 170, 173-174, 264, 269
neo-classical economists: 67
Nihonjinron
    "ideal" Japanese family: 20
    Japaneseness: 19, 165, 170, 173-176
    "myth" of ethnic homogeneity: 19, 173, 188
Nikkei: 117, 276
Nippon Television Network
    survey, January 2012: 124, 132
Noda, Yoshihiko
    administration (government): 46, 73, 246, 251, 253
    cabinet: 100
    Prime Minister: 13, 35, 72, 76, 92, 100-101, 118, 121, 125, 202, 208, 243, 273, 275-
        277
Northeast Asia
    exports: 266
    nuclear emergencies: 219
    region: 25, 219, 222, 237-239, 248, 258, 261, 278
Northeast Asian History Foundation: 211
Nuclear Industry Safety Agency (NISA): 39, 112, 126
Nuclear Non-Proliferation Treaty (NPT): 46

O

P

R